Dec '09

MAFIA SON

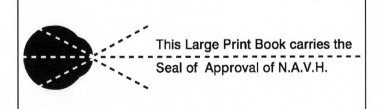

This Large Print Book carries the
Seal of Approval of N.A.V.H.

MAFIA SON

THE SCARPA MOB FAMILY, THE FBI, AND A STORY OF BETRAYAL

SANDRA HARMON

THORNDIKE PRESS

A part of Gale, Cengage Learning

GALE
CENGAGE Learning

Detroit • New York • San Francisco • New Haven, Conn • Waterville, Maine • London

GALE
CENGAGE Learning™

LIBRARY OF CONGRESS CATALOGING-IN-PUBLICATION DATA

Harmon, Sandra.
    Mafia son : the Scarpa mob family, the FBI, and a story of
betrayal / by Sandra Harmon.
        p. cm. — (Thorndike Press large print crime scene)
    ISBN-13: 978-1-4104-1855-5 (hardcover : alk. paper)
    ISBN-10: 1-4104-1855-3 (hardcover : alk. paper)
    1. Scarpa, Gregory. 2. Mafia—United States—Case studies. 3.
Gangsters—United States—Biography. 4. Criminals—United
States—Biography. 5. Organized crime—United States—Case
studies. 6. Large type books. I. Title.
HV6248.S3813H37 2009
364.1092—dc22
    [B]   2009020130

Published in 2009 by arrangement with St. Martin's Press, LLC.

Printed in the United States of America
1 2 3 4 5 6 7 13 12 11 10 09

For Deanne Barkley, my mentor
and best friend,
who has always stood by me with
unconditional love and support

CONTENTS

PREFACE

The story of Greg Scarpa Sr. — and, ultimately, the story of his son — is like no other mob story. Why? Because Scarpa was like no other mobster. Even in a world dominated by criminals, killers, and con men, Scarpa was uniquely qualified for the job. A sociopath who for thirty years was protected by the FBI from his enemies, other federal investigators, and local law enforcement authorities, Scarpa had nothing less than a license to kill. And he used it — sometimes for perfectly practical, economic reasons, and other times simply because he felt like it.

But Scarpa's greatest offense, perhaps, was the manipulation of his first-born son, Gregory Scarpa Jr., an innocent boy (at one time, anyway) who was transformed into a doppelgänger of his father. At least in part to please Greg Sr., Gregory Scarpa entered the family business and became a mobster;

he remained a "wiseguy" to the core until, betrayed by his father, he went to jail, where he became a government informant. He elicited in 1998 the incredible story of how Al-Qaeda terrorists were planning a horrific attack on American soil, which was ultimately carried out on September 11, 2001. But Gregory's information was either buried or ignored; he was sentenced to forty years to life at the ADMAX Prison in Florence, Colorado, and there he has remained for the better part of the past decade, virtually incommunicado, locked in his cell for twenty-three hours a day.

His story is one that reflects the complexities of life, especially a life lived outside the boundaries of legality. Gregory Scarpa is a hardened criminal; he is a murderer who spent virtually all of his adult life in a business for which killing was merely part of the territory . . . currency, if you will. But he was not an unrepentant or soulless monster. As is so often the case with men who walk in the footsteps of their fathers, Gregory was at once less and more than he appeared to be. If his actions regarding the acquisition of information that might have prevented the attacks of September 11, 2001, were on some level self-serving, they were nonetheless admirable.

Like most authors and journalists, I am intrigued by nothing so much as a fascinating story, and I found it in the twisted and sometimes tragic tale of the Scarpa family. While researching a project with Scarpa Sr.'s longtime mistress, Linda Schiro (about whom you will hear in this book), I was introduced to Gregory Scarpa Jr., the eldest child produced by the union of Greg Scarpa Sr. and his wife, Connie. Gregory was imprisoned at the time; nevertheless, Linda assured me, Gregory was a "great guy" who had worked for his dad since he was seventeen years old and knew precisely where the bodies were buried (and I am speaking quite literally).

Despite some reservations, I reached out to Gregory. I wrote him an introductory letter; to my surprise, he replied swiftly, and thus began a correspondence that I never envisioned. Instead of a hardened criminal, Gregory gave the impression of being a rather ordinary man who chattered incessantly about his children and grandchildren. In his very first letter he extended an invitation for me to visit, dangling an irresistible carrot in the process: "I'll tell you everything I know."

It was a sweet letter, oddly charming in its apparent innocence, and I found myself almost instantly drawn to its author. I knew that I wanted to meet Gregory. In the meantime, though, Linda changed her mind about encouraging my contact with Gregory, and my relationship with her ended shortly thereafter.

In the spring of 2004 I learned from a forensic intelligence analyst named Angela Clemente about undercover work that Gregory supposedly had done for the U.S. government, which in turn had rewarded him by burying him in ADMAX. This seemed almost incomprehensible. Could Gregory really have possessed information that might have averted the tragedy of 9/11? And could that information have been ignored by the United States government? The very thought of it made my head spin. I've never been much for conspiracy theories, but something about this story pulled me in and wouldn't let go. Eventually, through Clemente, I had an opportunity to read copies of FBI memos detailing Gregory's intelligence; the information was shocking. I told Clemente that I would help her in any way that I could, and sent her all of my research.

In May 2004, I wrote to Gregory at AD-MAX and told him that I believed his story and the intelligence that supported it. Our correspondence soon escalated in frequency and intensity. Because all of the nonlegal mail that Gregory sent or received was opened, read, censored — and often simply kept from him — we learned to communicate in code, sending much of our mail through a trusted attorney.

Like a homesick boy writing letters from summer camp, Gregory tried to mask his despair. Oddly, and endearingly, his letters were frequently adorned with smiley faces; rarely did he complain about prison life or draw attention to the brutal conditions faced by inmates. Later I would learn that this is not an uncommon characteristic of convicts — they can be enormously charismatic and manipulative — but I was drawn to Gregory, his story, and his plight. If he was trying to use me, well, perhaps I was using him as well. It was the truth I was after.

And so I became Gregory's conduit to the outside world. Typically, when a reporter or broadcaster attempted to interview him in prison, the warden would reject the request on the grounds that he was simply too dangerous. Consequently, these reporters (who discovered my relationship with Gregory) often spoke with me. It seemed ludicrous: Charles Manson could be interviewed, but not Gregory Scarpa Jr.

As I learned about the level of corruption surrounding the Scarpa family and various law enforcement agencies (including those of the federal government), the greater was my outrage. I pressed on, digging deeper despite the gnawing sense that I was putting myself in danger. The story took on a life of its own, and I felt almost powerless to set it aside. I began to lose sleep; I worried about how I could protect myself, until finally it dawned on me: I couldn't. But I could write a book.

Gregory was eager to cooperate, of course, since he wanted his story told. He sent me hundreds of letters about his life: tales of his youth, his father's control over him, and how he joined Greg Scarpa Sr. as both a Mafia member and an FBI informant. Crimes, scams, schemes, marriages, divorces, betrayal, and murder — here was the whole sordid, bloody history of the Scarpa family. Gregory, as far as I could tell, had nothing to hide. Most notably, he wrote extensively about what he always insisted was his father's corrupt and violent relationship with his FBI handler, R. Lindley DeVecchio.

Armed with the information that I had acquired from Linda Schiro, Gregory

Scarpa Jr., Angela Clemente, and Dr. Stephen Dresch (a highly respected Yale Ph.D., former Michigan legislator, Michigan Tech University dean, and forensic analyst), as well as my own extensive personal research, I began writing. I was confident that I had a thorough understanding of the puzzle in front of me, as well as a strategy for putting the pieces together.

Then the unthinkable happened. The Brooklyn District Attorney's office opened an investigation of former FBI Agent Lin DeVecchio, in part because of a confidential affidavit I had submitted to the office attesting to a murder that Linda had discussed with me — a crime allegedly involving DeVecchio. However, when the details of the affidavit were leaked to the press, all hell broke loose, with stories in major newspapers naming me specifically as the instigator of the DeVecchio investigation. This led to months of threats from Mafia types, intimidation by the FBI, ridicule in local newspapers for lacking the journalistic credentials of a "real crime writer," denigration in cyberspace (with the greatest venom generated on a Web site known as "Friends of Lin DeVecchio"), and denunciation in a book by a former undercover FBI agent. I was also warned that my phone line might

15

be tapped, and — through contacts in federal custody — that certain terrorist factions had gained access to my address and phone number. As a result, I was encouraged to exercise extreme caution in all correspondence. Finally, I was subpoenaed and called as a witness by both the prosecution and the defense in connection with the sensational murder trial of Lin DeVecchio.

This story is so remarkable — and my participation in it so unlikely — that it still feels somewhat surreal to me. And yet, even now, as I write these words many months after the trial, I remain the target of threats and intimidating behavior.

This, of course, only serves to reinforce the central thesis produced by my research. While some of the information in this book is based on the work of other writers, and on the accounts offered by secondary sources, the majority stems from personal interviews and firsthand research. I have thoroughly investigated every story in these pages — stories related to the Mafia, the FBI, and the justice system. Admittedly, some of the claims my sources have made appear, at first blush, to stretch the boundaries of credibility. But having immersed myself in this strange and brutal world for the better part of five years, I can say with complete sincerity that I believe all that I have written to be true.

Injustice anywhere is injustice everywhere.
— DR. MARTIN LUTHER KING JR.

1
SUPERMAX PRISON:
THE LAST WORST
PLACE

They call themselves "Cowboys." They love to threaten us, or deny us the simplest of requests. Some of them wake you up every hour throughout the night by shining a flashlight in your face, or throw flaming papers into your cell as a pretext for spraying you down with a fire extinguisher. Then there are the meals served with feces and urine in the food trays. And faces smashed into concrete walls; handcuffs clamped so tight that wrists and ankles are left lacerated and bruised; leg shackles that cut flesh to the bone when men are forced to run; and when we fall to the ground, we are kicked, hit, and slammed some more.

You learn to stay out of their way, except for the ones who just want to torture us, no matter what, the ones who get their kicks that way. And of course you have to watch out for the inmates, because most of them are totally nuts, because they have been locked up here for years, and this place is designed to drive you crazy.

— Anonymous inmate in ADMAX, Florence, Colorado

Welcome to the United States Penitentiary Administrative Maximum (ADMAX) facility in Florence, Colorado. The most secure federal prison in the country, Florence is specifically designed, and uniquely qualified, to keep every occupant in nearly total solitary confinement for his entire sentence. Gregory Scarpa Jr., fifty-eight, convicted of racketeering, will call this prison home until at least 2033, when he will be eighty-four years old.

Gregory has been a resident of ADMAX since 1998. He lives alone in a steel-and-concrete box approximately the size of your bathroom. For twenty-three hours a day, day in and day out, year after year, Gregory is confined to this space. His meticulously soundproofed seven-by-nine-foot cell includes a concrete slab and a thin mattress for a bed; a shower with a timer (to conserve water and prevent flooding); a sink with no taps (just buttons); a toilet with a valve that shuts off the water automatically; a light fixture; an immovable concrete desk and stool; a polished steel mirror riveted to the concrete wall; and a thirteen-inch black-and-white television encased in Plexiglas (to prevent tampering). The lights are controlled by the guards: Frequently they are left on throughout the night, leaving the prisoner disoriented and sleep-deprived, and thus keenly aware that he has forfeited his freedom, and that he is, in many respects, nothing more than an animal.

Motion detectors and cameras track his every move; fourteen hundred remote-controlled steel doors modulate his infrequent journeys throughout the facility; twelve-foot-high fences rimmed with concertina wire help ensure that he'll never take an unapproved vacation. Three times a day, like clockwork, small, tasteless meals are slid into his cell through a slot in the wall.

"You eat because you need to keep up your strength, but at night you dream about a thick steak, or a plate of spaghetti, or even a box of cookies," says Gregory. "I remember when I got a picture someone took of my mother in front of a tray of cookies, and all I could think about were the cookies. You see pictures of food on the TV and you begin to drool. You see beautiful women or happy families on TV and you try not to cry, because although you fear you will never be able to hold a woman or child in your arms ever again in your life, you have to be tough to survive."

Inmates have almost no physical contact with anyone: Corrections officers, for example, approach inmates' cells through a vestibule; bars separate the vestibule from the solid steel doors of the cell, providing a second barrier and allowing the COs to handcuff inmates safely before removing them from their cells for transport or exercise. As with food, mail and laundry are delivered through a slot in the steel bars. Meals are either typical American diner fare — casseroles, hamburgers, and blue-plate specials — or foods conforming to almost all religious restrictions: no pork; an abundance of beans and vegetables. During the month of Ramadan, Muslims are afforded certain courtesies, such as taking their meals in the evening hours. But these are the rare exceptions.

From the prison nerve center, officers and other staff maintain control through the use of a wide array of sophisticated electronic and surveillance equipment. Doors are opened and closed by remote control, and almost always from a safe distance. Corridors are lined with cameras and microphones, making it almost impossible for an inmate to escape the watchful eye of prison administrators. The goal here is not rehabilitation; the goal is confinement — punishment. The safety of staff and officers is paramount at all times.

Gregory Scarpa Jr. is five-feet-six-inches tall, with a thick, muscular build, gray beard, and an assortment of tattoos. Though short in stature, he is a physically impressive man (prematurely bald, he no longer sports the rather conspicuous and obvious toupee he wore in his youth); and yet, there is an undeniable sadness in his eyes, something in his demeanor that suggests nothing so much as regret. He passes the endless hours exercising in his cell, watching TV, and writing long letters to his four children: Kori, Diane, Gregory III, and Maria (the last, at twenty, his youngest). He says that he attempts to be a father to them through daily letters; to date, however, he has rebuffed their overtures to visit. He says he would love to hold his children, to feel their touch and to hear their voices, to feel their breath against his cheek. But even if they were permitted to visit, there is no assurance they would be allowed any sort of intimacy, and the longing he feels — the sadness that comes with isolation — is offset by the pain he imagines they would feel if they saw him in this cell, chained and shackled, their encounter mitigated by a Plexiglas barrier.

Five days a week, for one hour a day, Gregory is removed from his cell and transported to a small indoor steel-mesh cage about half the size of his cell. Inmates call it the "kennel" or "dog run," because that is precisely what it resembles. Leaving his cell for even this brief interlude involves an extraordinary ordeal for Gregory. Two guards enter his cell and order him to strip. After a cavity search, including a pointedly humiliating anal examination, he dresses again, and his hands are cuffed through a slot in the steel bars. Then the guards — with steel-tipped batons at the ready — accompany him down a long, narrow corridor. At all times, their movements are tracked by video monitors. Nothing is left to chance.

Exercise hour is exactly that — one hour. Afterward, the moving process begins again, including a second degrading cavity search. He then sits in his tiny cell for the next twenty-three hours, waiting for the next meal, for mail, for anything that will help interrupt the crushing monotony and sameness that typify his life. Gregory Scarpa has been incarcerated at several different federal penitentiaries over the course of the past seventeen years; he is no stranger to the boredom and indignity of prison life. Florence ADMAX, he readily acknowledges, is easily the worst. Guards wield authority and power to a degree not known at most prisons. It is a completely controlled environment, and nothing is allowed to put that control at risk. An inmate who is unhappy with his situation is well advised to keep his mouth closed. Corrections officers will meet force with force — tenfold — and as long as no one is killed or maimed, the muscular tactics are generally approved and encouraged. ADMAX is not supposed to be a warm and welcoming place. It is prison. In every sense of the word. And the inmates at ADMAX are never allowed to forget this fact. So long as an officer brings no unwelcome attention on the institution and its administration, his methodology is unlikely to be questioned.

The maximum security facility at Marion, Illinois, the model for Florence ADMAX, has been denounced by Amnesty International, a human rights organization, for violating the United Nations Standard Minimum Rules for the Treatment of Prisoners. But few people care, because "supermax" facilities such as Marion and Florence ADMAX are considered little more than repositories for society's scum. Garden-variety drug addicts and petty thieves do not find their way to Florence; one's criminal oeuvre must be decidedly more violent, and persistently high profile. Florence ADMAX is the end of the line for drug kingpins, gang leaders, hit men, snipers, and, more recently, international terrorists (for example, Al-Qaeda shoe bomber Richard Reid and four men convicted of involvement in the 1998 bombings of U.S. embassies are all residents of ADMAX).

High-profile American terrorists have also called ADMAX home, including Oklahoma City bomber Timothy McVeigh (who was executed in 2001) and his accomplice, Terry Nichols, as well as Theodore Kaczynski, the Unabomber. Together, for a time, this trio gave the prison's highest-security section its nickname: Bombers Row.

Another notorious Florence ADMAX inmate is Ramzi Yousef, who is serving a life sentence with no chance for parole following a conviction in 1998 for his involvement in both the 1993 World Trade Center bombing and the Bojinka bombing plot. In 1998, three years before 9/11, Gregory Scarpa Jr. risked his life to spy for the United States government, extracting from Yousef himself the incredible story of how Al-Qaeda was planning 9/11. Scarpa passed the information, in minute detail — including exact sketches of terrorist bombs — to then assistant U.S. attorney Valerie Caproni (now the FBI's head counsel), and to then AUSA Patrick Fitzgerald (later a U.S. special prosecutor). In return, Scarpa had believed that his sentence would be reduced, or perhaps even commuted. Instead, he was called a liar, his intelligence was buried, and he was sentenced to forty years to life at Florence ADMAX, where he has been held essentially without any contact.

One might reasonably wonder why Gregory has been kept in this hellhole of a prison, unable to tell his story — unless, of course, the United States government has something to hide. Certainly he is no choirboy; he is, by his own admission, a killer. But is it possible that even a murderer can be both more and less than he appears?

"It is an absolute outrage that Gregory Scarpa Jr. should be doing four decades in the same jail as the man behind the trade center bombing and Bojinka," says Larry Silverman, Gregory's former lawyer. "Especially when we only now have a full understanding of the quality of the intelligence he was furnishing to the feds."

2
WISEGUY

We are shaped as much by the world into which we are thrust as by those who serve as our guides.

Greg Scarpa Sr. was born in 1928, in Bensonhurst, a working-class neighborhood in south-central Brooklyn, to a traditional (i.e., poor) Italian-American family. In 1949, at the age of twenty, he married Connie Forrest, a pretty girl from the neighborhood who was just seventeen years old and already pregnant with the first of their four children (a girl they would name Debbie). The young couple moved into a small apartment in nearby Bay Ridge, and began their life together.

Connie Scarpa, now seventy-seven, still a blonde and working to pay the rent by filling pill bottles at a pharmaceutical company, insists she had no idea her husband was a gangster until she was in the hospital, waiting to give birth to Gregory Jr., her second child. She saw Greg Sr.'s picture in one of the New York tabloids, standing with a few other men, their hands pressed against a wall as a small army of police officers stood by, smiling. The cops had busted Scarpa and his buddies for burglary, which came as something of a shock to his wife. If she was angry at the time, though, she held it in check, for it was more important to stand by her man, and to see to it that he would be free to take care of his family. So Connie wrote a long letter to Scarpa's lawyer and to his judge, arguing, in the way that only a young, pregnant wife possibly could, that he was a good guy who had never gotten into trouble.

"I wrote that he had a daughter and that I was expecting another baby," Connie recalls. "The other girls in the maternity ward at the hospital used to ask me, 'Where's your husband?' but I used to say, 'He's a salesman. He travels.' They let him come out of jail just in time to pick me and Gregory Jr. up at the hospital."

Since everyone called the father "Greg Sr.," the little boy became Gregory. Greg Sr. lavished attention on his son from the moment he was born. Gregory was a happy and loving boy who naturally adored his father.

31

"When I was a kid, all I cared about was playing sports and always wanting to be around my dad," remembers Gregory. "I just loved him so much as I was growing up. I would wait and count the hours until he would come home. He usually didn't come home until late at night, but it didn't matter. I'd wait up all night for him."

Of course, the reason Greg Sr. came home late at night was because most of his business was conducted in the evening. Having long ago traded the workaday world for something more lucrative and exciting — not to mention dangerous and illegal — Scarpa had risen through the ranks to become a "made man" in the Colombo family, one of New York City's five Mafia crime families. (The others were the Bonanno, Gambino, Genovese, and Lucchese families.) The Colombo family was originally the Profaci family. Born in Sicily, Joe Profaci ruled the family for nearly thirty years, until an upstart crew headed by Albert, Larry, and "Crazy Joe" Gallo, based in Brooklyn's Red Hook section, launched an open revolt, kicking off what came to be known as the Gallo–Profaci war. Greg Sr. originally sided with the rebelling brothers; never one to confuse loyalty with stupidity, though, Greg Sr. ultimately shifted his allegiance to Profaci, who, upon emerging successfully from the conflict, rewarded Greg by helping him gain a foothold in myriad illegal business endeavors. With Profaci's backing, Scarpa became a successful and wealthy mobster. When Profaci died of cancer in 1962, he was replaced by then underboss Joseph Magliocco, who ultimately was forced to retire as the head of the family. Magliocco was replaced by capo Joe Colombo and the family was rechristened as the Colombo family.

Although Greg Sr. never rose above the rank of soldier — the lowest rank among made men — he was considered a "good earner" (in the parlance of the Mafia). Scarpa had his own fifty-man crew, based out of a storefront club on Thirteenth Avenue in Bensonhurst, which he jokingly named the Wimpy Boys Social Club. They made their money through a wide variety of illicit (and time-honored) undertakings: bookmaking; securities and credit card fraud; auto theft; illegal slot machines; joker poker games; stickups; burglaries; bank robberies; truck hijacking; and drug dealing. Scarpa also fronted cash to loan sharks and served as banker to the Brooklyn mob's vast illegal numbers racket. On the side, when the mood struck, he fixed horse races. Over the years Greg Scarpa Sr. earned millions of dollars for the Colombo family.

But Scarpa was more than just an extraordinary earner; he was also one of the Mafia's most feared and gleefully efficient killers. Known for his sense of humor, his remarkable run of good fortune (indeed, it is nothing short of remarkable that he avoided prison for so many years), as well as his brutality, Scarpa was a man of many monikers: Among his more popular nicknames were the Grim Reaper, the Mad Hatter, and, near the end of his career, by which time his work had become famously bloody, Hannibal Lecter.

It would be a gross simplification (as well as a mitigation of the crimes) to suggest that murder was simply a cost of doing business with Greg Scarpa Sr. While this may have been occasionally true, it would be erroneous to paint Scarpa with a romantic brush (as Mario Puzo did so elegantly with the Corleone family — "it's only business"). In reality, Scarpa may have had as much in common with the good Dr. Lecter as he did with Don Vito. By most accounts, he was a particularly unrepentant killer who enjoyed the violence of the Mafia life even more than he enjoyed the money or the power or the women. Here, after all, is a man who once so relished whacking a hated rival that some weeks later he professed a desire to exhume the dismembered corpse and kill him all over again.

Clearly, this was no ordinary wiseguy.

"Greg loved killing," explains Lou Diamond, Scarpa's former attorney. "He was a sociopath. He would smile at a guy, take him out to dinner, and blow his brains out."

If the method varied, the outcome was preordained. Scarpa would end a seemingly benign meeting at Wimpy Boys by pulling a pistol from beneath a table and shooting someone in the face; he'd plug a victim in the back of the head as he sat behind them in a stolen car. More than once, like a gunslinger in the Wild West, he'd pull up alongside another car, lean out the window, and pick off his target with a rifle. Then he'd drive away, without a moment's remorse.

For all his violent proclivities, Greg Scarpa Sr. was hardly a hoodlum archetype; while some mobsters compensated for their insecurities by projecting an image of snarling menace, Scarpa, more often than not, greeted the world with a disarming, friendly smile. He dressed impeccably (and expensively), favoring designer labels and elegant jewelry, and always carried at least five thousand dollars in his pocket — emergency money, he called it, in case he had to make a payoff (which, in Scarpa's world, was an omnipresent possibility). He sauntered through the streets of Bensonhurst with his chest thrust forward, head held high, looking and feeling less like a criminal than a local celebrity — or even royalty.

And if Greg Scarpa Sr. was in some fashion the king of Bensonhurst, then his son Gregory was a prince in waiting. Every day after school, from the time he was eight years old, Gregory would walk the few blocks to Wimpy Boys; not only did he enjoy spending time with his father, but even then, at such a young age, Gregory was enthralled by the toughs and thugs who hung out at the club. To him, of course, they were not criminals, or even "bad guys" (at least, not according to an eight-year-old's definition). They were big, boisterous men who filled a room with their laughter, as well as with their physical presence. To Gregory, they were not so different from the thickly muscled heroes of his comic books; best of all, they answered to his dad, which had a predictable impact on Gregory: It impressed the hell out of him. The boy was young but attentive — he noticed a lot of money changing hands, with most of it going to his father. He didn't understand why, but he figured, quite reasonably, that it had something to do with his father's stature in the neighborhood. He noticed that the respect accorded his father extended beyond the walls of Wimpy Boys to the street corners, where kids would hang out, and to the shops and stores, where proprietors would shake his hand and thank him. Why they were so grateful, the boy had no idea. But it made him proud; it made him feel special.

When business did not interfere, Greg Sr. made time for his son. He'd spend hours teaching Gregory the finer points of baseball — how to hit a curveball or slide into second, spikes high, in the tradition of the toughest ballplayers. There were frequent outings to Yankee Stadium, where father and son would watch the game, cheer on the Yanks, and stuff themselves with popcorn and hot dogs and soda. In this sense, of course, they were no different than other fans. Sometimes, though, after the game had ended, Scarpa would take his son onto the field or into the locker room, where the superstars of baseball's golden era — guys like Mickey Mantle, Roger Maris, and Yogi Berra — would throw an arm around Gregory's shoulder and pose for photographs; they'd sign cards, caps, and pictures —

37

anything the boy wanted. And before they'd leave, his father would thank the ballplayers, who simply nodded and smiled in the same deferential manner Gregory saw in the shop owners of Bensonhurst. If he didn't quite comprehend his father's reach, he appreciated it nonetheless.

Boxing was Gregory's other passion, largely because it was the sport that most appealed to his father. The sweet science of Greg's youth enjoyed a place in popular culture that might seem odd to a modern audience. Indeed, there once were no bigger stars in the sporting world than the champions of professional boxing — men like Sugar Ray Robinson and Rocky Marciano, and later, when Gregory was growing up, Muhammad Ali. From an early age Greg Sr. tried to instill in his son a similar appreciation for the fight game, even going so far as to buy Gregory his first pair of boxing gloves when the boy was only three years old. Greg Sr. would get down on his knees and playfully spar with Gregory, envisioning a day when his son might fight for a title — or at least be capable of defending himself.

Greg Sr. was almost fanatically devoted to fitness in general and sports in particular, and this passion was transferred to his family. There were three children in the Scarpa household: Debbie, the oldest ("my second love," Greg Sr. called her); Gregory, the middle child and first-born son; and Buddy, the baby of the brood. Greg Sr. tolerated neither laziness nor apathy in any of his children; he even devised an exercise program, which all of the children were required to complete on a daily basis — usually with their father watching closely and intently, commenting on their form and offering both criticism and support.

By 1960 Greg had become rather flush with money, and although he still ran his rackets in Bensonhurst he moved his family to a rambling old house on Staten Island (which by this time had become a popular spot for up-and-coming mobsters, made men in particular, to establish familial roots). Each night, like any other successful workingman, he'd return to Staten Island, to the five-bedroom house with a swimming pool that Connie had found and decorated. The Scarpas were a happy family, living in the "country" in a style that reflected Greg Sr.'s growing success. The fuel for that success was unrecognized and unimportant.

One day, though, Gregory, Debbie, and Buddy were playing hide-and-seek when Gregory ducked into his father's closet and was surprised to find guns, holsters, and fedoras. After that he began nosing around his parents' bedroom, and he found stacks of money in drawer bottoms, as well as badges and other sophisticated, supposedly proprietary material from the New York Police Department (NYPD) and Federal Bureau of Investigation.

"I began to wonder what my dad was doing with all that stuff," recalls Gregory. "But I kept my secret to myself and went about the business of growing up."

Many of the men whom Gregory had seen at Wimpy Boys would now visit the house on Staten Island for pool parties and barbecues, often with their wives and children in tow. Approximately once a month a group of men would come to the Scarpa house unaccompanied, for what Greg Sr. called his "homework." Interestingly, business was conducted in the open, with the men emptying duffle bags filled with gold chains, diamonds, watches, rings, and other jewelry one at a time onto a large dining-room table.

"I always noticed that the guys were having a great time, laughing and hugging one another while they separated and sorted the jewelry," Gregory remembers. "One time I picked up a bowl of diamonds and started shooting them on the floor, like marbles. When one of Dad's friends, John Sapanaro, found me in the living room playing with the diamonds, he began to tease my mom and say that I was going to be 'bad.' My mom got angry. She told John that I was a 'good' boy, and was going to be a doctor or lawyer."

Greg Sr. instructed his son not to discuss the "homework" being done at the house. He said that if anyone asked what his dad did for a living Gregory should tell them that he was a jeweler.

When each of the Scarpa boys reached the age of ten, Connie registered them for any available athletic activity. Little League baseball became a big part of the family's life. Connie attended all of her sons' games (and most of their practices, too). When Gregory would walk to the plate, he'd invariably hear his mother shouting, "Hit that ball, Junior."

Although Greg Sr. couldn't make it to all of Gregory's baseball games, he made sure to be there whenever his son pitched. The night before a game he'd sit Gregory down and go over the pitches that he had taught him: a curveball, a knuckleball, and a changeup.

"Our sit-down would be him showing me secret signals on what pitch to throw at what time," recalls Gregory.

The next day Greg Sr. would volunteer to sit high in the scorer's booth behind the backstop, in order to have a better view of the entire field. When Gregory was on the pitcher's mound, he would study the batter carefully, and then peek up at his dad, who would signal which pitch to throw. Gregory would nod in response. When Gregory did well, he and his dad would celebrate. His father's approval meant everything to him.

Gregory was twelve years old when the family welcomed a new member: a baby boy who came to be known as Frankie Boy.

"I loved this little guy dearly," Gregory says. "As I grew up, I always felt that Frankie Boy was like a son to me, rather than a little brother. I still feel the same way today. I taught him how to play ball, and I showed him how to draw Woody Woodpecker, and I listened to all his problems and helped him figure out the best solutions."

By the time he was fourteen, Gregory had developed into a formidable adolescent package. He enjoyed working out and running on the beach and boxing with friends; in many ways he felt like the luckiest kid in the world. Gregory's teenage years were only marred by the occasional wave of bad publicity and notoriety — for example, articles in the *Staten Island Advance* characterizing Greg Scarpa as a Mafia big shot. If Gregory had once been proud and unquestioning when it came to the power and influence wielded by his father, now he felt something less pure. He was older, smarter, and no longer limited by the lens of childhood. On some level, at least, the adolescent Gregory was aware that his father was an unconventional businessman; but he responded to the taunts and epithets of classmates with a confrontational attitude. Anyone who disrespected Greg Scarpa Sr. would have to deal with Junior as well. Indeed, more than once Gregory was provoked into defending the honor of his father. But that was okay — the kid didn't mind a good fight.

These same newspaper reports alarmed Debbie greatly, who had never shaken a frightening memory of picking up the phone one evening, while her parents were out, when she was ten years old. On the other end of the line had been a sinister voice informing the little girl that her father was going to be murdered. When she told her parents Greg Sr. had kissed his daughter on the forehead and tried to calm her fears: "Just some crazy person who dialed the wrong number; don't give it another thought. Daddy isn't going anywhere."

From that night on, however, Debbie suffered terribly from vivid, bone-chilling nightmares in which her parents were often victims. Debbie turned to her little brother in search of the truth.

Because Gregory felt so close to his dad, he felt comfortable asking him about the newspaper articles. Greg Sr. took his son for a walk on the beach one day and promised to reveal the truth. Theirs was a special bond — unbreakable, Greg Sr. explained — father and first-born son. There would be no secrets, no lies. Gregory was growing up quickly, and soon he'd figure things out for himself, the father reasoned, so why not get it out in the open.

"At that moment," recalls Gregory, "I really loved having this private conversation with my father. I looked up to him with love and respect, and always listened to him."

Greg Sr. told his son that the stories were true — to a degree. He was indeed a member of the Mafia, but that was only one of the hats he wore. Scarpa looked into his son's eyes and told the boy that his real job — the one that mattered most — was as an undercover agent for the FBI. He never wavered in his story, never averted his glance out of embarrassment or shame.

Rather, he reveled in the embellishment, telling Gregory to think of him not as a mobster or a criminal, but as a hero.

"Like Elliott Ness," Scarpa said with a smile, invoking the name of one of Gregory's personal crime-fighting favorites.

Untouchable. Yeah. Gregory liked the sound of that.

Greg Sr. explained that his job was complicated and clandestine, that his primary function was to learn everything that went on in the Mafia, and then to inform the FBI of his findings. It was dangerous, thrilling work. Lucrative, too. Or so it seemed, given the way the family lived and the cash that always seemed to be on hand. The important thing, Greg Sr. explained to his son, was that the work was truly important. Unlike most people, Greg Sr. had an opportunity to serve his country; he was one of the *good guys*, you see. There was right and there was wrong, and if Daddy sometimes veered into the wrong lane, well, that was merely in search of a greater good.

"But what about all the money, Dad?" Gregory remembers asking. "The jewels on the dining-room table?"

"Rewards for a job well done," Greg Sr. replied. "And richly deserved." He told the kid not to sweat it. The FBI knew all about

Greg Scarpa Sr., and endorsed his activities on every level. "Come to think of it," Greg Sr. said, "I really am untouchable."

Gregory took it all in, let it soak into his marrow. And then he did what any son would do: He rationalized his father's behavior.

"I now understood that my father *was* in the Mafia," Gregory says. "But only as a way to help the government."

But as he listened, another, more palpable fear enveloped Gregory. Suddenly he became terrified that if the Mafia ever found out what his dad was doing, they would kill him. The mob was pretty good at that sort of thing, Gregory knew, and if his father was some sort of double agent, well, surely his life was in danger.

Ever the cool customer, Scarpa merely smiled and shook his head. He put a single finger to his lips.

"As long as you keep my secret," Greg Sr. told his son, "the Mafia will never find out."

Gregory naturally agreed — what else could he do? This, after all, was his father, a man Gregory adored and worshipped. He would die rather than betray his father's trust. Greg Scarpa nodded approvingly and hugged his son tightly, solidifying their bond.

"The walk I took at the beach with Dad was an experience that left me often daydreaming and thinking a lot," Gregory says. "More than anything else, I wanted to work and be just like him. I told Debbie that Dad wasn't in the Mafia and not to worry about what was in the papers."

Even now, as an adult, Gregory suffers from episodes of melancholy as he recalls the complexities of his relationship with his father. If there was betrayal and manipulation on the part of the father, and undying loyalty on the part of the son, well, maybe there was love as well.

"At family affairs, Dad would keep the chair next to him empty and wait for me to sit down next to him," Gregory explains. "All my life he showed me how much he cared and loved me, so much so that still to this day I find myself talking to myself with disbelief at the truth of his betrayal of me."

But one man is not surprised at the arc of the father-son relationship, nor at the degree to which Greg Scarpa was willing to use every tool at his disposal — including his own family — to meet his own selfish needs.

"Greg was Machiavellian," says Lou Diamond. "He was the puppeteer. He lived to manipulate people against people, even the people he loved."

3
TOP ECHELON
INFORMANT

Sometimes it seemed as though Greg Scarpa Sr. had been born under a lucky star. Both the men in his crew and his bosses in the Colombo family often marveled at Scarpa's ability to evade apprehension by the authorities; he seemed gifted that way, always one step ahead of the latest bust. Six times Scarpa was arrested, on charges ranging from bookmaking to vagrancy to assault. Almost miraculously, each charge resulted in dismissal or acquittal. But it wasn't the stars that dictated Greg Sr.'s good fortune. Rather, it was a willingness to compromise his principles (such as they were).

In the Mafia code of conduct, unwritten though it may be, there is nothing worse than a "rat," no form of life more deserving of contempt. In fact, Scarpa, a mobster to the core, would have been the first to say as much. In point of truth, however, he lived a dual life for more than thirty years, dating back to March 1962, when federal agents seized him outside New York State following an investigation into an armed robbery. Scarpa was given a choice: "Keep your mouth shut and go to jail, or feed us information and remain a free man (relatively speaking)." This, of course, was a defining moment in Scarpa's life and career. Busts and jail time had long been associated with the Mafia lifestyle — indeed, it was considered nothing less than a rite of passage. *Omertà,* the Mafia vow of silence, was considered the greatest sign of loyalty and strength, and it was violated only by those who had some sort of death wish. Most people, looking in from the outside, would have considered Greg Scarpa Sr. an unlikely candidate to succumb to the temptation of ratting out his colleagues and coworkers. He was a strong, charismatic leader, fearless and unyielding. But he was also selfish and greedy, and in the end these proved to be the traits that dictated his life. Following a brief negotiation, Scarpa began cooperating with the FBI, first as a confidential informant, and then as a top echelon informant.

In other words — a rat.

Scarpa was a rare and valuable source, high enough in a criminal enterprise to provide what the bureau called "singular" information, such as a detailed organizational chart of the Colombo crime family. Among other things, he provided the FBI with a detailed history of the Mafia's origins, structure, methods, leadership, and its secret rites and rituals. He did the unthinkable, handing over vital information against his own boss, Joe Colombo, just as he had told the secrets of prior Colombo family bosses Joseph Profaci and Joe Magliocco. Later, Greg Sr. gave agents ammunition against Jerry Langella, the capo, or "captain," for whom he worked, and Carmine "Junior" Persico, his immediate boss.

Greg Sr. held nothing back. He told the FBI which mobsters were on their way up, and which (unfortunate) ones were on their way out. His tips led to the indictments and convictions of dozens of gangsters and corrupt lawyers. Scarpa once informed simultaneously on three people proposed for Colombo family membership, including one whom he himself had sponsored.

None of this bothered Scarpa in the least. As it turned out, he was uniquely suited to the amorality of his new role. He avoided prison, got revenge against those who had betrayed him (or those he wanted to dispose of), and, best of all, he was compensated for his services. Not only did the FBI give

Scarpa a pass when it came to running a criminal enterprise, but it paid him more than $150,000 in informant fees over the years. What is most important and disturbing is that the FBI had given Scarpa a virtual license to kill. Greg Sr. would ultimately admit to murdering more than fifty people, many with the assistance or knowledge of his FBI handlers. The thought of being arrested or serving time in prison (the usual deterrents to such behavior, at least when one's moral compass has been shattered) had no impact on Scarpa. Typically, the FBI warned him of upcoming investigations; on those rare occasions when a lapse in communication resulted in Scarpa being arrested, he would spend only a few days in jail. Somehow, it seemed, the charges were always dismissed.

The Top Echelon program was initiated in 1960 by then FBI director J. Edgar Hoover, who had famously (and not convincingly) argued for years against the very existence of an organized crime syndicate known as the Mafia. Three years earlier on November 14, 1957, titular figures of the Mafia's most prolific and influential families gathered in the small upstate New York town of Apalachia to conduct strategy sessions aimed at quelling the violence and turf wars that were threatening to shatter their world and their way of life. The meetings were held in supposed secrecy at the farm of Joseph Barbara, a senior captain in the Buffalo mob. But the hundred-plus mobsters from across the country were discovered when an alert New York State Police trooper, who saw that Barbara had booked an unusually large number of rooms at a local motel, drove out to the estate. When a squad of New York troopers descended on the farm, the mobsters scattered in all directions. A few escaped, but many were rounded up and detained long enough to be identified as the bosses of the American La Cosa Nostra. This left Hoover with no choice but to acknowledge, at least within the framework of the FBI, that the Mafia was indeed a living, breathing organization, with tentacles and influence throughout the country.

As Ralph Ranalli, a Boston-based journalist, wrote in *Deadly Alliance: The FBI's Secret Partnership with the Mob:*

Hoover fired off a memo to all his field offices on November 27, 1957, ordering them to compile lists of the Top Ten organized crime figures within their jurisdictions. He specifically instructed his agents to recruit murderers, mob associates, and crime bosses as informants who had reliable information. The top hoodlums were supposed to receive priority for investigation and prosecution and the order sent FBI agents scrambling to find anyone they could possibly classify as a "Top Hoodlum."

A substantial obstacle to the FBI's efforts was *omertà,* a code of honor and silence that forbade mobsters from speaking of the Mafia, even in their own defense. Suspicion of being an informant invited death by execution. There would be no trial, no discussion. A rat was dispatched with precisely the same level of contempt as the vermin he represented. Consequently, agents deployed an array of illegal tactics in their pursuit of information, including wiretapping, improper surveillance, break-ins, and searches. Since breaking and entering was, of course, an illegal act, the agents installing the bugs were ordered to leave their credentials at home and, if discovered, deny that the FBI had any knowledge of their activities. In a way, this drew them closer to the criminals they pursued, for both were inching closer to the gray area that separates right from wrong. And under Hoover's jurisdiction, their territories and activities would eventually overlap.

For years mafiosos claimed that the FBI engaged in unethical and even criminal tactics. A popular complaint was that the feds were fond of installing illegal bugs at places frequented by the mob — nightclubs, for example, or private meeting halls. Agents would listen patiently to conversations, sometimes for months on end, in order to acquire the names and activities (often illicit) of particular targets. Once armed with this information, the FBI would arrange meetings with its targets and threaten to prosecute to the full extent of the law — implicit was the understanding that the mobster would spend the better part of his adult life in jail if he did not cooperate with the authorities. And cooperation did not involve something as simple as the passing of a name or place — it meant accepting the burden and responsibility of forming an ongoing partnership with the very people most despised by the mobster and his cronies: the cops.

Through the employment of such questionable — albeit effective — tactics, the FBI forged relationships with organized crime figures throughout the United States.

Then, in 1965, according to Ranalli,

One of the bugs installed in a Washington, D.C., hotel room started picking up information on Robert Baker, a former top aide to President Lyndon Johnson when he had been in the U.S. Senate. When President Johnson learned of this, he ordered all the Bureau's illegal bugs be not only turned off, but physically removed from their locations. That meant that Organized Crime Squad agents broke back into the Mafia-controlled social clubs, restaurants, and wherever else they had been installed, and tore their eavesdropping equipment out.

Not one to be easily dissuaded by orders from the Oval Office, Hoover pressed on. His next step was the Top Echelon Informant Program, in which the director brazenly allowed his reach to exceed his grasp. Top Echelon bypassed the street-level thugs and soldiers who did much of the mob's dirty and bloody work, and focused instead on the importance of recruiting sworn Italian Mafia members to the ranks of FBI informants. Agents were exhorted to develop at least four such informants a year. In New York alone, twenty-five FBI officers were assigned to a newly formed Organized

Crime Squad. Among the charter members of this unit was a young man named Anthony Villano, a smart, Brooklyn-born FBI agent who was Greg Scarpa Sr. FBI liaison (or "handler") during the 1960s and 1970s. In 1976 he would co-author a book (with Gerald Astor) entitled *Brick Agent: Inside the Mafia for the FBI*. In that memoir, Villano admitted that he paid little attention to regulations while pursuing and protecting his sources: "As an agent, I had to break almost every rule in the book to do my job. The Bureau never wanted to know about such transgressions, so, in the reports we filed, they were either not mentioned or covered up by lies."

As an author, Villano was nothing if not proud. Portraying himself as a man who "had the guts of a Serpico and the steel nerve of Intrepid," Villano painted a vivid, self-aggrandizing portrait of a good cop fighting the good fight — against all odds. But there is another side of the story, and it is all but absent in the pages of *Brick Agent*. According to two people who have more than passing knowledge of the situation — Gregory Scarpa Jr. and Linda Schiro, Greg Scarpa Sr.'s common-law wife for more than thirty years — Anthony "Nino" Villano was also on the take.

Whenever Greg Sr.'s crew pulled off a big score, Nino received a kickback. This was not done covertly, at least not on Scarpa's end. Greg Sr. would explain to the boys in his crew that paying off the cops was just another cost of doing business; a piece of the pie was always presented to his law-enforcement buddy, whom he derisively labeled his "girlfriend." Scarpa's crew naturally presumed that the boss's law enforcement "source" was a cop on the inside looking out for Greg Sr. and his pals. This was hardly unusual in Mafia circles. Indeed, in the world of organized crime there frequently existed a circle of benevolence that permitted everyone to do their jobs and to make money. The mob would run illicit enterprises, cops would be paid to turn a blind eye, and all was well and good. Of course, every so often the cops had to throw a bad guy in jail, or otherwise flex enough muscle to keep the brass happy and the civilians comfortably unaware, but generally the machinery of mutual mistrust hummed along smoothly. Typically, though, these arrangements existed on the local level, between neighborhood mobsters and cops walking a beat. The feds? That was a different matter entirely; no one could have imagined that Greg Scarpa Sr. was deeply involved in a partnership with an FBI agent. But he was. After a job had been completed and the cash divvied up, Scarpa would wait for his crew to depart for the evening. Then he would sit back in anticipation of the arrival of Nino Villano, who invariably stopped by to claim his percentage of the haul.

Sometimes Scarpa would share information with Villano about robberies (some involving his own crew). This invariably led to Villano recovering stolen merchandise, and subsequently receiving reward money from the insurance company. Here's an example of how the mobster and the FBI agent executed their scam. Scarpa would hear of a particular heist or hijacking; in turn, he would tell Villano where to find, say, a $200,000 load of imported perfume. Villano would then tell whoever was liable for the loss (typically, an insurance company) that the perfume could be returned for $20,000, which Villano then kept for himself. Or, perhaps, he might kick some of the cash in Scarpa's direction. Not often, though — Scarpa's remuneration came primarily in the form of cash payments for information that led to arrests, or in the form of indifference on the part of the FBI. The quid pro quo, simply put, was this: As long as Scarpa remained a valuable and productive informant, he would be allowed to conduct business without fear of interference or retribution.

The FBI under Hoover also initiated a secret system of cash bonuses to reward agents on particularly important cases. If, for example, an informant provided the bureau with valuable intelligence that led to wiretaps and arrests, the informant's agent also benefited. This capitalistic invasion of an organization founded on the principles of public service naturally had its proponents and detractors. Bonuses ranged from a few hundred to several thousand dollars on some occasions, which obviously opened the door to temptation and exploitation. To a federal agent earning $225 a week before taxes in 1970, these were not insignificant numbers; even a few hundred dollars was a princely sum. Clearly, the mixing of wealthy, immoral gangsters and righteous, underpaid federal law enforcement officers — the FBI's starting annual salary in the mid-1950s was $5,500 — was a volatile practice, carrying with it the potential for corruption on a grand scale.

In the late 1960s, rumors about Greg Scarpa Sr. began to percolate through the underworld and the halls of the Federal Bureau of Investigation. There were stories about questionable tactics and behavior, and his uncanny ability to avoid prosecution. Perhaps, it was speculated, Scarpa had been rendered untouchable by the FBI. If true, the rumors would have greatly upset both Scarpa's colleagues in the Mafia and the majority of agents within the bureau. Most law enforcement officers, after all, still believed in doing their jobs the old-fashioned way: through research, investigation, arrests, and prosecution. Programs such as Top Echelon cut to the core of the FBI's philosophy of law enforcement, blurring the lines between good and evil, right and wrong, criminal and cop. To put the rumors to rest, Scarpa's Mafia bosses purposely gave him murder contracts, figuring, quite reasonably, that even the FBI had standards of ethics, and that these standards would preclude permitting an informant to commit the most heinous of crimes: the killing of another human being.

As it turned out, the mob had greatly overestimated the FBI's innate goodness.

"How very wrong the Mafia was," notes Gregory Scarpa. "Dad would go out and kill someone; then, afterward, he would inform his FBI handler of what he had to do and why. His handler would then sway anyone who was investigating the murder to another direction away from my dad. It was the perfect setup."

4
BLIND RAGE

In modern parlance it would probably be said that Greg Scarpa Sr. suffered from an "anger management" disorder. In the Mafia of the 1960s and 1970s, he was merely a powerful man with a bad temper, which wasn't such an unforgivable offense; indeed, a short fuse sometimes came in handy. Usually amiable and laid-back, at least around friends and family, Scarpa was capable of spontaneous violent eruptions. He was always ready for a fight; not surprisingly, he encouraged his son to be the same way. There was, in Scarpa's eyes, no more vital and accurate measure of a man than his ability to defend himself.

"I remember when I was about fifteen, a few of my friends and I got into a fight with some older guys at a bar who had said something disrespectful to us," remembers Gregory Scarpa Jr. "One big guy started choking me until the bar owner came out and pulled the guy off me yelling, 'Are you crazy? Do you know who that kid is?' "

The following day, when Greg Sr. saw the marks on Gregory's neck and learned what had happened, his face turned crimson and his eyes narrowed. He looked hard at his son.

"Come with me right now!"

With the aforementioned bar as their destination, they drove together in silence, father and son, with Scarpa's knuckles tight on the wheel, his eyes staring out the window at the cars whizzing by but his mind clearly focused on something else altogether. Gregory knew what was coming: The only thing left unanswered at this point was the intensity and resolution of the confrontation.

They entered the club together; within a few moments Gregory had fingered the man who had assaulted him the previous night. He was chatting amiably and loosely with a large circle of men, blissfully unaware of what was about to happen. Greg Scarpa Sr. stepped in front of his son and began walking purposefully toward the circle of men. As he approached, their heads turned. Most of them knew exactly who Scarpa was and quickly stepped aside. They may have been friends with the man who had accosted

Scarpa's son, but they weren't willing to die for him. In an instant Scarpa was on the man, raining blows on his head like a prizefighter until the man crumpled to the floor; then Scarpa began kicking him, beating the poor bastard to within an inch of his life.

And then he summoned his son.

"To this day, I have never seen anyone receive a beating like the one this guy got from my father," Gregory remembers. "After the guy was out cold, my dad told me to kick him in the face. I said, 'He's out, Dad.' He then yelled with his deep voice, 'Kick him, I said.' So I did what he told me to do, and then we left."

If Gregory's taste for bloody violence did not yet match his father's, he remained, nonetheless, a tough and passionate fighter. He preferred the boxing ring to the streets; although smallish in stature, he was tough, and had sound tactics, characteristics that helped him win far more often than he lost. Gregory dreamed of winning a national title and eventually becoming a professional boxer. When he was nearly sixteen, he informed his father that he wanted to enter the Golden Gloves tournament, sponsored by the New York *Daily News.* Greg Sr.

responded enthusiastically, hiring Richie Hall, a former boxer, to train his son. For much of the next year, Gregory lived the life of a Spartan, training several hours a day, traveling to gyms, churches, and smoky clubs in search of competition. Greg Sr. rarely missed one of his son's fights, and his presence — screaming, cheering for his son to end each bout with a knockout — was unmistakable.

There was, in Greg Scarpa Sr., a bit of the Great Santini. He was proud of his son's accomplishments and ashamed of his failures and flaws. The notion that another fighter might hurt Gregory in the ring incensed Scarpa on multiple levels. It wasn't just that he couldn't bear to see his son bleed; it was also that the blood represented some weakness on the part of the son, and thus cast an unflattering reflection on the father.

Once, following a bout in which both Gregory and his opponent had landed numerous shots to the head (Gregory lost by decision), he was confronted by his father before he even stepped out of the ring.

"Now go back and break his face in the locker room," Scarpa shouted.

Luckily, the kid had left before Gregory

found him.

Richie Hall wanted Gregory to train extensively at a Brooklyn gym to prepare for the Golden Gloves tournament in late July. Gregory dutifully followed his trainer's prescribed regimen; but if his body was in the gym, his mind often wandered. The daydreaming usually revolved around a girl named Diane Dimino, who lived in Tottenville, a small town five miles away. She was a pretty girl, with long dark hair, a warm smile, and hypnotic blue eyes.

"And a body that could make a guy talk to himself," Gregory adds with a smile.

Lacking a car, Gregory and his friends walked or hopped the train to Tottenville so they could hang out at the candy store or listen to music, or play ball at the high school. Really, though, these were all excuses to be within proximity of Diane. His was a classic teenage infatuation — the first of Gregory's life — and when it hit, it hit hard.

Gregory's father was surprisingly understanding: Shortly after hearing of his son's predicament (lusting after a girl who didn't live within walking distance of their home), Greg Sr. pulled a few strings (attached to Nino Villano, of course) and arranged for his son to get a driver's license, even though he was underage. Before long Gregory was driving to Tottenville in style, behind the wheel of his very own 1968 burnt-orange Corvette convertible. This, too, was a gift from father to son.

When Gregory wasn't with Diane, he usually could be found hanging out with his buddies. They were not exactly Boy Scouts. They drank hard and often, and once sufficiently fueled by alcohol would go off in search of a good fight. Neither did Gregory ever shy away from a confrontation, and the skills he had learned in the gym now served him well in the far less egalitarian world of street fighting. One night, while hanging out with a couple of his friends in a Staten Island club, Gregory and his pals got into an argument with the club's owners. Discretion suggested that the boys keep a safe distance in the future, but Gregory and his friends soon returned, where they were soundly (and predictably) beaten by the owners and a gang of sympathetic thugs.

Again, though, Greg Sr. came to his son's defense with an almost religious zeal, escorting Gregory and his friends, along with a meaty cross section of his Brooklyn crew, to the Staten Island club.

"Dad told me to go into the bar alone and call these guys out to fight," Gregory remembers. "I did what he said, and on the way out, I saw my dad hit one of the guys over the head with a pipe."

Several of the men associated with the club were hurt seriously. Greg Sr. was arrested a few days later and charged with felonious assault. Accounts of the incident reported in New York newspapers referred to Scarpa as a Mafia capo. Both the arrest and the publicity surrounding the incident worried Gregory. But not his father. Greg Sr. told his son not to be concerned. "Nino will take care of everything," he said. And, in fact, ultimately the charges were dropped. As always, Greg Scarpa remained a free man.

Eventually Gregory got a chance to meet his father's benefactor. It happened on the way home from one of his boxing matches, at a Chinese restaurant on Staten Island. There, Greg Sr. introduced Gregory to Anthony Villano, a good-looking, well-dressed man whom he identified as Nino, "my boss at the FBI."

Villano played along smoothly, setting Gregory at ease by chatting with him about the teen's favorite subjects: sports and girls. Then, surprisingly, he told Gregory that he had been ringside at his fight that evening. Nino complimented the boy, told him he moved well and seemed to have a pretty good understanding of the sport. He was tough, too, which was important for any aspiring champion. But the truth, Villano told him, was that the world was filled with talented, hungry boxers, and that the odds were deeply stacked against Gregory rising to the top of the heap. And anyway, he said with a shrug, there are easier, less painful ways to make a living. A good living.

"Like what?" Gregory asked.

"Like working secretly for the FBI," Villano said. He paused and smiled, and nodded toward Greg Sr. "Just the way your dad does."

Villano continued to flatter the kid. He could tell by watching Gregory in the ring that he had the right stuff to work for the federal government — right alongside his father. You'll be helping your country, Nino said. And you can get rich in the process.

Gregory thought a lot about what Villano had told him that night, and soon decided to put boxing on the back burner. Almost all of his free time — and there was an abundance of it now — was spent with Diane.

"That," Gregory recalls, "was one of my first mistakes."

With no formal outlet for his aggression

and anger, Gregory began fighting on a more recreational basis, with predictably disastrous consequences. After school one day he got into a fight with a classmate who had been disrespectful toward Gregory's sister, Debbie. (This, of course, was an offense that could not go unpunished in the Scarpa household.) The brawl ended only when police intervened, although no arrests were made. Afterward, Debbie and Gregory snuck into the house and went to the basement, where Debbie applied ice to Gregory's forehead. That evening, when Greg Sr. came down to say hello, he saw the bump on Gregory's head and became enraged. Not concerned, as most parents might be, but furious.

"Gregory, tomorrow, when you go to school and when you see this guy," he said, "whether it is inside, outside, the principal's office, I don't care where — if you don't send him to the hospital, don't come home."

Gregory did not question his father's authority, nor the wisdom behind his order. He simply nodded and promised to do precisely as he was told. The next day Gregory tracked down the kid and beat him so badly that the boy required hospitalization for his injuries. Gregory was suspended from school, arrested, and charged with assault. Although the charges were later dropped, Gregory never returned to school.

Not that this bothered him in the least. He wasn't much of a student anyway, and, practically speaking, he felt it was a waste of time. Now that he had lost interest in boxing, his goal was to enlist in the Army. At a time when most young men were trying to figure out ways to avoid the draft, Gregory wanted nothing more than to wear the uniform of the United States into the jungles of Southeast Asia — despite the fact that one of his cousins had been drafted and killed in Vietnam. Far from being deterred or frightened by his death, Gregory clung to the notion that military service — particularly in a time of war — was noble, and that somehow he might avenge his cousin's death.

Interestingly enough, this view was not shared by Greg Scarpa Sr. Whether he disagreed with the war in Vietnam on some political or philosophical level (unlikely) or simply wanted to shield his oldest son from the battlefield (more likely), Scarpa used all of his considerable influence to ensure that Gregory would never serve in the military. Ignoring his son's desires, and utilizing the services of a corruptible Brooklyn physician whose name he had gotten from Villano,

Scarpa managed to have Gregory diagnosed (though he was never actually seen by the doctor) with back and knee problems that precluded service in the Army. Gregory's draft classification was altered to 1-Y, meaning he could only be drafted in the event of a national emergency.

With few other available options, Gregory entered the family business and began working for his father. His job description was unusual and came with a lengthy period of apprenticeship. Really, in the early months, Gregory was expected to do nothing more than hang out at Wimpy Boys, demonstrating, in the process, that he was capable not only of the friendly banter that helped mobsters pass the day, but of keeping a secret as well. In reality, of course, secrets were shared with his father.

"Everything you learn, you bring to me," Greg Sr. said. Gregory was happy to oblige. All his life he had wanted to be like his dad — to have his father's trust and respect. Now the opportunity had presented itself. That the fulfillment of this promise involved dangerous, duplicitous, soul-crushing work was not even a mild deterrent.

Less enthusiastic about Gregory's indoctrination into "the life" was his mother. Connie wanted something more for her oldest son — a better and safer life, if not necessarily a more prosperous one. But Greg Sr. assuaged her fears with a promise to look after their son — and an assurance that Nino Villano would take care of him as well.

"My mom still didn't agree," says Gregory, somewhat wistfully. "But there was absolutely nothing she could do but go along with Dad."

5
THE EDUCATION OF A
WISEGUY

Wimpy Boys became Gregory's second home. With almost preternatural ease, he slipped into the wiseguy's routine, hanging out with the crew, sharing jokes and stories, partying, fighting, flexing muscle when necessary. For six days a week, from Monday through Saturday, this was Gregory's life. On Sunday he reported back to his father; in turn, Greg Sr. would either use the information for his own benefit, or pass it on to Nino Villano. To protect his son from the mob, Scarpa never permitted Gregory to meet personally with Villano (aside from their initial introduction); rather, the father acted as intermediary, prioritizing information and placing a dollar figure on its value.

Gregory was a quick learner. He figured out the basics of running a numbers game in just a few months, and soon assumed stewardship of his father's racket. It was a relatively small operation, and Greg Sr. liked it that way; to Gregory, though, it seemed as though he had stumbled upon buried treasure.

"On average," recalls Gregory, "my dad cleared ten thousand dollars a week; eventually, when I began to control the whole numbers racket, which meant that I added up the work every night, my dad told me to take out approximately two thousand dollars a week for myself. To me, that was a lot of money. I mean, I was seventeen years old."

Gregory, as smitten as a teenage boy could be, spent most of his cash on Diane.

"I was so in love with her," he remembers. "She was a virgin, and she wasn't giving me anything but hugs, kisses, and smiles . . . but she was so beautiful, and so much fun to hang out with, I didn't care. Throughout that first year we were dating, I bought her lots of gold and diamond jewelry. I would have given her the world if I could."

As much as he enjoyed hanging out at Wimpy Boys and collecting easy money, Gregory couldn't wait to leave each afternoon so that he could rush over to Diane's house. When he was with her, he felt like a different person. He fantasized sometimes about leading a more normal existence, a nine-to-five life, perhaps, with little kids and a nice house. It bothered Gregory that his father sometimes seemed to be an extraordinarily mean and violent man — especially as someone who supposedly was working with the federal authorities.

"He would yell at people who owed him money and didn't pay on time," recalls Gregory. "He would also hit and beat up someone or have one or two other guys do it for him. I also heard conversations about my dad killing people. I was surprised at what I was hearing, because I thought we were with the FBI."

The rumors of bloodshed — of murder — became persistent, and they sickened Gregory. Eventually he summoned the courage to confront his father.

"Is it true?" he asked. "Are you a murderer?"

Scarpa smiled, and for a moment Gregory's stomach loosened. He prepared for his father to tell him that everything was all right, that he had never killed anyone. Remember — he was one of the good guys. Instead, Scarpa's smile gave way to a laugh — a boisterous, dismissive, full-throated cackle.

"The feds are fine with my murders, as long as we keep giving them good information," he said. "Don't worry about it."

So there it was. As a top echelon informant, Greg Scarpa quite literally had a license to kill. And he was more than willing to use it. Moreover, he no longer felt any need to hide the "truth" from Gregory.

They were a team now: father and son. School, officially, was in session.

"He showed me how he killed people," remembers Gregory. "He told me he would always put a bullet right behind the ear. He seemed to enjoy telling me this. He seemed to be bragging."

Gregory was glad when the conversation was over, although it never left his mind. Thoughts of the victims interrupted his conversations during the day; images flashed through his mind and sparked nightmares when he fell asleep.

Angst notwithstanding, Gregory made no effort to slash the cord that bonded him to his father and the strange, violent world they inhabited. Instead, Gregory's immersion deepened, and became more complex. As with any corporate enterprise, Scarpa's fifty-person crew was populated by men who possessed a broad array of "talents." About ten men were pure killers, on call whenever a hit was required. The order to kill was most often issued by Scarpa; sometimes, purely for pleasure (or because he was good at it), Scarpa carried out the execution himself. More than a dozen other members of the crew could be classified as shylocks (or loan sharks). Greg Sr. would seed a bankroll for each of them with approximately $80,000. His job was to push the money onto the street — to engage desperate, cash-poor souls in a partnership that was certain to end badly for the borrower. Typically, this meant lending money to people who could not possibly procure a loan from a traditional source (such as a bank), and charging an exorbitant interest rate.

"If Dad gave a shylock $10,000, he would have to pay my dad $100 a week and always owe the principle of $10,000," explains Gregory. "The shylocks would then push it out for three to five points, which means that at four points, the shylock would be collecting $400 a week, give my dad his $100, and make $300 a week."

Some of the hired killers in Scarpa's crew also doubled as drug dealers or shylocks. Some were merely muscle, adept at collecting cash either through threats and intimidation or, failing that, by breaking a limb or two. The crew also employed a handful of auto specialists who reaped enormous profits by stealing high-end, late-model cars, altering their vehicle ID numbers, procuring new license plates, and selling them to wholesalers. There were electronics specialists — engineers without degrees, really — who could defuse and deactivate almost any alarm system, enabling the crew to rob banks and retail establishments.

Another group specialized in hijacking trucks and tractor trailers; in this the crew captured and resold great quantities of TVs, VCRs, coffee, and designer clothes. Gregory often helped unload the hijacked cargo at the warehouse and then load it onto smaller trucks and vans for delivery.

"I was given $1,500 to $2,000 a truck while the actual hijacking crew was making $5,000 to $10,000 a truck," says Gregory. "Often Nino would be on the lookout, and would warn us if police were nearby."

But Villano sometimes went even further than merely warning the crew. There was the night, for example, that they intercepted a tractor trailer carrying a full load of J&B Scotch. Gregory had just finished helping unload the last few cases at the warehouse docks when a fleet of some two dozen state law enforcement officers crashed into the crew's getaway vans, imploding the scene, splattering glass and scotch throughout the area, but ensuring that multiple arrests would be made.

Leading the raid was a detective assigned to the squad of then Manhattan district attorney Elizabeth Holtzman. Greg Sr. quietly offered the detective a bribe on the spot; the detective, however, demurred. "Too many big shots in the neighborhood," he whispered. "Let's settle it later."

They met in a public place — a casual neighborhood bar. Scarpa, with a microphone and a yard of wire taped to his torso with adhesive tape, compliments of Villano, calmly chatted with the detective for a few minutes, shared a couple of drinks, and then invited the detective to meet him in the men's room, where they could continue their conversation in private. One would think that the detective, an experienced law enforcement officer, might have known better, might have suspected something was amiss. But greed apparently got the better of him, as he accepted Scarpa's terms for a deal — including a quiet exchange of cash from the mobster to the cop. The next day Nino Villano visited the compromised detective and told him that Scarpa had been wired. The detective, of course, was stunned, but utterly helpless. Shortly thereafter, the hijacking and possession charges were thrown out of court on a "technicality." In reality, of course, this was merely a euphemism; cases against high-level informants were often dropped on technicalities, either because the benefits of keeping the informant on the street outweighed the benefits of locking him up, or because someone in a position of authority stood to gain by ensuring the informant's freedom.

One might reasonably wonder why Anthony Villano, a respected, long-tenured FBI agent, would go to such lengths to help and protect a known killer such as Greg Scarpa Sr. Certainly financial gain played a role in this process, but there is a more complex subtext. Michael Levine, a thirty-five-year veteran of the Drug Enforcement Administration who has written two best-selling nonfiction books, *Deep Cover* and *The Big White Lie,* and who has testified extensively on relationships such as the one that existed between Scarpa and Villano, offers a suggestion.

"As a street agent and as a supervisor, one of the biggest problems was agents falling in love with informants," says Levine. "They [the agents] literally become part of the crime. It's just flat-out conspiracy. Agents often work long hours at low pay in dangerous surroundings for little appreciation, and can rationalize that accepting a gift or a loan from an informant is okay."

But, of course, it isn't okay. It's merely that the twisted, symbiotic relationship of the informant and the law enforcement officer wreaks havoc on the emotions and the ethics of a cop.

"The illegal use of sleazy criminal informants is tantamount to firemen starting fires to get themselves headlines," adds Levine. "It has made a mockery of the justice system and costs the taxpayers tens of billions each year. With protectors like these, who needs enemies?"

Gregory, meanwhile, found himself sinking deeper into the muck of the family enterprise. Confident and comfortable in his new surroundings, he developed close friendships with many of the guys who hung out at Wimpy Boys. Some he already knew — they were the same men who had divided up cash and jewelry with his father at the Scarpa home on Staten Island. But now he was no longer a kid looking in from the outside; he was part of the crew. Despite the friendships, Gregory's primary function — and he was told never to lose sight of this — was to absorb as much information as possible about not only the crew and the various factions of the Colombo family, but the entire five crime families as well, and then report any developments or changes to his father. Scarpa, in turn, kept the FBI up to speed.

In many ways Greg Scarpa was the ultimate mercenary, a solitary, amoral gangster with no allegiance to anyone but himself. The FBI for the most part turned a blind eye to the criminal activity of Scarpa's crew; only when it would have appeared obvious that something was amiss if they did not act aggressively did law enforcement officers create trouble for Scarpa's gang. Consequently, most of the crew took little pinches for minor crimes, and many of them did short bids in jail. While still in his teens, for example, Gregory did three months in the Brooklyn House of Detention on Atlantic Avenue for possession of a stolen car. He had been apprehended with the vehicle in his possession — red-handed, as it were — so rather than waste a favor from Villano and the FBI, Greg Sr. told his son he would have to bite the bullet. Gregory dutifully did as he was told, keeping his mouth shut during his entire sentence. Anyway, it was a rite of passage for a mobster to spend a few months (or years) behind bars, and now Gregory had been properly indoctrinated. If anything, the bid only served to enhance his reputation and deflect any suspicion that he or his father might have been cooperating with the feds.

6

THE PRINCESS OF BENSONHURST

Although Greg Scarpa Sr. was a married man with four children, he believed, like most wiseguys, that it was practically his birthright to have as many girlfriends on the side as he deemed appropriate. What was life without a "gumare" (or two — or three)? It was important to raise a family and to support a wife — to provide a safe and secure shelter. But a man had needs, and if a wiseguy was willing to risk his life to put food on the table, well, didn't he deserve to have a little fun once in a while, too?

Debbie recalls being a teenager and running into her father one evening when he was out with one of his girlfriends. "Don't call me dad," he had whispered shamelessly. "Call me Greg." Implicit in this reaction was the belief that Debbie would play along — that she would understand. It didn't mean that her father didn't love her, or that he was going to run off and leave the family behind. It was about sex, and nothing more.

But when Scarpa met Linda Diana in the summer of 1964 at the Flamingo Lounge, a Bensonhurst club that he had just opened, Scarpa took one look at her and found himself shaken from his moorings. Linda was barely seventeen years old, five-foot-five, and slim and fit, with a button nose, sparkling eyes, and a happy laugh. Dangerously, intoxicatingly attractive, she was the kind of woman that men and boys fought over (and, indeed, she liked having them fight for her affections). They found her irresistible and showered her with gifts and attention. The lovesick, hormone-crazed teens of Bensonhurst could barely summon the courage to speak when Linda was in their midst. Not that it mattered; they had neither the cash nor the cachet to win her affections. Linda knew what she wanted out of life, and she knew how to get it, so she routinely dated "up," in terms of both age and social standing. In Bensonhurst, the men who qualified were wiseguys, men in their thirties, even forties, who knew how to treat a beautiful girl, and how to throw cash around in a way that would impress her.

Linda was a climber; she was also a survivor, having endured a tough, poverty-stricken childhood. She had been raised by her parents in an unhealthy, claustrophobic setting ruled by an abusive, alcoholic grandfather (her father's father) who would drink mightily, and chase after anyone who came through his door. It was the grandfather's home, and he ran it like a sadistic king. Linda was the only one in the family who was not afraid of him. She merely hated the man.

Linda was eleven years old when she dropped out of school to stay at home and help care for her mother, who had been diagnosed with terminal stomach cancer. The family lacked the funds for any sort of long-term private care, so Linda's mom had been discharged from a hospital and sent home to die. Linda sat by her bed in the living room, day after day, holding her mother's hand and listening to her anguished cries, wishing that she could do something to relieve her pain. That feeling of helplessness, born of poverty and abuse, never left her, and indeed became the driving force in Linda's life.

Shy and withdrawn until her teenage years, Linda became, in her adolescence, a wild and unpredictable young woman — one who lived as if every day might be her last. She gave up her virginity to a neighborhood boy when she was fourteen, and found that she enjoyed sex. She liked the way it made her feel when a boy held her in his arms; she liked the power and control it offered. Linda was naturally attracted to bad boys, and began hanging out with a motorcycle crowd. She loved the feeling of riding on the back of a bike, of roaring down the streets of Brooklyn, the wind in her face, the road dangerously close to her feet. Even then, however, Linda knew that they were merely a prelude — small-time toughs and hoods who lacked either the brains or the balls (or the bank accounts) to provide her with the life she desired.

Linda had been attracted to wiseguys all her life. The neighborhood mobsters would sometimes shoot craps in the back hall of her maternal grandmother's house, which was also in the neighborhood. Grandma was a piece of work: a widow; a devout Catholic who worked the six o'clock mass every morning of her life — and a numbers runner. Linda would pick up the numbers from her grandmother at the church in the morning and drop them off at a local pool hall at night.

The pool hall was an intoxicating place to Linda, with its musky air of smoke and power. Wiseguys from the Colombo and

Gambino crime families hung out there on a regular basis. They favored expensive suits and fancy jewelry; they drove nice cars and spent money freely, as if it spouted from a ceaseless well. These men filled Linda's dreams and fantasies. She had returned to school after her mother died, but quit for good at the age of sixteen, when she lost all interest in algebra and geometry — and anything else she deemed too abstract to be of relevance to her life.

After her grandfather sold the house, Linda, her dad, and her older sister Mary-anne moved into a small apartment. Impatient to join the adult world, Linda took a job as a clerk typist for a Wall Street brokerage firm, earning forty dollars a week. The pay, obviously, wasn't great, but that was alright. The job was merely a vehicle, she had been assured by her sister, Maryanne, that there was no shortage of rich, eligible bachelors on Wall Street.

And, in fact, it wasn't long before the money men were lining up for a chance to compete for Linda's affections. She briefly dated a very nice (and very wealthy) stockbroker whose apartment overlooking Central Park had a foyer larger than Linda's home. He treated Linda well, taking her to nice restaurants, and spoiling her with expensive gifts. But she found him physically unattractive, and their relationship was never consummated. Later, she dated one of the firm's partners. He was even wealthier, and just as cordial and respectful, and Linda got the sense that he might even be falling in love with her, and perhaps might one day propose marriage. Again, however, there was no spark for Linda, no passion, and soon she put an end to their relationship.

So despite where she worked, and despite the affections of wealthy suitors, Linda remained a poor girl from Brooklyn. Most of her meager salary was passed on to her father. Lacking the resources to buy new outfits, she borrowed dresses from Mary-anne, or from her friend Annie, whose father owned a Bensonhurst poolroom.

A lot of wiseguys hung out at the poolroom. Sometimes they visited Annie's father at his house; it was during one of these visits that Linda met Larry Pistone, a married big shot in the Gambino family. Larry had a well-deserved reputation for being tough and vicious. Violent confrontations were his forte, and he never shied away from conducting business, regardless of the audience. On more than one occasion he beat down men who were delinquent on their payments — in full view of their spouses and children.

A curious thing about mobsters, though: They often keep the darker side of their personalities (and their work) hidden from those they love. Pistone was unfailingly polite and gracious to Linda. Among the fronts for his illicit enterprises was a butcher shop, and Pistone frequently brought the finest cuts of the day for Linda and her family: filet mignon and sirloin — the choicest meats — the ones her father could never afford. Larry also kept a boat docked at Sheepshead Bay; on weekends and evenings, he and Linda would go there to escape the withering summer heat and humidity. Thanks to Larry's influence and wealth, Linda became a fixture at trendy Manhattan restaurants and nightclubs such as the Copacabana and the Peppermint Lounge. Some stealth was required for a teenager to live this sort of exotic life, but Linda was nothing if not resourceful. Usually nothing more was required than a simple lie to her father: "I'm saying at Annie's house tonight, okay?" Dad was often too tired, and loved his daughter too much, to argue or investigate. Linda was seventeen going on thirty, and she found herself enormously attracted to Larry and the lifestyle he provided.

Moreover, she found him physically attractive, and before long the two of them were involved in a romantic relationship. That Linda was still not yet a legal adult was of no concern to either one of them.

If, on some level, Linda was falling for Larry Pistone, she remained a free spirit nonetheless. On opening night at the Flamingo Lounge, Linda was in the crowd, enjoying a night out with Annie. The atmosphere was exciting, intoxicating. Go-go girls danced on a small stage; music and cigarette smoke filled the hall; well-dressed men threw money around with reckless abandon. Seated at the bar were two men Linda recognized: They were regulars at the pool hall where she and Annie hung out; they were also friends of Linda's father. The girls knew the men only by their nicknames: "Sonny Squint" and "Linguine." As Linguine was doing his best to flirt with Linda, Greg Scarpa Sr. walked into the club. Linda spotted him instantly. He was tall and handsome, with thick hair and olive skin. Linda was transfixed. She stared at Scarpa until she caught his eye. Finally, while shaking hands and moving elegantly, smoothly through the crowd, Scarpa spotted Linda. He gave her a big smile and immediately began walking in her direction.

Sonny Squint, who ran numbers for Scarpa, quickly introduced Greg Sr. to the two young women. Greg Sr. bought each of them a drink.

"So what do you do?" he asked Linda.

"Oh, I work on Wall Street," she said, trying to instill an unmerited measure of importance into her forty-dollars-a-week job. Scarpa, of course, knew better, but didn't let on. He merely listened and nodded attentively as Linda raved about the excitement of Wall Street and complained about the long, sweaty, daily commute from her home in Brooklyn.

Scarpa smiled. "If you were with me, I'd air-condition your subway car." Linda laughed like a nervous schoolgirl. Although he was old enough to be her father, she found Scarpa extremely attractive. And clearly the feeling was mutual.

"You have eyes like black olives," Scarpa said at one point. "So dark and beautiful."

"Oh, I never heard that line before," Linda replied, laughing.

The truth was — she hadn't. At least, not from anyone whose opinion mattered.

As Sinatra sang on the jukebox, Linda asked Greg Sr. to dance. The mobster was unaccustomed to such initiative on the part

of a woman — especially one so young —
but he didn't mind in the least. With a
disarming smile, he took Linda's hand in
his and led her onto the dance floor. They
danced slowly, gently, romantically, with
Scarpa singing along softly. Linda felt
herself moving her body closer to his as they
swayed gently to the music, content to be in
his arms.

Scarpa drove Linda home at the end of
the evening and asked for her telephone
number.

"No, you give me yours," Linda countered. If this seemed like merely a bit of the
mating dance — acting coy on the first date
— it was actually something else entirely.
Linda figured, quite reasonably, that Larry
Pistone probably wouldn't like the idea of
Linda dancing with Greg Scarpa Sr. at the
Flamingo; certainly he'd be unhappy to hear
that she had given Scarpa her phone number — an act of implied intimacy.

Scarpa seemed disappointed by Linda's
reluctance, but acquiesced anyway. He
withdrew a pack of matches from his jacket
and wrote down his phone number. Then
he gave it to Linda.

She looked at the number and smiled.

"I'll call you," she said. "Promise."

True to her word, Linda contacted Greg

Sr. a few days later, and the two of them arranged to have dinner at Romano's, an old-world Italian restaurant not far from Scarpa's club. Not normally one to drop his guard quite so quickly, Greg Sr. found himself so captivated by Linda that he began sharing his deepest desires. She had been haunting his dreams, he explained. When he closed his eyes at night, he saw her face, staring down at him. Linda reached across the table and touched his hand. In that moment, he seemed almost vulnerable.

After dinner they went to the Flamingo, where Scarpa introduced her to several members of his crew, including the Sapanaro brothers, John and Joseph (they were known, of course, as Johnny Sap and Joey Sap); Nicky Bianco; Bobby Zambardi; and Fat Jo-Jo. The men all admired Linda's radiant beauty, and Greg Sr. beamed proudly in her presence. The guys in the crew — killers and burglars and drug dealers — could see that their boss had fallen hard for the new girl. And they didn't blame him one bit.

In the early morning hours, when Linda arrived home, she was surprised to find her father awake, sitting at the kitchen table. He'd been waiting up for her.

"What's wrong, Daddy?" Linda asked, trying to sound as though she hadn't done anything wrong.

Her father waited a long time before responding. Then he told Linda about a recent conversation he'd had with Sonny Squint — something about Linda dating a gangster (a married gangster, no less!) named Greg. Linda shook her head. Then she embraced her father. Sonny Squint, she said, was a damn liar. Yeah, she'd met a nice, older man, but he wasn't married and he wasn't a mobster. His name was George, and he was as sweet and good-natured as a puppy dog.

And that was all Linda's father needed to hear. Whether he believed her or not was irrelevant. He wanted to believe. And that was enough.

From that day on, Greg Scarpa Sr. became "George" to Linda's family. Lavish, overflowing baskets of fruit and bouquets of flowers would arrive at the house; invariably they would be accompanied by a thoughtful card signed by a man named George. Linda's father accepted the gifts at face value, and never trafficked in skepticism.

"You really hit the jackpot," he'd say to Linda. "That George sure is a great guy."

But he wasn't the only guy.

Linda secretly and separately maintained

relationships with both Larry Pistone and Greg Sr. Oddly enough, she continued to have sex with Pistone but wouldn't allow Greg Sr. to make love to her. Why? The longing — the anticipation — made them both feel like kids. Greg Sr. and Linda took long walks in the park, held hands, and shared previously untold secrets. Although they made out in his car, Scarpa never pushed Linda into having sex. Although impulsive by nature and impatient in most other aspects of his life, he was willing to wait for Linda. One night he said, "You know, sweetheart, when you're ready to make love to me, just tell me you want to get drunk."

Linda laughed. "You got it."

There was something exciting about balancing two relationships — keeping two men happy while never letting on that the other existed. For a while, Linda pulled it off without a hitch, until one Friday night, while leaving the Copacabana with Larry Pistone, the couple was confronted by Pistone's wife.

Most wiseguys' wives knew what was going on behind their backs. As long as the mafioso was discreet and didn't do something stupid (like fall in love with his gu-

mare, or, God forbid, run off with her), no
one seemed to mind too much. But Mrs.
Pistone was a philandering husband's nightmare. Rather than turn a blind eye to
Larry's affairs, she followed him to the
Copa, then waited outside for him to emerge
with his girlfriend. There, with Pistone's
mob buddies (and their gumares) looking
on in horror, Mrs. Pistone threw a temper
tantrum in front of Larry's Brooklyn mob
cronies and their girlfriends.

Linda stayed just long enough to hear Pistone's wife call her a whore; humiliated by
the spectacle, she flagged down a cab and
went straight to the Flamingo Lounge. She
rushed inside, found Greg Sr., and began
unburdening herself of her secrets. She told
Scarpa all about her relationship with Larry
Pistone. She told him what had happened
at the Copacabana. To her relief, Scarpa
seemed remarkably understanding. In fact,
he seemed moved by her confession — it
was almost as if it had brought them closer.

Later that night, as Scarpa drove Linda
home, they ran into Larry Pistone. He had
been searching for Linda, and now that he
had found her, he wasn't about to let her
run off. Pistone knew of Scarpa's reputation, of course, but he didn't care. Embold-
ened by alcohol, furious at having been

embarrassed by his wife, he projected an almost suicidal air of defiance.

"Get out of the car," he instructed Linda.

Scarpa leaned forward and reached beneath the seat of his car, where he always kept a baseball bat. Linda, sensing something horrible about to happen (and feeling responsible for it as well), suddenly began to weep. She begged Scarpa to remain calm, to ignore Pistone's rage.

Just about any other time Scarpa would have beaten Pistone bloody. But with Linda by his side, imploring him, begging him, he softened. With one hand on the bat and the other on the steering wheel, he cursed at Pistone, who finally (and fortunately) drove away. As the taillights of Pistone's car faded in the distance, Greg Sr. pulled Linda close and brushed away her tears.

"Be my girl," he said. "I'll take care of you."

Linda nodded, tucked her body into the crook of Scarpa's arm. For the first time in memory — maybe for the first time in her life — she felt safe.

7
SCARPA'S MISTRESS

When it came to keeping his gumare at a safe and manageable distance, Greg Scarpa proved to be an utter failure. In reality, Linda was the great love of Scarpa's life, and their relationship can be viewed as proof that even mobsters and killers are subject to human frailties and emotions.

Their bond was cemented one evening as they sat together at the Flamingo Lounge. When Linda stared at Greg Sr., holding court as usual, she felt an overwhelming surge of desire and passion. So Linda smiled at Greg, put her arms around his neck, and whispered in his ear, "Let's get drunk." He smiled back, nodded, and kissed her gently.

A few hours later they checked into the Lincoln Hotel on Staten Island; at once nervous and excited — like teenagers on their first date — they toasted each other with champagne, smoked a little weed to ease the tension, and began to make love.

Greg Sr. tried to take his time, but when he started to penetrate Linda, he came too quickly. For a man who prided himself on control and patience, this was a disturbing and embarrassing development, and Scarpa did not hide his disappointment.

"After all this time," he said, "I can't believe that happened."

Linda merely smiled and pulled him close.

"Don't worry," she said. "We have the rest of our lives."

The tender intimacy of this moment was short-lived, as Linda suddenly realized something was wrong. Even in a dimly lit hotel room, she could see the blood, and the sight caused her heart to race. Frightened, she ran into the bathroom to get some towels, but the menstrual flow was so heavy now that she began to feel light-headed.

"What's wrong, baby?" Scarpa asked when she emerged from the bathroom.

"Take me home," Linda answered. "Please."

Linda spent the night in the bathroom of her apartment, trying unsuccessfully to stanch the flow of blood. The next morning, after wobbling into her bedroom and passing out, she was discovered by her father, who picked her up, put her in the car, and drove her to the hospital. There, of course, Linda received the news that she had both feared and anticipated: The bleeding had been caused by a miscarriage. As it turned out, Linda had been nearly three months into a pregnancy, the result of her relationship with Pistone.

When she awoke from the dilation and curettage medical procedure, the first person Linda saw was Scarpa. He stood at the side of her bed, tears welling in his eyes.

"I understand what happened," he told her. "And I don't want you to worry about anything. I'll take care of you."

By this time Scarpa had already paid the hospital bill.

Rather than return to her apartment, Linda recuperated at the home of her sister, Maryanne, who had recently married, and her brother-in-law, Morris. Greg Sr. called often and sent flowers nearly every day. Eventually Linda felt well enough to agree to a lunch date. When Scarpa pulled up outside in a late-model Cadillac, Maryanne was practically speechless. She watched as Scarpa slowly emerged from the car and snuffed out a cigarette. He was attired elegantly, his skin bronzed, and the brim of his fedora adjusted perfectly.

"Oh, God," Maryanne said, putting a hand to her mouth and trying to stifle a laugh. "He looks like a gangster."

Linda smiled, and nodded. "He is — and by the way, his name is Greg."

Scarpa's visits became more frequent. He'd bring her flowers, jewelry, sometimes even malted milk shakes ("I'm trying to fatten her up," Scarpa joked) to help Linda regain her strength. One evening, while dropping Linda off at her sister's house, they saw Larry Pistone's car parked in front. Pistone wasted little time in confronting his wayward girlfriend.

"I thought I told you to stay away from Scarpa," he shouted.

This was not the type of thing one did in front of a man like Greg Scarpa Sr. — unless, of course, one possessed a secret death wish. But Scarpa barely had time to react, since Linda immediately jumped to her own defense.

"Shut up, Larry!" she yelled. "It's all over between us! Leave me alone! I'm with Greg now."

If only things were decided so easily and swiftly (and bloodlessly) in the Mafia. Two made men from competing crime families embroiled in a dispute over a beautiful young woman — was there a more volatile situation? Or one that was worse for business? Linda might have been laboring under the impression that she was free to choose her paramours. To mob elders, however, the young woman's feelings and concerns were among the very least important factors. They cared about one thing: money. If the machinery of mob business was threatened by the jealousies of two high-ranking mafiosos, then no one stood to gain. A peaceful, reasoned solution was required.

To that end, Scarpa and Pistone were summoned to a meeting (a "sit-down") with the heads of the Gambino and Colombo families to settle their beef over Linda. Hostilities provoked by territoriality regarding women was nothing new to the mob; indeed, throughout history men have fought battles large and small over the affections of beautiful women. The Mafia, however, had long prided itself on encouraging rational thinking when passion raised its ugly head. This, however, was a particularly delicate situation: the first time that two senior members of major gangs had threatened to come to blows over a teenager. In every way, it was an ugly, dangerous situation, and one that required careful disposition.

In the end, it was neither strength nor seniority that won the day for Greg Scarpa, but rather an ability to convince family leaders that his love for Linda was genuine. The

Mafia bosses officially ruled that only Scarpa would be permitted to date Linda, a decision that thrilled both of them.

To celebrate their victory, Greg Sr. bought Linda a new Buick Riviera and encouraged her to quit her job so that he could take care of her. She did. She also moved back in with her father. On her eighteenth birthday Greg Sr. gave her a beautiful gold bracelet inscribed with the words "I love you 4 Ever, G," and then took her to the Copacabana. He invited a group of friends to share the celebration. A dozen of Greg Sr.'s pals, including Joe Colombo, the titular head of the crime family, joined them at a table filled with flowers and champagne as they listened to singer Tom Jones. Linda was now officially Scarpa's girlfriend, and his friends acknowledged their relationship by presenting her with gifts — envelopes stuffed with cash, for the most part.

Less sanguine about Scarpa's victory was Linda's father; upon learning that his daughter's new beau was not merely a handsome older gentleman named "George," but rather the notorious Mafia gangster Greg Scarpa Sr., Linda's dad was outraged. A man of limited means who wasted a large portion of his meager salary betting on the ponies, Linda's father was at once envious of Scarpa and frightened of him; mainly, he feared for Linda's safety. Again, though, Scarpa proved remarkably adept at winning the affections of someone who at first seemed skeptical. He shared a few drinks with Linda's dad, bought a few things for their home, gave him some tips on picking winners at the track, and generally ingratiated himself in a way that surprised even Linda's father. How bad could he be, this smiling, charming pied piper of a gangster?

Soon enough, Scarpa became a fixture at Linda's home, so comfortable in his surroundings, and so sure of the family's allegiance, that on one occasion he would use her apartment as a temporary warehouse for stolen goods.

Linda's father arrived home from work one evening and discovered that he couldn't gain access to his own living room — the door had been wedged shut. With some effort he pried it open just a crack, and then peered into the room, where, to his shock and dismay, he discovered dozens of large boxes. At the center of the great pile of swag was Linda, smiling beatifically.

"What in the hell is this?!" her father yelled.

"Calm down, Daddy," Linda responded.

"They're color TVs." Linda ran a hand along the top of one of the boxes, then smiled at her father. "Greg says you should pick one out for yourself."

And that was that. Like most everyone else who stood in Greg Scarpa's way, Linda's father had become an obstacle cleared. Sometimes, Scarpa knew, charm worked as well as muscle.

Scarpa would stop by late at night and they would lie in her bed together and make love. Linda was young, beautiful, and passionate, as unbridled and desirable as any woman he'd known. Certainly she stood in marked contrast to Scarpa's wife, Connie. Scarpa had once taken Connie to a hotel in an attempt to break the routine of their love life. She reacted with dismay: "Why in the world would you want to waste money on a hotel room when we have a perfectly good bed at home?"

And so he turned to Linda, who was not only young and beautiful, but appreciative of such gestures. That the lifestyle he provided was funded by crime and violence was a trivial detail, one that excited her. Once, Greg Sr. and his crew had broken into a bank vault and came to Linda's apartment late at night, dumping three large canvas sacks of cash and jewels onto the dining-room table, and admiring and evaluating everything before turning it over to be fenced.

As Greg Sr. sorted through the gems, remarking on the continued good fortune of his hardworking crew, he held a man's ring up to the light. It was large and encrusted with diamonds, almost ostentatious in its girth. Suddenly he paused and frowned.

"Damn it," Scarpa snarled. "We can't keep this one."

"Why not?" Linda asked.

"Because it belongs to Whitey Ford."

Indeed, this was no ordinary bauble, but a World Series ring engraved with the name of the great New York Yankees left-handed pitcher. This was 1964, when the Yankees owned New York, and Ford was among the finest players in baseball; he was, in fact, Scarpa's favorite ballplayer.

"We have to send it back," Scarpa said, tucking the ring into his pocket, illustrating, once again, that mobsters live by their own particular, peculiar code of conduct. (It should be noted, however, that Whitey Ford says he never recovered the original stolen ring; instead, a new one was later provided by Yankees owner George Steinbrenner.)

Another evening, when Linda was home

alone waiting for Scarpa to arrive, detectives broke through the front door.

"Where is he?" they shouted. "We know he's here."

When Greg Sr. walked in and saw the detectives, he laughed and asked, "What the hell is going on?"

"We've got you now," said one of the detectives.

Scarpa didn't even blink. While other detectives ransacked the apartment, apparently in a haphazard search for evidence of some random criminal misdeeds, Scarpa calmly opened a desk drawer and withdrew a small, black, leatherbound notebook. With a smile, he reached out and opened the jacket of one of the detectives, and then slid the notebook into the cop's breast pocket.

"See me tomorrow," Scarpa said with a wink.

The following day the cop and the gangster met for lunch. Scarpa traded a stack of money for the notebook, the pages of which included detailed information about his numbers racket. The amazed detective thanked Scarpa, and added, "If you ever decide to teach a class, let me know. I want to be the first one there."

Everything Scarpa did for Linda — and the

laundry list of favors included showering her with gifts (stolen and legitimate); fixing a beauty contest in which she was a contestant; arranging a fashion modeling and cosmetic contract — had the rather obvious and predictable (and perfectly human) effect of making Linda feel special. It was impossible to be in Greg Scarpa's orbit and not be subject to the effects of gravity.

One evening at the Flamingo, Linda and Greg Sr. were standing together at the bar when one of the club's scantily clad dancers sidled up to him and began flirting, casually and expertly brushing Scarpa's arm with her breasts.

"I want her fired," Linda said, after the dancer had departed.

Scarpa smiled and raised a hand, as if to say, *Consider it done.*

The dancer was gone by morning; she never worked at the Flamingo again.

Males who displeased Linda were dealt with more harshly, regardless of whether their transgressions were intentional or deliberate, perceived or real. There was the time, for example, that an unfortunate Flamingo bartender named George let the pressure of a busy night cloud his judgment, and he made the mistake of speaking curtly to Linda. When Scarpa found out he sum-

110

moned George to the men's room, where he proceeded, in grand school yard fashion, to immerse the poor bartender's head in the toilet. He, too, never worked another day at the Flamingo.

Although tradition dictated that women were to be kept largely ignorant of Mafia activities — regardless of their relationship to a made man — Linda found herself exempt from the usual operating procedures. Almost from the moment she met Scarpa, Linda was privy to information most Mafia girlfriends (or wives, for that matter) never knew — or wanted to know. In many ways Scarpa regarded her less as a trophy than a partner.

"We can talk about anything in front of Linda," Scarpa once proudly proclaimed to his attorney, Lou Diamond. "I don't keep secrets from her."

Over time Scarpa began to reveal not just the more glamorous aspects of his work (if stealing and hijacking can be considered glamorous), but the grislier aspects, as well. One night, following a heist, Scarpa showed up at Linda's apartment with two guys from his crew. Greg Sr. was in a buoyant mood. As he tossed a thick steak into a cast-iron pan and cranked up the heat, Scarpa began to laugh.

"You should have seen the look on this guy's face when I pulled out the gun," he said to Linda. A short time later, as the crew sat down to eat, Scarpa shared the gory details of the heist, which apparently included blowing off the head of one of the victims. Scarpa's gleeful depiction of the incident so resonated with the crew that one poor guy dashed off to the bathroom to vomit. This, too, Scarpa found rather amusing. Weren't mobsters supposed to have strong stomachs?

For her part, Linda was neither repulsed nor amused. She simply accepted Scarpa for what and who he was. In her eyes, the good outweighed the bad — even if she knew, on some level, that the bad was particularly heinous. Having become rather savvy about the ways of the Mafia, Linda understood killing to be part of the contract — implicit or stated — when one became involved with a made man. If Greg had to kill someone, Linda figured he must have good reason for doing it. At least, that is the rationalization she chose to embrace. And anyway, it wasn't like this was the first time she'd been regaled with tales of murder and mayhem (although it was a bit more graphic than usual). Not long after they first met, Scarpa had revealed to Linda that he had personally murdered at least twenty people. He hadn't bragged about it, hadn't attempted to explain or otherwise mitigate the circumstances surrounding their deaths. He just tossed it out there — another little tidbit of information to help her fill in the gaps as their relationship blossomed. Maybe it was a test, to see how she'd respond. If so, Linda passed. In Scarpa's world, killing was a route to respect as well as riches.

That respect rubbed off on Linda. And she liked the way it felt.

8
MISSISSIPPI BURNING

When it came to Linda, Scarpa's trust was complete. There was no detail of his life, professional or otherwise, that he was unwilling to share. She was his friend, lover, confessor.

Only a few months after they began dating, Scarpa took Linda to Romano's. Over dinner, he held her hand and told her the deepest of secrets — a secret that would cost him his life if she repeated it.

"I have this other thing I do," he said. "I help the government — the FBI and the CIA. Sometimes they need special help, and that's where I come in."

Scarpa paused to let the information sink in. This revelation, of course, was an affront to the unwritten Mafia code of conduct. But there was more to it, Linda knew, and she waited for his full explanation.

"Please don't think I'm a rat," he continued. "I do work for them. After all, I really love my country."

Whether this was true or not, Linda could never say for sure. Nor did she particularly care. Perhaps Scarpa did see himself as some sort of noble hero — a double agent serving his country. Or, more likely, that is the fantasy he concocted to gain acceptance from those he loved — and to find a measure of peace in his life. His was a self-aggrandizing, amoral existence, and it required a bit of myth making.

To that end, Scarpa told Linda that he often accepted the federal government's dirtiest and most dangerous jobs — assignments even the FBI and CIA found too distasteful or risky to undertake on their own. Among Scarpa's "missions": helping the government frame members of Israel's Mossad; setting up a sting operation for the CIA; and gathering intelligence on Howard Hughes and his connection to the Mafia.

Scarpa spun these tales with great gusto, twisting his role as an informant into something else entirely. And, once rolling, he found himself unable to stop. *Omertà,* apparently, was a concept that did not apply to Scarpa. To bolster his case — or perhaps simply to feed his own version of the fantasy — Scarpa even introduced Linda to Tony Villano. Linda became fond of Villano; the two men often used her apartment as a place to conduct business, and sometimes Villano would arrive early and drink coffee with Linda until Scarpa arrived.

In those days, Greg Sr. wore numerous hats, often contradictory in nature. For example, he served as a public spokesman for the Italian-American Civil Rights League, generally regarded as a daring role for a Mafia member. The league, set up by Mafia don Joe Colombo, was a none-too-subtle attempt by the mob to legitimize itself while simultaneously earning enormous income from the league's membership, which included hundreds of thousands of dues-paying Italian Americans who objected to being stereotyped as gangsters because of their Italian descent. The league was an overwhelming financial (and public relations) success, its legitimacy stamped by the endorsement of politicians who routinely spoke at league rallies.

Greg Scarpa Sr. was a potent and charismatic fixture at these events. A natural politician and leader, he would incite and inflame the constituency with all manner of theatrical antics: climbing aboard a flatbed truck; or grabbing a microphone and delivering an impromptu, rousing speech attacking the federal government's "bias." He also spoke at the league's weekly protest rallies outside the FBI's New York offices on East Sixty-ninth Street. Television coverage of these events often included clips of Greg Sr., wearing his signature dark glasses, denouncing the anti-Italian investigators.

If Linda was impressed by Scarpa's confidence and courage, she also couldn't help noticing that he sometimes seemed almost reckless. In retrospect, of course, Scarpa's behavior can be seen as narcissistic, if not downright delusional, but at the time it was more exciting than anything else. After one particularly heated rally, he took Linda to a Chinese restaurant, where he spotted Tony Villano sitting at a table. Greg Sr. brazenly greeted his friend: "Hey, *paisan*, you like that speech?" He and Linda joined Villano for dinner, and Linda spent most of the evening anxiously scanning the restaurant's entrance. Of the several hundred people who had attended that afternoon's rally, many were from Bensonhurst and knew Greg Sr. personally. They had just watched him deliver an angry speech against the FBI and the government. What if some of those same people saw him now, sharing dinner with Villano? What if they walked into the restaurant and saw Greg Scarpa Sr. laughing and chatting amiably with a federal law enforcement officer?

The thought so frightened Linda that she could scarcely touch her food, a fact that did not escape Scarpa's attention. He reached over and put a hand on Linda's shoulder.

"Don't worry," he said. "It's okay."

Scarpa then proceeded to tell Villano all about the rally: the names of gangsters who had been in attendance; how they hoped to exploit league contacts; and about Joe Colombo's upcoming plans. Important, deeply privileged information, the sharing of which was surely an egregious violation of Mafia protocol. Linda could only marvel at Scarpa's bravado.

And this was only the beginning.

One day Scarpa excitedly told Linda that he had a new assignment from the FBI, one related to a case that had garnered national attention. His job, Scarpa explained, was to find the bodies of three civil rights workers believed to have been murdered in the summer of 1964 in Philadelphia, Mississippi, by the Ku Klux Klan. Michael Schwerner, a white graduate of Cornell University, had gone to Mississippi with his wife, Rita, to work for the Congress of Racial Equality. After opening a community center in Meridian, Mississippi, the young couple had undertaken a variety of altruistic causes, including teaching young African American children to read and write, and encouraging their parents to register and vote. James Chaney, twenty-one, who was black, was a frequent visitor at the center, and had become Schwerner's friend and confidante.

In June, Schwerner and Chaney had driven to Oxford, Ohio, to help train volunteers for a Mississippi voter-registration drive known as Freedom Summer. There they befriended Andrew Goodman, a twenty-year-old white New York college student. After reaching Mississippi on June 20, the three men had spent a day inspecting the ruins of a black church near Philadelphia, Mississippi, that had been firebombed by the Ku Klux Klan. Local police acknowledged that they had pulled over a Ford station wagon carrying the three young men. Their explanation: The vehicle had been traveling at an excessive rate of speed. Authorities later said the men were then detained at a local lockup because of suspicions that they had been involved in the church burning. According to the police, the three were held until nightfall, and then released unharmed. But the men were never again seen alive. Mississippi politicians, including United States senator James Eastland, had said that their disappearance was probably just a "publicity stunt" staged by the three civil rights workers to call attention to their cause.

It was widely believed that Ku Klux Klan members had murdered the three young men; their bodies, however, had not turned up, despite the largest FBI manhunt in history. FBI director J. Edgar Hoover, under tremendous pressure from Attorney General Robert Kennedy and President Lyndon Johnson, had authorized the full weight and force of his agency in the service of this investigation, to find the bodies and solve the case. And yet, it had proved fruitless.

And now Greg Scarpa, like some sort of superhero, supposedly had been summoned to solve the mystery.

Scarpa wanted Linda to join him on this mission, and the invitation both shocked and excited her. Linda had never ever even flown on an airplane, so this would be a real adventure. Greg Sr. laid out the itinerary. They would first visit the Gulf Coast near Mississippi, where Greg would conduct his investigation; then they would fly to Miami to visit Linda's uncle. Linda, naturally, was more excited about the trip than the mission. To her this was just another fringe benefit of being Greg Scarpa's mistress —

their life together was becoming increasingly surreal.

They flew first class. Linda wore an expensive new print dress and matching hat that Greg had purchased for her prior to the trip. Not even a bumpy flight and a bout of air sickness could spoil the trip for Linda, who clung to Scarpa's arm throughout. A seasoned traveler, Scarpa drank and ate heartily, even as the plane was buffeted by turbulence. Every so often he would pull Linda close and tell her not to worry, that they'd be on the ground soon and everything would be all right.

They landed in Mobile, Alabama, and took a cab to their hotel, a magnificently preserved, antebellum resort that reminded Linda of something out of *Gone with the Wind.* As they walked into the lobby, Linda and Greg Sr. noticed more than a dozen federal agents on the mezzanine above, carefully watching their every move. Scarpa told her not to worry — they were all on the same team.

As Linda unpacked her bags in their luxurious suite, a man with close-cropped hair wearing a black suit came into the living room. Linda watched as he spoke briefly with Scarpa. Before leaving, the man nodded grimly and handed him a gun. Scarpa escorted the man to the door, then walked over to Linda. His face betrayed a hint of trepidation, something Linda rarely saw in Greg.

"I'm going out with these men," he explained. "If I'm not back, there's a return ticket on the bureau." Scarpa reached into his pocket and withdrew a stack of bills. "Here — take this."

Despite the tone of seriousness in Scarpa's voice, Linda was only mildly concerned. In her eyes, Greg Sr. was invincible. He had survived — even thrived — in the toughest milieu around: the Mafia world of New York City. What harm could possibly come to him here, in the bucolic South? Surely these people were no match for a man like Greg Scarpa Sr. He was the most fearless person Linda had ever met, and she simply could not imagine any situation with which he would be unable to cope.

After the agents briefed him, Greg Sr. drove a rented car to a small appliance store owned by a Klansman named Byrd. Scarpa concocted a story to gain favor with Mr. Byrd, telling the store owner that he had recently arrived from Chicago, would be working in town for some time, and that he wanted to buy a TV set. They haggled over the price, but finally came to terms. Scarpa then instructed the man to hold the set while he arranged for a place to live. He said he would be back before closing time that night to pick up the merchandise.

As promised, Scarpa returned to the store shortly before 9:00 P.M. The place was empty, save for the proprietor.

"Would you put the set in my car, please?" Scarpa asked Mr. Byrd. "I have a bad back and can't lift anything." Mr. Byrd obliged, carrying the set out to Scarpa's car. The manager opened the car's back door and pushed the set in. As Byrd leaned in to secure the television, Scarpa shoved him hard to the floor and jumped onto the backseat. He stuck a pistol in the man's ribs and told him to lie still and keep his mouth shut. An FBI agent who had been hiding in the front seat suddenly sat up and began to drive the car.

They drove south for several hours, a second car filled with federal agents tailing them every inch of the way. When they arrived at the appointed safe house, a lonely country cabin tucked deep in the Mississippi woods, the agents took up positions around the house to guard against any unexpected interruption. With the barrel of a gun pressed against his back, Mr. Byrd was led into the house. Scarpa directed him to a small room that passed for a kitchen, and then bound the man's legs and arms to a chair. Then, as FBI agents stood outside, listening through open windows, Scarpa began to administer a brutal beating. Between blows Scarpa would interrogate the man, asking pointed questions about the three missing civil rights workers: "What had happened to them? Who killed them? Where were the bodies?"

Fearing for his life, and wanting only for the beating to end, the man offered an account of the murder and burial. But the waiting agents responded with skepticism.

"He's lying," they told Scarpa.

"Are you sure?"

"Absolutely."

At first, Scarpa kept his cool, even as the interrogation continued. But as hours passed and the FBI continued to dismiss Byrd's information as fraudulent, Scarpa grew frustrated and began beating the man savagely. He slammed a gun barrel into Byrd's mouth; pulled down the trembling Klansman's pants; put a razor blade against his penis, and made a few preliminary cuts.

"Tell me the fucking truth or I'll blow your fucking brains out, and cut off your dick," he said.

Byrd, terrified and weeping, finally began

to talk. He admitted that after Deputy Sheriff Cecil Price arrested the three civil rights workers six weeks earlier, he had sent out word that those arrested included a young man referred to as "Goatee," the Klan's code name for Schwerner, who had been marked for death by the Klan's imperial wizard, Sam Bowers. Deputy Price had detained the civil rights workers long enough for Edgar Ray Killen, a preacher and local Klan leader, to round up a posse. As Schwerner, Chaney, and Goodman headed down Route 19 that evening, Deputy Price tailed them in his cruiser, followed by two carloads of Klansmen, including Mr. Byrd himself.

After a frantic chase, the three men were caught, taken to an isolated spot on Rock Cut Road, murdered in quick succession, and buried below an earthen dam on the farm of Olen Burrage, one of Philadelphia's wealthiest citizens. Their Ford wagon was set ablaze.

Scarpa returned to his hotel early the next morning, just in time to leave for the airport. In the cab, Linda nestled close to Greg Sr. and asked if his mission had been successful.

"Everything worked out just fine, sweetheart," he said. "We got the guy to talk, no problem."

Scarpa and Linda arrived in Miami that evening and checked into the Fontainebleau Hotel, where they stayed for two days before flying back to New York. The entire tab for the trip was picked up by the United States government. By the time they returned, the FBI had recovered the bodies of the three missing civil rights workers — at precisely the spot where Byrd had said they were buried. The discovery of the bodies was front-page news all over the country, and the case received widespread media attention for months to come. Linda and Greg Sr. watched the reports with bemusement (and maybe a trace of satisfaction). Not once was Scarpa linked to the case or the investigation. His involvement had been clandestine, his role that of hired muscle — professional interrogator.

And he had executed the task to perfection.

Near the end of the year, federal agents arrested eighteen men for conspiring to deny Schwerner, Chaney, and Goodman their civil rights. After numerous delays, a federal jury convicted seven defendants, including Deputy Sheriff Price. Three more went free when the jury deadlocked. The rest, including Byrd, were acquitted.

Byrd told anyone who would listen about how he had been kidnapped by the FBI and beaten viciously by a nameless "thug." His story was generally dismissed as unworthy or unbelievable. Although the state of Mississippi failed to charge the defendants with murder, and most are still free men, this incident in Philadelphia, Mississippi, changed the course of the civil rights movement and caused new laws to be enacted.

For his brutal and unrepentant (although thoroughly professional) handiwork in Mississippi, Greg Scarpa Sr. was paid several thousand dollars and given a virtual lifetime "get out of jail free" card. He continued to run his Mafia enterprises, without fear of retribution or prosecution. In a very real sense, Scarpa had been given a license to kill.

9
MARRIED TO THE MOB

Inevitably, perhaps, the relationship between Linda and Greg Scarpa evolved to a level of intimacy and comfort that was bound to cause problems. Against her better judgment, Linda had fallen deeply in love with Greg. And it wasn't just the money and power she found attractive; Linda knew a side of him unrecognizable to others. With her he was sensitive, thoughtful, and generous.

What Linda wanted, of course, was a more traditional, monogamous relationship. Like many a gumare, she tired of the mistress's role — with its layers of secrecy and shame. What once was exciting now seemed tawdry, even humiliating. Eventually Linda asked Greg Sr. to divorce his wife, Connie; then, presumably, Linda and Greg would wed and live happily ever after. There are, however, no fairy tales in the Mafia. When it came to affairs of the heart (and flesh), mob protocol was explicit and unforgiving: A made man could never divorce his wife; nor was he permitted to fool around with the wife of another made man. There were no exceptions, and one violated these rules under penalty of death.

Scarpa proposed a compromise: He would separate from Connie and move into an apartment with Linda. Although unrecognized by the church or government, theirs would be a "marriage" nonetheless. Greg even agreed to start a family with Linda, something she had long desired. There was just one problem: Linda considered herself Catholic (personal moral transgressions notwithstanding) and wanted her children to be baptized in the church. So she devised her own rather twisted and unorthodox solution: She would marry someone else and have Greg Scarpa's children. The offspring would bear the surname of her husband and be baptized properly. Then, her babies having been blessed by the church, Linda would divorce her husband; she and the kids would live together under one roof with their stepfather and her one true love, Greg Scarpa Sr.

To say that Scarpa disapproved of this plan would be an understatement. He recognized it as the impractical, overwrought, and potentially disastrous scheme that it was, and pleaded with Linda to accept his compromise. (To some extent, of course, Scarpa was simply jealous of the idea that Linda would marry another man; in his world, what was acceptable for a male was not necessarily acceptable for a female.) Linda, though, was not to be dissuaded. So she went off in search of a husband (if not necessarily a mate).

In short order Linda ensnared and released a series of potential suitors: a chiropractor who had been treating her father (Linda seduced him on the floor of his office while her father was in the next room, strapped into some sort of therapeutic device); Joey, a former boyfriend from the neighborhood who still carried a torch for Linda and was helpless at resisting her charms; and a handsome, diligent young man named Charlie Schiro, who worked full-time as an insurance agent and moonlighted as a waiter at a pancake house.

Of this trio, two were quickly frightened away by the exploits and efforts of Greg Scarpa, who wasted no time in flexing his muscle in defense of what he perceived to be his own territory. (The former boyfriend was a quick and understandable casualty, as he had the misfortune of working in the

130

crew of a rival wiseguy; when Joe Colombo got wind of Linda's intention to wed him he quickly called Scarpa and reminded him of the rules: If Linda were to marry Joey, her relationship with Greg Sr. would have to end. Not surprisingly, Scarpa made sure that the wedding plans were aborted.)

Charlie Schiro was a more persistent and safer paramour, and ultimately his resilience paid off. On March 25, 1968, Linda and Charlie were married at city hall in New York and flew to Miami for a honeymoon. The phone rang almost as soon as they set their bags on the floor of the bridal suite. On the other end was an agitated Greg Scarpa, calling to tell Linda that he was on his way to Miami; the honeymoon, he said, was over.

"No, no, don't do that," Linda said. "Look, I'll come back early, I promise." Without waiting for a response, she hurriedly hung up the phone.

"Who was that?" asked Charlie.

"Oh, that was just the hotel," Linda lied. "They wanted to send up free champagne. I said we'll have it with dinner."

Later, Charlie, the poor, hapless newlywed husband, became embroiled with the hotel maître d' after demanding the free champagne they'd been promised.

Charlie and Linda returned home earlier than originally planned and went directly to the apartment of Linda's sister, Maryanne, where they had arranged to stay until they found their own place. As soon as Linda arrived, Maryanne told her that Greg Sr. had called.

"He wants to meet you — now," Maryanne said.

So Linda fashioned an excuse, which love-struck Charlie swallowed without question or complaint, and ran off to see the man she loved, leaving her new husband behind. Linda and Greg spent the afternoon and evening at a Brooklyn hotel, making love and talking, and trying to figure out how to make the best of their strange situation. It was Greg's contention that Linda had made a terrible mistake, and that the most sensible way to rectify that mistake was to leave Charlie Schiro — immediately. They'd been married only a few days; it was still possible to have the union annulled. Linda rejected that proposal out of hand. Why should she leave Charlie if Greg wouldn't leave Connie?

"But I will leave Connie," Scarpa promised. "I just can't divorce her."

Not good enough, Linda said. Either she would have Greg all to herself, legally and romantically, or she would remain tied to Charlie Schiro. She would take his name while bearing the children of Greg Scarpa. Just as she had planned.

Charlie and Linda rented a small apartment on Brooklyn's Ocean Avenue, and they built a life that at least gave the presentation of some degree of normalcy. Dutiful and diligent, Charlie would rise early, make coffee, give his new bride a kiss good-bye, and head off for a long day of work. Linda would wish him well and promise to have dinner ready when he returned. Sometimes only a few minutes would pass before Greg Scarpa pulled up in his car and entered the apartment. He and Linda would have sex, and then go out for breakfast. Often, they would spend the entire day together; before long, the days melted into the nights, and soon they were practically living together, just as they had before Linda met Charlie. There were trips to nightclubs, and to the racetrack, with Linda's father in tow. Scarpa, not surprisingly, often benefited from insider information — it would be naïve to suggest they were merely "tips" — and routinely dropped thousands of dollars on a single race. Sometimes he went to the window alone, quietly placing his bets; if the information was solid, however, he'd nudge Linda's father to tag along. Regardless, the booty was always shared.

Sometimes Greg Sr. and Linda would take a room at the Golden Gate Motel, a gangster hangout on the Belt Parkway, or at one of the hot-sheet motels on Staten Island. The active pursuit of pregnancy was a linchpin of their relationship, so sex, recreational or dutiful, was practically a part of their daily routine. Odd as it may seem, Charlie Schiro never questioned this arrangement, and never complained about his very public status as a cuckold. Whether he was utterly clueless about the nature of his wife's relationship with Scarpa (this seems doubtful), or simply too frightened and lonely to face the truth of her infidelity (a more reasonable assessment) is impossible to say. Only this much is certain: The bizarre triangle endured for a few years, and eventually produced the child Linda always wanted.

Gregory remembers his astonishment the day that Linda came by for lunch with Greg Sr. and Gregory noticed the unmistakable belly bump beneath Linda's shirt.

"I wondered if the baby was my dad's, or whether it was the guy Linda married," Gregory recalls. "She told Charlie that my dad was an old, longtime friend of the family. I found this to be very mean to do to Charlie. I put myself in his shoes, and it didn't feel good. But again, this was my dad. Who was I to say anything? Maybe if my dad would have been a regular working guy I could have said how I felt. But the kind of guy Dad was, well, nobody, including me, could or would say anything."

Gregory's escape from the madness of his Brooklyn environment came at the end of the working day, when he'd drive out to Staten Island to hang out with his little brother, and to spend time with Diane. Weekends were even better.

"On Sundays, the whole family would hang out at our house, and we would watch sports on TV and eat my mom's meatballs and spaghetti," Gregory remembers. "Then Dad would get a call from Nino, telling him that he had to meet him in Brooklyn. That gave Dad an excuse to leave and go to meet Linda."

Whatever hostility Connie might have felt toward her philandering husband, she kept it largely to herself. Whether she still cared deeply for Greg Sr., no one could say for sure, although it was hard to imagine anyone sustaining such an unrequited love. More likely, Connie had simply grown accustomed to a certain degree of comfort in her life, and she wasn't about to threaten that lifestyle with a display of moral indignation. Connie carried herself with an air of sophistication and means. Her closet was filled with beautiful clothes and furs, and the finest designer shoes. A generous weekly stipend ensured that she would never be relegated to window shopping. And, of course, she had her family — four children she adored, and who in turn loved her. Was Connie going to risk forfeiting all of that over her husband's gumare?

Not likely.

Scarpa seemed in some sense to be keenly aware of the selfishness that governed his own lifestyle, and to make amends, both moral and practical, he bestowed upon his family all manner of riches. Courtesy of his illegal ventures, he moved Connie to a sprawling horse farm in Lakewood, New Jersey, which was, coincidentally, far enough away from Brooklyn for Scarpa to use the distance as a good excuse for not taking the drive home most nights. By this time Debbie had acquired a husband and home of her own, and Gregory was preparing to marry Diane. So Connie moved to Lakewood with her two youngest sons, Buddy and Frankie. To keep them happy, Scarpa stocked the ranch with five robust new horses and hired a friend to help the boys learn the basics of training and grooming.

The complications escalated with the birth of Linda's daughter. Her name, too, was Linda — they called her "Little Linda" to differentiate between mother and daughter — and while her surname was Schiro, there was no question as to the child's paternity. Greg Scarpa Sr. was the father. Shortly after the baby's birth, Scarpa provided the means for Linda to buy a new house for her burgeoning family; he gave her a large cash gift rather than purchase the house himself, in order to avoid further raising Charlie's ire or suspicion. When Linda explained that the money had been a gift from her father, Charlie cast aside skepticism (*where did the old man get that much money?*) and eagerly embraced the job of house hunting. The newlyweds picked out a modest one-family, detached house in Bensonhurst, and Greg Sr. continued his practice of stopping by nearly every day after Charlie had left for work. The little house became a base of operations for Greg; he'd make phone calls from the kitchen, and sometimes even host meetings with Anthony Villano.

For the longest time, all of this flew under

the unreliable radar of Charlie Schiro. Eventually, though, even the nicest of guys grow suspicious (or perhaps, in Charlie's case, he'd simply grown tired of playing the fool). Charlie hired a private investigator to determine his wife's loyalty — or lack thereof. The stakeout, of course, required little effort and quickly yielded unpleasant results. Coming home from another late-night encounter with Scarpa, Linda found her father at her home and Charlie in an unusually foul mood. Linda's father, of course, had been keenly aware of Linda's second life, and had benefited from the arrangement. His presence in the house now after being summoned by Charlie, was merely to serve as peacemaker in what was sure to be an ugly and heated confrontation.

Before Charlie could say anything, Linda's father approached her and whispered in her ear: "He knows."

In a startling and uncharacteristic outburst, Charlie began screaming at Linda, calling her names and threatening her. Linda stormed out of the house, though her exit stemmed less from any fear that Charlie might actually hurt her than from concern over her unborn child. She was pregnant again (and again Scarpa was the father), and wasn't about to risk a miscarriage by becoming involved in a heated emotional dispute. Practically speaking, Linda had little cause for concern. Charlie was not about to kick her out of the house, especially since it belonged to her. Also, Charlie was no match for Linda, let alone Scarpa, when it came to acting on impulse. He was a cautious, measured man; given time, he would come to understand (if not appreciate) Linda's situation. And the more he learned about his wife's lover, the less he wanted to engage in any sort of dispute — whether over the custody of Little Linda, ownership of their home, the parameters of their marriage, or anything else. He would quietly accept the indignity of being married to Greg Scarpa's mistress, or he would suffer the consequences, most likely at the hands of Scarpa himself.

Only after the birth of their second child, a baby boy named Joey, did Linda begin to seriously question the durability of her current arrangement. It happened one day while all three adults were in the house, and a nurse was taking care of Joey. As the nurse changed the baby's diaper, and cleaned and caressed him, she let out a little chuckle.

"You know, Mr. Greg, this baby has your ears and your eyes," the nurse said, not quite understanding the wound she had opened. Charlie sat mute. Scarpa, however, started laughing. Linda, meanwhile, tried to change the subject, but she knew in that moment that it was time to end the charade; it was time to end her marriage to Charlie and to begin her real life with the man she loved.

10
MURDER, INC.

Joseph "Joe Brewster" DeDomenico was, in Mafia parlance, a stand-up guy. Quick with a joke, a reliable and loyal friend, and a remarkably skilled and efficient killer. Joe Brewster was among the most valued and popular members of Greg Scarpa's crew. Their friendship reached deep into the past and transcended the usual boundaries of business. Of course, not even Joe Brewster knew of Scarpa's secret life. He trusted and admired Greg Sr., and over the years had become one of the top earners in the crew — an energetic and inventive worker who could always be counted on to generate new schemes and crimes.

One of Joe Brewster's buddies, for example, had devised a pick that was remarkably efficient at popping the locks of pay phones. Scarpa thought it was an ingenious little gadget and loved putting it into practice — sometimes he would go several miles out of his way just for the thrill of stealing fifty bucks in dimes. He used the pick in hospitals, airports, restaurants — once he even cracked the box of a courthouse phone. For months, Scarpa and some of the crew (with Linda in tow) drove up and down the Eastern Seaboard — Boston, Baltimore, New York, New Jersey — picking locks and disgorging pay phones. They would stay overnight at a nice hotel, relax, go swimming, take a sauna, have an expensive dinner, get a good night's sleep — and repeat the routine the next day.

On one of their excursions, Linda and the boys stopped for the night at a Baltimore motel. Scarpa, as he did on occasion, reminded everyone of the importance of maintaining a low profile. Fueled by too much whiskey, however, Sonny Squint became rambunctious and argumentative. Unhappy with the service at a rooftop bar, he tossed a waiter holding a tray of drinks off the roof and into a pool.

Scarpa immediately left the scene and returned to his room, where he summoned Sonny Squint and chewed him out. Poor drunken Sonny apologized profusely, broke down in tears, and then slunk away for the night. Alone with Linda, Greg Sr. exploded with laughter, recalling the strange and wondrous sight of the waiter, still holding his tray, plummeting from the roof to the pool, screaming all the way down. A few days later authorities caught up with the crew in New Jersey. Scarpa, Joe Brewster, and Sonny Squint were arrested; as usual, their time behind bars was laughably brief — all three men walked out of the police station within a matter of hours, and charges were soon dropped. The pay phone scam ended rather predictably, and suddenly, with the phone company installing new and more rigorous lock boxes on its equipment.

A more traditional venture — stealing cars — followed the phone scam. The versatile crew proved adept at this as well, and soon everyone was driving late-model "mob mobiles": Cadillacs, Lincolns, and the like. For his trouble and tolerance (and probably to ensure his silence), even Charlie Schiro got a new car. As fate would have it, poor Charlie, ever laboring under a dark cloud, was soon pinched by the cops and charged with auto theft. What could he do but reach out to his former nemesis? Scarpa took the call from Schiro while hanging out at Wimpy Boys. He drove straight to the precinct house, and within an hour, after speaking with detectives, walked out with Charlie. All charges were subsequently dropped; Charlie was innocent: and, ironically, he even got to keep the car!

Owing in large part to his chummy relationship with the feds, Scarpa naturally came to think of his crew as invincible. Predictably, the heists grew bigger, and the accompanying risks greater.

Through Joe Brewster, he heard about a place in Manhattan's Diamond District that seemed ripe for the picking. The store's jewelry stands, adorned during daylight hours with diamonds and gold, were stripped each evening, and the gems were stored in safe-deposit boxes in a locked rear room. Joe Brewster had recruited a safe-cracker familiar with the store's locks, so the heist seemed simple — at least, on the surface. But there was one significant drawback. Actually there were two drawbacks: the massive windows at the front of the store, which offered an eyeful to anyone passing by; and its proximity to a police station, which was located almost directly across the street.

Undeterred by these obstacles, Scarpa devised a plan. The crew would utilize a large shade adorned with an image of the store's interior; a casual glance would tell passersby that that all was normal inside. Behind the shade, however, the crew would be hard at work, unlocking the safe-deposit boxes and stealing the gems.

For this particular heist, Scarpa recruited his son, despite a comparative lack of experience when it came to burglary.

"My dad told me that I would be going, but I'd be outside using the corner pay telephone to watch for any problems, and wait for the guys to bring out the jewels," Gregory Scarpa explains. "He told me not to worry about anything, because Nino would be in the vicinity for my protection. And he was. Approximately one hour into the burglary, I heard Nino honk his car's horn to let me know he was there."

The heist was an unqualified success. Each member of the crew received $165,000 after the goods were fenced successfully. A similar fee was paid to the Colombo family (which always got its cut). And then, of course, there was the payoff to the FBI.

"My dad took $10,000 from each of us for Nino," Gregory recalls. "I knew where it was going, but the other guys figured it was going to a guy named 'Charlie Moose' Panerella, who, at that time, was my dad's captain. Nobody ever questioned my dad."

As Gregory would soon realize, not only did Nino Villano receive kickbacks for serving as a lookout, he also aided Scarpa in ways far more nefarious and immoral. Indeed, according to Gregory, Villano provided information that enabled his father to execute certain mobsters; moreover, Villano tacitly agreed with the killings. There was the time, for example, that Gregory asked Joe Brewster about a crew member named Jamsie (nicknamed "Mut"). The guy usually hung around with Joe, but Gregory hadn't seen him in a few weeks and wondered what had become of him. Joe Brewster casually told Gregory that his father had ordered Jamsie's execution; Joe Brewster had completed the deed. By way of explanation (not that one was necessary), Scarpa had said that Jamsie was about to give the FBI information related to Scarpa and the crew. There was no choice, Joe Brewster had been told. Jamsie was a rat and had to be exterminated.

The source who revealed that Jamsie was about to inform on Scarpa: Greg's buddy, FBI agent Anthony "Nino" Villano.

Something about this particular murder bothered Gregory, and so he asked his father about it. The response?

"You worry too much, kid. Just try to have fun."

In truth, Greg Scarpa Sr. wanted much

more than that for his son. He had been preparing Gregory for a Mafia life almost from the day Gregory was born. Scarpa's logic was shameless but irrefutable: With Gregory in the family (as well as the *family*), Greg Sr. would have someone in whom he could place all of his trust; someone who would never betray him.

To fulfill his (or his father's) destiny, Gregory was compelled to take another man's life. Murder was the cornerstone on which the Mafia foundation was built — the mob's way of dealing with difficult problems. In order to become a made man, Gregory would first have to accept a murder contract, and then successfully complete the terms of the agreement. The order typically came from the family boss or the capo. A wiseguy could not decline a contract simply because he had some personal relationship or connection with the target; indeed, it wasn't at all unusual for a murder to be carried out by someone close to the victim (as with Jamsie and Joe Brewster). A wiseguy pledged allegiance to the mob and vowed to exact retribution against anyone who crossed the family. No discussions or debate allowed. Once completed, the murder would clear the path for membership. The newly made man, in a secret and solemn ceremony, would be inducted into the family.

Greg Scarpa Sr. arranged his son's first hit. The target was a local restaurant owner who had run afoul of the mob. Early in the evening of the planned murder, Greg Sr. and Linda were dining at the café, having a good time, seemingly oblivious to the impending violence. In reality, Scarpa was trying to monitor the owner's routine in order to tip off his son. Eventually Scarpa paid the bill and left the restaurant with Linda. Shortly thereafter, Gregory walked through the front door, numb with fear but prepared to do his duty. He pulled a revolver from his jacket and steeled himself. But he couldn't do it. Upon seeing the owner, Gregory froze. He'd known this man for years, and was friendly with his wife and children. Gregory had been dining at this restaurant almost his entire life, and when he thought about the family that would be left behind, he was overcome with sadness.

Gregory tucked the gun into his coat pocket, turned, and walked out the door.

After driving around the neighborhood for the better part of a half hour, Gregory found a phone booth and called his father. He fully expected Greg Sr. to be furious — this failure of nerve, after all, reflected poorly on Scarpa and his crew, and on the entire Colombo family. To his surprise, though, Greg Sr. expressed no anger, in part because he'd already heard about his son's inability to pull the trigger — he'd assigned a few guys to watch the restaurant while Gregory was inside.

To Gregory's surprise and relief, Scarpa acted more like a father than a mobster.

Sort of.

"The first time is hard for a lot of guys," he said. "But I'm not worried about you, son, you'll be fine."

There was a pause on the other end of the line. Then a chuckle. "You might even learn to enjoy it as much as I do."

11
THE GOODFELLA LIFE

In 1971, at the age of twenty-one, Gregory Scarpa Jr. married Diane Dimino. It was a large and lavish affair, underwritten by Greg Sr., who wanted only the best for his son (it should be noted, however, that Gregory paid for the $20,000 engagement ring that adorned Diane's left hand). Greg Sr. had urged Linda to attend the wedding, escorted by one of his friends, but she had politely and reasonably declined: Going to a wedding hosted by Scarpa's wife was not exactly Linda's idea of a good time.

Still, it was a star-studded bash, with scores of Mafia big shots drinking and eating and toasting — and stuffing great wads of cash into Gregory's pocket. Later, when he bought a house on Staten Island and had to explain to the Internal Revenue Service where he got the cash to pay for it, Gregory merely smiled: "wedding gifts."

Joe Brewster, who had become one of

Gregory's closest friends, served as best man; he and his girlfriend even joined Gregory and Diane on their honeymoon (in Hawaii and Las Vegas). Everyone had a blast and, for a while, all seemed well in the Scarpa circle.

But soon the marriage began to fray, weakened by a combination of Gregory's late hours and Diane's youthful jealousy.

"I opened a nightclub on Staten Island, and every weekend the joint would be full of guys and girls drinking and having fights," recalls Gregory. "Because of that, I felt that it wasn't a place for Diane; when she was there, I would constantly have to watch out for her. I asked her not to come to the club on the weekends, but she didn't want to have to stay home while I was at the club until 4:30 in the morning. Although I never cheated on her, she constantly accused me of seeing other women."

Faithful or not, there is no denying that Gregory thoroughly enjoyed life as a gangster. It was, he discovered, a life of leisure: Indeed, one of the great obstacles for any career criminal who hopes to go straight is overcoming the pathological fear of the nine-to-five world.

"In my years on the street, from when I was sixteen to thirty-eight, I never had to work a regular job," Gregory says with some satisfaction. "I went to sleep when I felt like it and woke up when I felt like it. It was a real good-time party life."

Although the young newlyweds were at first thrilled to learn that Diane had become pregnant, the physical changes in his wife's appearance provoked an odd psychological response in Gregory: He began to feel uncomfortable making love to her because his child was so "visible."

Like most mafiosos, Gregory hoped that his first-born child would be a male, to carry on the family lineage. Imagine his surprise when the baby turned out to be a girl; imagine, too, the way the disappointment lasted not even a moment, as Gregory, standing by his wife's hospital bed, fell in love with the little girl they named Kori.

Unfortunately, the expansion of his family did little to improve Gregory's relationship with Diane. Two years later, despite Gregory's lack of enthusiasm, they had another baby girl — this one named after her mother. But the marriage by now was disintegrating in a cloud of jealousy and frustration. When Diane became angry (which was frequently), she threw things at Gregory; his response, typically, was to walk out of the house without saying a word, and to not return until the next day, if then. Eventually they began sleeping in different bedrooms. Diane accused Gregory of having a girlfriend on the side — and she was right. By this time, in fact, Gregory was juggling four gumares at once.

What was good for the goose, though, was not good for the gander, not in the Mafia. And so it was that the marriage imploded upon Greg Jr.'s suspicion that Diane was cheating on him. When he told his father of his suspicions, Greg Sr. responded with a predictably moblike display of paternal affection: He offered to whack the guy for Gregory.

A nice gesture, Gregory thought, but perhaps a bit extreme. Instead, he settled for tossing Diane out of the house.

"My father told me to give Diane $10,000 and kick her out," Gregory recalls. "I did what he said, but I soon felt so guilty that I began slipping her money every week, without my dad knowing." He also paid for their divorce and made certain the girls were well taken care of.

Diane's place was quickly taken by Lilly, one of the four girls Gregory had been dating on the side. She was pretty and shy, and seemed to understand her role in Gregory's life. At the time Gregory was still merely a

Colombo family associate in his father's crew. Greg Scarpa Sr. answered to "Charlie Moose" Panarella, who was, according to Gregory, "a mean, strict, and very tough guy. Luckily, he took a liking to me, and to Lilly. Lilly had class, and goodfellas always admired and respected classy women."

Charlie asked Gregory if he could hold his monthly mob meeting at Gregory's house. This meant that Charlie trusted Lilly to serve coffee and pastries for the boys and to be respectful to them. Gregory, like the other associates in the crew, was expected to remain in the kitchen while Lilly was in the living room with the made men. In effect, then, she was privy to more inside information than Gregory himself. But such was Mafia protocol, and Gregory accepted it without complaint.

Lilly eventually gave birth to a baby boy they named Gregory III. The baby looked just like Gregory, who adored his new child and embraced the responsibilities of fatherhood with renewed vigor. But his life was complicated, and not merely because of the nature of his work. On weekends, when Gregory also had custody of his two daughters, the Scarpa home was a congested, tense place, and Lilly grew to resent the division of her boyfriend's loyalties.

"She had a point," recalls Gregory. "We would all sleep together in our bedroom. In the morning, the kids were up early and they would start giggling and jumping on my back, which they knew I loved. As long as my babies were laughing and happy, that's all that mattered to me."

As always, though, the ugliness of business interfered with any tranquillity Gregory might have known. A beloved cousin (and a member of the Scarpa crew), Gus Faraci, in the process of screwing up a drug deal, killed a DEA agent. Such transgressions were not treated lightly — federal law enforcement typically responded with overwhelming force when one of their members was killed in the line of duty. Faraci would draw considerable attention and heat until he was brought to justice; in the meantime, any arrangements between the FBI and informants would likely be suspended or strained. In other words, Gus Faraci had to go.

To Greg Scarpa this was no big deal. A bit of internal house cleaning was necessary on occasion to preserve the greater good. And so he gave the order authorizing the killing of one of his own crew members (who also happened to be his nephew; Greg's sister — Gus's mother — appears to have had no knowledge of Greg's involvement). Faraci was gunned down, gangland style, shot eleven times in the face, chest, and neck. Gregory took the news hard. This, he thought, was a line that shouldn't have been crossed. Wasn't family the most important thing in the world?

Greg Sr. shrugged, said he loved the kid, too. But:

"Business is business."

The son, at this point, had yet to acquire the father's hardness, his resolve to do whatever was necessary. He became haunted by nightmares, visited in the depths of the night by the memory of his cousin.

"I was very upset," Gregory says. "I couldn't sleep. I kept seeing Gus's face. I just didn't know how my dad could kill him. I loved him."

To ease the pain and encourage the onset of sleep, Gregory began drinking heavily. Predictably, his relationship showed signs of strain. Lilly found his drinking distasteful, particularly with a baby in the house; she also accused him of fooling around. Her suspicions, of course, were well-founded: If Gregory wanted to be faithful, he lacked the resolve and commitment, in part because the wiseguy lifestyle hardly encouraged monogamy. Attractive, available women were always hanging around — women who liked to drink and party; women who had no use for commitment or love. Ultimately, Gregory and Lilly separated.

Gregory helped expand his father's burgeoning empire by opening another nightclub, this one called On the Rocks. Greg Sr. and capo Anthony "Scappy" Scarpati were his partners. The lounge was a solid moneymaker but turned out to be a bit of a headache, primarily because it was located within the territory of a Staten Island crew run by a mobster named Alfred Longobardi. Mafia turf wars were nasty and often bloody, and this one was no different. One night, as Gregory parked his car outside the club, he felt something cold against his temple. It was Longobardi, holding a pistol.

Gregory tried to remain calm.

"Take it easy, Al," he said. "What do you want?"

"For now," answered Longobardi, "any time one of my friends comes to this place, they don't pay for nothing."

Gregory nodded slowly. "You got it, Al."

"And my friend who lives upstairs from the bar?" Al added, "he don't have to pay rent no more."

"You got that too," Gregory said, speaking

quietly, calmly.

By cooperating and keeping his cool, Gregory was able to defuse the situation. Sufficiently appeased, Longobardi put away his gun, got into his car, and drove away. Gregory, of course, immediately reported the details of this encounter to Scappy, who became so enraged that he ordered the lounge closed and put a contract out on Longobardi's life for disrespecting Gregory. Nearly a full year passed before the contract was executed successfully. Al Longobardi died of a gunshot wound to the head, at close range. Gregory was charged with the murder, but not convicted. He claims to this day that it was Greg Scarpa Sr. who pulled the trigger.

12
MÉNAGE À TROIS

The inevitable dissolution of the union between Linda and Charlie Schiro occurred less than a year after the birth of Linda's second child. For her there was no sadness or grief associated with the separation — after all, it allowed for the fomentation of a life she had always wanted; a life with Greg Scarpa Sr., the two of them living an American dream (or some version of it, anyway) together under one roof, the patter of tiny feet bringing them closer, giving their lives purpose and clarity.

To that end, Scarpa bought a new home in Brooklyn and moved there with Linda and the children. Of course, he never bothered to tell Connie about his new arrangement. Although she generally saw her husband only on weekends, Connie, by now practiced in the art of self-deception, presumed that Greg Sr. was still a resident of their home and a member of the household;

and he was, if only as a technicality.

As for Linda, she finally had things precisely as she wanted them. She had Greg Sr., two children, and a beautiful new home. Scarpa was a surprisingly devoted "husband." It wasn't unusual, for example, for him to excuse himself from a mob sit-down to take a call from Linda. And these were not emergency calls; rather, they were requests from Linda: "Can you stop by the grocery store on your way home? We need milk and eggs." Far from being annoyed by these interruptions, Scarpa happily obliged. Each year, like clockwork, he presented Linda with the keys to a new car (usually a Cadillac or a Mercedes) so that she could roll through the neighborhood in style. For shopping excursions to Manhattan, Scarpa provided a limousine.

And plastic, of course. Plenty of plastic.

Among the crew's many illegitimate businesses was the procuring and selling of counterfeit or stolen credit cards, some of which were used to feed Linda's prodigious appetite for shopping. To ensure that Linda would never arouse suspicion, Greg Sr. never allowed her to use the fake plastic on her own; instead, she would go to a store, pick out what she wanted, and then one of Scarpa's crew would be dispatched to close the deal. That way, if a clerk became suspicious and a pinch was made, Linda would be protected.

The bogus credit cards were also used whenever the couple went out to dinner, which was practically every night. Often Joe Brewster and his wife would join the Scarpas (as they came to think of themselves). The foursome would go primarily to restaurants where the owners were in on the scam — and what a beautiful scam it was! The diners would eat lavishly and pay the bill with fraudulent plastic; the restaurant owners would collect their money from the credit card companies, and then plead ignorance or victimization. Everyone was happy — except, of course, the credit card companies.

Killing and thieving aside, Greg Sr. and Linda enjoyed a relatively "normal" life of marital convenience and companionship. On a typical day the couple would wake at 7:00 A.M. and have coffee together. They would chat until 9:30 A.M., when Scarpa liked to eat breakfast. He loved to cook, and often would whip up pancakes or scrambled eggs for the whole family. Greg Sr. liked this domestic routine, and interrupted it only for the most urgent of business. One morning, for example, a crew member stopped by the house and informed Scarpa that a long-standing target had been spotted in the neighborhood, at a nearby luncheonette. Linda did not know what the poor guy's transgressions might have been, but they must have been serious, for upon hearing the news Greg Sr. dressed quickly and left the house. Within an hour he had walked to the luncheonette, shot the victim in the head, and returned to finish his breakfast.

Life was good.

As the years passed, the bond between Greg Scarpa Sr. and Linda Schiro deepened. Unconventional though it might have been, their relationship was born of love and respect. It was genuine. But, like many married couples who had been together for some time, they found the passion draining from their union. Rather than ignore this development, however, Linda took action; once again, her approach was decidedly unique.

To keep the fires stoked, Linda introduced another man into her marital bed — and she did so with the full knowledge and (eventually, at least) cooperation of Greg Scarpa Sr. The object of Linda's affection (perhaps "recruitment" would be a more appropriate term) was a young man named

Larry Mazza, who delivered groceries to Linda's home.

As was the case with Linda's decision to marry Charlie Schiro, Greg Sr. initially disliked the idea of Linda seducing another man, but he quickly came to appreciate it as a solution to their problem. Moreover (as with the marriage to Charlie), even if Scarpa had loathed the idea, he would have gone along with it just to keep Linda happy — she had that much influence on him. In reality, though, Scarpa was titillated by the thought of Linda making love to someone else, particularly a handsome, naive young man. Their relationship was secure enough that Greg Sr. wasn't concerned about her falling for another man.

The seduction was effortless. Larry Mazza had been impressed with Linda from the first time they met — even though she was several years older than him. He had blushed the first time she subtly flirted with him; the next time Larry showed up to deliver a few bags of groceries, Linda was more direct.

"So, do you fool around, Larry?" she asked.

Larry blushed again. "Yeah, sure I do."

Linda, in full control of the situation, pressed on. "Well, why don't you drop by tonight?"

Larry arrived around 9:30 P.M. Linda brought him into the living room and immediately took charge, removing his clothes and seducing him on the floor. For Larry, who was in his late teens, this was nothing less than the realization of a fantasy. What the boy didn't know (and a good thing, too, since it surely would have scared him into impotency) was that Linda's partner, the infamous mobster Greg Scarpa Sr., was barely a wall away, listening to their every word.

The seduction completed, Linda quickly sent Larry home and went upstairs to file a report with Greg Sr. (not that one was necessary, since he'd been eavesdropping the entire time). Then they made love. Linda and Greg Sr. kept this sexual stew boiling for weeks, without Larry knowing that he was a prime ingredient. When Larry began to ask questions about her "husband," Linda told him not to worry, that Greg Sr. was in Florida and had no inkling as to what was happening under his roof. Mazza, though, was understandably skittish: Exciting as his relationship with Linda might be, it was not worth risking his life over. To calm the young man's nerves, Linda and Greg Sr. decided that a meeting was in order. Linda explained to Larry that she had told her husband about this bright young man, and that Greg Sr. wanted to meet Larry; perhaps, Scarpa had suggested, he could help Larry get into business.

The three of them dined at Romano's. Scarpa naturally did most of the talking; among other things, he proudly told Larry all about his farm in New Jersey, where he raised horses. When he asked Larry about his future plans (surely he wasn't content to deliver groceries for the rest of his life), the young man said he hoped to one day be accepted into the New York Fire Department. His dad had been a fireman, as had several other family members, and Larry thought it might be nice to follow in their footsteps.

Noble work, Scarpa said, but there were easier and far more lucrative ways to earn a living. Perhaps, he suggested, Larry might prefer working in a company that manufactured fire extinguishers. Scarpa happened to own just such a venture. Mazza accepted the gracious offer, but lasted only a few weeks in the job. He was a restless kid, uncomfortable behind a desk or making sales calls. So Scarpa got him a job at one of his auto repair shops; this, too, proved unsuccessful. What he really wanted, Larry admitted, was something more profitable and less demanding — something more exciting — a job that didn't involve punching a clock — a job like Greg Scarpa's.

Indeed, Mazza had something more in common with Linda than merely an interest in sex: He, too, was dazzled by the mobster life; proximity to Greg Sr. and Linda had the predictable effect of greatly diminishing the allure of becoming a firefighter. Suddenly, Larry realized, that was a job for a chump.

With Scarpa's financial support, Larry set up a numbers racket and quickly began earning more money than he had ever imagined. A few weeks later Scarpa invited Mazza to a private dinner at Sorrento's. These types of dinners were regular events that Greg Sr. hosted for his gang to show his appreciation for their hard work. He figured that Larry would soon graduate into being a crew member, so why not begin the initiation process? To Scarpa's surprise, though, Larry failed to show up at the party; over the next few days and weeks, Scarpa noticed that Larry was enormously agitated and nervous whenever the two of them were together. Scarpa, of course, understood the cause of Mazza's anxiety, and decided to put the young man's mind at ease. One night at Wimpy Boys, after Mazza dropped off a pile of cash from his numbers business, Scarpa shook the kid's hand and gestured toward a chair.

"Have a seat," he said.

Larry looked like he was about to faint.

"Listen," said Scarpa. "I know about you and Linda, and it's okay. Really, it's okay. See, whatever makes Linda happy, makes me happy. I love her and she loves me. Have your fun. It's not going to change anything between us."

Mazza was shocked almost to the point of disbelief. He fully expected that Scarpa would kill him; truth be told, Mazza felt that Scarpa probably should have killed him, his transgression had been that severe. Instead, here he was, sitting at the boss's club, receiving not merely dispensation or forgiveness for past misdeeds, but permission to continue screwing the boss's "wife."

It was almost too much to comprehend. And for a while Larry continued to tread delicately around Scarpa, and to express reluctance when it came to sleeping with Linda. Eventually, though, Larry grew more comfortable, and before long there developed a strange but surprisingly successful love triangle between Linda Schiro, Greg Scarpa Sr., and young Larry Mazza.

Linda and Greg Sr. would often lie in bed

167

together, smoking pot and listening to music before making love. Afterward, when Greg Sr., satiated and suitably high, inevitably fell asleep, Linda would turn her attention to Larry Mazza.

Oddly enough, it was neither Linda nor Greg Sr. who allowed emotion to distort the nature of this arrangement; for them the presence of a third person in their relationship represented nothing more than an accoutrement, a way to heighten arousal and recapture some of the spark of their younger days. Larry Mazza saw things differently. He was younger, less experienced, and more prone to flights of fancy. Inevitably, perhaps, he fell in love with Linda; late-night conversations turned to unmet expectations and irrational, dangerous desires.

"Run away with me," Larry begged Linda. "Have my baby."

The possessiveness deepened, clouding Mazza's perceptions, and even his ability to do his job. In public, watching Scarpa holding Linda's hand (something he was not permitted to do) or kissing her, he would be gripped by a jealous rage. Once, at a wedding, Larry watched Greg Sr. and Linda dancing closely together, swaying to the music, smiling at each other, and he went into a deep funk. From across the room,

Scarpa watched in amazement as Mazza sulked.

"Is this kid fucking crazy or what?" he asked Linda. "I can't dance with my wife? I shouldn't hold your hand?"

If Scarpa was unmoved by Mazza's broken heart, he was nevertheless concerned about the kid's desire to have a baby with Linda. After all, Scarpa had been down this road before; he knew all about Linda's fondness for both sex and babies. And so he took this threat seriously. Scarpa asked Linda to have her tubes tied, and she agreed. Larry, who was asked to drive Linda to the hospital for the operation, was visibly upset.

"Don't do this," he pleaded with Linda. "Let's run away; you don't have to do it."

It was only then that Linda realized the depth of Mazza's infatuation. She liked the kid and found him to be a nice diversion in the bedroom, but clearly, he had no clue as to his actual role in her life. After the operation Linda told Greg Sr. about her conversation with Larry, how he wanted her to run off and live happily ever after. To Linda's surprise, Scarpa merely laughed. He knew Linda would never leave him — and certainly not for a lightweight like Larry Mazza.

Incredibly enough, this strange erotic arrangement continued for the next fifteen years, as Larry Mazza moved up in the mob, effectively becoming Greg Scarpa Sr.'s right-hand man. One might reasonably ask how Scarpa could trust a man who was sleeping with his "wife." Then again, one could also argue that there was almost no one on the planet to whom Scarpa was more closely aligned. Years later Mazza would become a rather spectacular informant, not only blowing the whistle on his colleagues, but selling the tawdry story of his relationship with Linda to the *National Enquirer*.

Even then, it seemed, Larry Mazza didn't quite get it. The relationship "wasn't just [about] sex," he told the newspaper. "It was love."

13
FATHERLY LOVE

If Linda and Greg Sr. were devoted parents, theirs was, at times, an admittedly unorthodox approach — and not simply because of their peculiar living arrangement. This was particularly true of Greg Sr., whose no-nonsense approach to dealing with the trials and tribulations of boyhood grew out of his own rather harsh outlook on life. There was, for example, the time that five-year-old Joey came into the house, his eyes red, his cheeks stained with tears. Joey was a sweet and sensitive little boy who had just experienced the trauma of an encounter with a neighborhood bully. The other kid, a bit older and larger, had yanked Joey off his bike. And now Joey was visibly shaken.

Unsympathetic (or, at least, unwilling to express sympathy), Greg Sr. grabbed a baseball bat from the closet and handed it to his son. The bat was bigger than the boy, which lent an air of silliness to the scene, but that, too, escaped Scarpa.

"I want you to go outside with the bat behind your back," Scarpa told his son. "And when you see the other kid, hit him on the head until he bleeds."

Joey did as he was instructed, cradling the bat with both hands and waddling awkwardly out the door. He returned an hour or so later, informing his father that the beating hadn't been necessary. The two boys had made peace with each other and decided to resume playing.

A mobster, it seems, is made, not born.

Given the recklessness of her own life (and a well-documented track record of courting trouble), Linda was a surprisingly strict and protective mother. She rarely let Joey out of her sight; on the cusp of adolescence, he suffered the indignity of being told he wasn't allowed to cross a street on his own or leave the block while riding his bicycle.

"But Ma," he'd shout, "I'm twelve years old!"

Before Linda could respond, Greg Sr. would intervene.

"Listen to your mother!" When Linda smiled and looked away, Scarpa would give his son a conspiratorial wink. And off he would go, exploring the neighborhood in a manner appropriate for a twelve-year-old boy.

If Greg Sr. was more lenient than Linda when it came to child rearing, he was not a man without boundaries. The one unbreakable rule in the Scarpa household was this: no drugs. (This, of course, was hypocritical, given the long-standing fondness for marijuana displayed by both Linda and Greg, but, as with most parents, they feared less for themselves than they did for their kids.) The Scarpa children were expected to obey this rule without debate, but when Little Linda was thirteen, she came home one evening and ran straight to the basement, neglecting to pause and hug her father, as she ordinarily did upon arriving home at night. Suspicion aroused, Linda trailed her daughter down the stairs and found her in the bathroom, flushing water into her blood-shot eyes. Caught red-handed, as it were, Little Linda admitted the obvious: She'd been smoking pot.

When Linda told Greg Sr., he went ballistic. He rounded up some of his crew, and they quickly found the unfortunate fourteen-year-old boy who had supplied Little Linda with her first taste of marijuana. They administered a beating severe enough to hurt and frighten the kid, but not so severe as to cause any long-term damage. Nevertheless, a few days later the boy's father showed up at the Scarpa house, his bruised and bandaged son in tow. Clearly, the man had no idea who he was dealing with, although he soon found out. Scarpa allowed the father to speak his piece, then responded with a brief retort of his own. He was curt and unrepentant.

"If your son ever gives drugs to my daughter again," he said coldly, "I'll kill him."

When it came to his daughter, all transgressions incited the ire of Greg Scarpa Sr. According to Lou Diamond, Little Linda was once molested by a cab driver on the way to school. Naturally, she informed her father, who dispatched Gregory and some of his buddies to teach the guy a lesson. They beat the cabbie badly, but that turned out to be insufficient retribution for Greg Sr., who determined that the man must pay for his sins with his life. Disguised as a feeble old man, with an appropriate cap and ill-fitting suit, Scarpa arranged to ride with the cabbie. He took a seat in the back and said little as the cabbie drove on. Then he directed the driver to stop at a deserted place. There, he pulled a gun from his jacket and killed him with a single shot to the back of the head. Scarpa then calmly exited the cab and stepped into a car driven by one of his crew members, who had been following at a safe distance.

Such was the penalty for disrespecting the daughter of Greg Scarpa Sr.

Neither Joey nor Little Linda understood exactly what it was their father did for a living. Oh, they knew, on some level, that he was a criminal — a gangster — you couldn't share a home with Greg Scarpa Sr. and not be aware that his was a life lived outside the margins of normal, law-abiding behavior. Not until they were well into their teenage years, however, did they begin to recognize precisely what it meant to be a mobster. Certainly they had no idea that their father routinely killed people to maintain order in his business. To them he was not the Grim Reaper; they saw him as strong, loving, and successful. They knew that they lived well; they had money and a nicely appointed home. They saw the visible evidence of the respect commanded by their father. And it wasn't merely the mobsters who bowed before him.

Scarpa protected the local merchants, and while they said they loved him, they also feared him. And with good reason. One shopkeeper at a local drugstore ran afoul of Scarpa when he brazenly (or just stupidly) decided to install a lottery machine on the premises. The device, of course, was essentially nothing more than a legal version of a numbers game, and as such was viewed by Scarpa as an infringement on his territory. In response to the shopkeeper's temerity, Scarpa instructed one of his crew members to drive a truck through the front window of the store.

The owner, no fool, repaired the window himself and had the lottery machine removed from the premises. And not in that order.

This was the man who raised Little Linda and Joey: a man as frightening as he was generous; cold-blooded one moment, benevolent the next. A soulless monster to those who stood in his way; a father who would walk through fire for those he loved.

Or so it seemed.

But then, nothing about Greg Scarpa was ever quite what it seemed.

14
THE HITMAN AND
THE G-MAN

Over the years, Anthony "Nino" Villano developed a drinking problem that sometimes impacted his work as well as his personal life. This, to Greg Scarpa, was an inexcusable and disgusting display of weakness. His own recreational drinking and fondness for the occasional joint notwithstanding, Scarpa detested drug addicts and alcoholics, and he tolerated neither in his inner circle. Villano was useful to Scarpa — together they had forged a lucrative and mutually beneficial partnership. But Scarpa was something of a control freak, and Villano's escalating dependence on alcohol was nothing if not unpredictable. To Scarpa, it was a simple matter of practicality: When Villano drank on the job, he was not only useless, but dangerous.

"The guy is getting stupid and talking too much," Scarpa complained to Linda. And he vowed to take matters into his own hands. According to Linda, Scarpa claimed that a top FBI official had given him permission to execute Villano. But before Scarpa could carry out his "orders," Villano, acting on a previous tip from Scarpa, reported to his superiors that another FBI agent had taken a $10,000 payoff from a mobster. This byzantine series of accusations and threats led to an investigation by the FBI into Villano's actions (a self-proclaimed whistle-blower), as well as the agent who allegedly accepted a bribe. In the end, neither agent was charged formally with a crime, or even with a breach of professional conduct. Instead, each was shipped out of New York. Villano finished out his career in Philadelphia; the other agent was transferred to Boston.

Anthony Villano died in 1988. The official cause of death was heart disease; however, there is no shortage of people who believe his end came, either indirectly or directly, at the hands of Greg Scarpa Sr., who allegedly murdered his friend and former colleague to ensure that he would never reveal the true nature of their alliance, and the extent of Scarpa's crimes.

The FBI by this time felt no obligation to protect Scarpa's life or interests; indeed, his file had been ordered closed in 1975, following a dispute with the bureau over $20,000 Scarpa believed was owed to him for his "undercover" work. When the FBI withheld payment, Scarpa withheld services — and information.

"Dad told me that we would be on our own for a while," Gregory remembers. "But he assured me that the FBI would be back to work something out."

This was no idle boast; nor was it wishful thinking. Scarpa was nothing if not shrewd. Keenly aware of his own value in the marketplace of information, he had reason to believe that once things cooled down a bit, the FBI would be back, seeking a new and profitable relationship. And he was right.

Agent R. Lindley "Lin" DeVecchio was six foot five, with sharp features and curly hair. An attractive, well-dressed man who favored double-breasted suits and bold silk pocket squares, he was an impressive physical presence. Respected by his peers and superiors alike, DeVecchio was a seasoned veteran who had been with the FBI since the reign of J. Edgar Hoover; he'd risen through the New York office as a colleague of Louis Freeh, the former FBI director. DeVecchio had led an interesting, cosmopolitan life; the son of a decorated Army colonel who was buried at Arlington National Cemetery, DeVecchio had lived in Italy, Japan, and Bermuda, as well as several American cities — all before he he'd even graduated from high school. He received an undergraduate degree in political science from George Washington University, and in 1963 was poised to accept a full military commission when the FBI offered him a clerk's job, the first step toward becoming an agent. DeVecchio jumped at the offer, setting aside (permanently, as it turned out) his military career.

In 1966, having completed preliminary agent training and a "personal inspection" by J. Edgar Hoover (who was famously, and rather oddly, fixated on the appearance of his agents), DeVecchio was assigned to a post in upstate New York. One year later, in April 1967, he was transferred to the New York City office, where he specialized in organized crime. He later earned a master's degree in criminal justice from Long Island University.

By most accounts, DeVecchio was a formidable and ambitious young agent; a quick study, he soon became one of the bureau's most admired experts on dealing with informants. Interestingly, his close friend and mentor at Manhattan's Organized Crime Squad was Anthony Villano, thirteen years DeVecchio's senior.

"Tony had a very good way with wise-guys," DeVecchio has said publicly. "I learned a lot by watching Tony."

DeVecchio came across the name of Greg Scarpa Sr. one day while rummaging through the files of informants whose cases had been closed (or so he claimed). In 1980, intrigued by Scarpa's history and the potential for exploiting his current role within the Mafia, DeVecchio requested, and subsequently received, permission to activate the file. This was no simple matter, however; DeVecchio first had to entice Scarpa to cooperate — no small matter, given the manner in which the mobster's previous relationship with the FBI had ended. But DeVecchio was eager to make his own mark and saw Scarpa for what he was: the Holy Grail of mob informants.

DeVecchio began his courtship with a "chance" encounter on the street. He introduced himself to Scarpa as the mobster left the apartment of a friend. Quickly and smoothly (for DeVecchio was a terrific salesman), he ingratiated himself, heaping praise and flattery on Scarpa for all of his years of service to the bureau. DeVecchio explained to Scarpa that the Colombo family fell under his purview, and while he was not looking for anything in particular that day, he suggested that they get to know each other; perhaps, DeVecchio said, they might work together at some point in the future. DeVecchio handed Scarpa a business card bearing the agent's private FBI telephone number.

DeVecchio didn't have to wait long for a response. Scarpa, seeking a return to the lucrative, freewheeling days of Anthony Villano, agreed to assist the FBI. In short order he was reinstated as a top echelon informant; R. Lindley DeVecchio would be his new handler.

To ensure a reasonable system of checks and balances, FBI protocol now dictated that informants were to be handled by two agents at a time; moreover, the bureau discouraged supervisors from operating informants. These guidelines, however, were waived for DeVecchio, who had argued persuasively that Scarpa would trust no one else; Scarpa was considered such a valuable resource that the FBI granted DeVecchio's request. In the beginning, at least, DeVecchio was extraordinarily cautious about his encounters with Scarpa, meeting privately at a bureau-rented apartment, hotel room, or some other nondescript location. Scarpa soon proved to be every bit the prize catch

DeVecchio had anticipated; the mobster was a veritable font of inside information, and DeVecchio received praise and commendations from his superiors for his role as conduit.

Sometimes DeVecchio (referred to by Scarpa as "Dello"), delivered cash to Greg Sr.; at other times, as prosecutors later alleged, Scarpa delivered cash to DeVecchio. The men communicated frequently via a special telephone in the FBI building called the "hello phone," which could not be traced. When DeVecchio visited Scarpa's home on Avenue J in Brooklyn, he was greeted with warmth and hospitality — more like a friend or business associate than a cop holding the reins. Linda would give the agent a hug and fix trays of eggplant parmigiana to take home.

But it had been rumored through the years that DeVecchio soon succumbed to the lure of the Mafia. And as prosecutors later claimed, he became a partner in crime, and received kickbacks from the Scarpa crew. Sometimes the agent was paid in cash; other times he accepted gifts — jewelry, for example, that he passed on to his wife and mother. If DeVecchio's intentions were once noble and pure (with career ascension the primary selfish motivation), they now became something else entirely. Scarpa, ever the astute judge of character, had figured correctly: DeVecchio was as easily corrupted as his predecessor.

The first time Linda claims to have seen Greg Sr. give DeVecchio money was in their kitchen. While telling DeVecchio about a major score his crew had recently pulled off, Scarpa extracted a wad of cash from his pocket and handed it to DeVecchio, who slid the money into his pants pocket as the men went on talking; to Linda, his reaction was as cool and emotionless as it might have been if Greg Sr. had just passed him a cup of coffee. Clearly, she realized, this was not an unusual transaction.

With comfort came sloppiness, and soon there were others who claimed to have witnessed the illicit relationship between the agent and the killer. Debbie Scarpa, Greg Sr.'s oldest daughter, had a surprisingly strong relationship with Linda, and visited often. One day, when Debbie came over unannounced, Greg Sr. told her that Linda was out shopping. He introduced Debbie to DeVecchio and asked her to wait in the kitchen. As she passed the living room, she says she saw her father hand a thick stack of bills to DeVecchio. The image stayed with her. She knew that her father had a special relationship with his money (and this was a large quantity changing hands). Scarpa always kept his cash in a large roll of bills, folded over and held together with a rubber band. He was obsessive about money: The bills had to be going the same way, head to head, each one perfectly straight and smooth. No wrinkles, no corners turned up.

"I talk to my money," Scarpa would say with a laugh. "And my money takes care of me."

A less cryptic view of the Scarpa–DeVecchio show has been offered by Gregory Scarpa Jr., who had a front-row seat for many years.

"Whenever Dad's crew did a big job, like bank robbery, with a take of a few million dollars," Gregory claims, "DeVecchio was always in on it. He would be parked in a car a few blocks away from the bank, with a high-frequency police radio and a high-tech walkie-talkie. This enabled him to hear if anyone got word of the bank robbery and warn the crew in time to make a quick getaway. If law enforcement became aware of the crime while it was in progress, De-Vecchio would prevent arrests by claiming that the participants included FBI informants."

(It should be noted here that while Gregory claims to be certain that DeVecchio was involved in these heists, he acknowledged to prosecutors that he never actually witnessed DeVecchio at the site; rather, the involvement of DeVecchio, he says, was confirmed for him by Greg Scarpa Sr.)

According to Gregory, DeVecchio gave his father the addresses and phone numbers of delinquent borrowers from Scarpa's loan-sharking activities, as well as the identities of informants who might be a threat. With DeVecchio's knowledge and consent, Gregory says, Scarpa murdered, or attempted to murder, numerous individuals deemed oppositional to his various criminal enterprises. Greg Sr. then dutifully reported the killings to the FBI, attributing the murders to others. According to Gregory, committing murders and blaming others, always with DeVecchio's knowledge, became his father's modus operandi.

Albert Nacha was a particularly vivid example of this devil's pact. Gregory claims that DeVecchio informed his father that Nacha, a young neighborhood thug with far more balls than brains, had bragged of his plans to confront the great Greg Scarpa Sr. The kid's strategy was woefully simplistic: He would walk up to Scarpa, put a gun in his face, and demand some of that great wad of cash the mobster always seemed to be carrying. If Scarpa refused, then Nacha would shoot him in the head. That way he'd have a pile of money and a newfound reputation for toughness.

Tragically (almost pathetically), Nacha was in way over his head. With DeVecchio's assistance, according to Gregory, Greg Sr. quickly learned of this feeble plot and figured out where Nacha lived, and where he liked to hang out. Accompanied by a couple of his crew, Scarpa shot and killed Nacha. Initially, Gregory Scarpa Jr. was indicted for the murder, but he was eventually acquitted. Another crew member ultimately took the rap for the killing, and spent twenty years in prison for a crime he didn't commit.

As Greg Sr. dispatched his enemies and muscled, murdered, and ratted his way up the ladder of organized crime, he enjoyed extraordinary protection from the FBI. As it had been years earlier, when Scarpa reported to Anthony Villano, the arrangement proved fruitful for criminal and cop. According to prosecutors, Scarpa provided DeVecchio with sophisticated inside information that helped the FBI build cases against the mob brass of all five New York families. And as Scarpa ascended the ranks of organized crime, DeVecchio found his career on a similar trajectory. In 1983 he was promoted to squad supervisor; five years later, in 1988, he was put in charge of the entire Colombo crime family squad of the FBI's New York office. By 1990 DeVecchio's duties had expanded to include the Bonanno crime family. That he had compromised his integrity, broken the very laws he had sworn to uphold, and blurred the line between right and wrong apparently mattered little to DeVecchio, if Greg Jr., Linda Schiro, and prosecutors in the Brooklyn DA's office are to be believed.

15
DR. SCHOLNICK AND THE BEAUTY QUEEN

Gregory Scarpa Jr. made his bones in a highly personal and familial manner: by executing the jealous lover of his father's mistress. The twisted road that led to this killing had begun with an affair between Greg Scarpa Sr. and a former beauty queen from Israel named Lili Dajani.

Lili was a partner with Dr. Eliezer Scholnick, the beleaguered owner of a New York abortion clinic who had lost his medical license in 1976 for incompetence. Lili had worked as a nurse receptionist at the clinic before and after Dr. Scholnick lost his license. She and Scholnick had become lovers, a development that later contributed to a messy divorce and necessitated Scholnick placing the clinic in Lili's name — even as he remained its "administrator."

Profits from the clinic had left Lili financially secure. She owned a home in California, a condo in Las Vegas, and an apartment on Manhattan's Sutton Place. She traveled around Manhattan by chauffered limousine and was rarely seen in public without sporting a treasure trove of jewels.

Scarpa fell hard for Lili Dajani, in part because she was so different from Linda. Lili was not only beautiful, but exotic and rich, as well. Scarpa didn't have to take care of Lili, to throw money at her. She had resources of her own.

A three-week trip to Vegas, ostensibly to conduct mob business, evolved into a year-long affair between Scarpa and Dajani, during which the couple married. This, of course, left Scarpa with the equivalent of three wives: Connie, Linda, and Lili (of which only Connie was the legal wife). When he finally returned to New York, he alternated among three homes. Remarkably, while they might have been agitated by this arrangement, not one of Scarpa's wives tossed him out. As always, they tolerated his wandering, philandering, and criminal ways, figuring, perhaps, that a piece of Greg Scarpa was better than none at all.

Among those less sanguine about Scarpa's prodigious appetite for womanizing was the unfortunate Dr. Scholnick, who, unable to shake his infatuation with Lili, foolishly sought revenge against Scarpa. To facilitate his fantasy, Scholnick solicited the aid of an old friend who happened to be a made man in the Genovese crime family. Scholnick asked his mobster pal to intervene on his behalf, to convince Scarpa that the clinic was owned by the Genovese family; by extension, of course, this would have meant that Dr. Scholnick and Lili Dajani were, in essence, Genovese "property," and thus off-limits to members of the Colombo family.

There was just one problem: None of this was true. It was a complete fabrication, and no one would believe it. The mobster sympathized with the doctor, but there was nothing he could do. "Best leave it alone," he told his friend. "Get on with your life."

Sadly, the good doctor was not so easily dissuaded. Lovesick, broken-hearted, and gripped by a sort of madness, he made what could generously be termed a "tactical error." Vowing to take matters into his own delicate hands, Scholnick told his pal he was going to the FBI. Through Lili he had learned intimate details of Scarpa's illegal activities; surely this would interest the feds, Scholnick reasoned. (If necessary, he'd even testify in open court.) They'd swoop down on Scarpa, toss him in prison, and the doctor would be free to resume his affair with Lili (whose opinion in this entire matter was apparently irrelevant).

This, of course, was a plan not rooted in reality. In the world of the Mafia, such threats are not made idly, and rarely are they successfully executed by a novice. The five families were all engaged in similar and sometimes overlapping ventures; the last thing the Genovese capo wanted was to have the FBI cracking down on Scarpa through the use of information provided by one of his own friends. That would be bad for business; it would be bad for everyone. The mobster told Scarpa of the doctor's plan. Scarpa reached out to DeVecchio, asking for the usual pertinent information.

"Within the week," Gregory recalls, "DeVecchio gave my father Scholnick's home address, a picture of him, and his daily routine, without asking Dad why he needed the information."

A contract was put out on Scholnick; the job was assigned to Gregory. Greg Sr. had confidence in his son, but to ease his own mind and make Gregory feel more comfortable, he asked Joe Brewster to tag along. Joe was a pro — if anything went wrong on a job, you wanted him by your side.

By this time Gregory was a hardened criminal, more savvy about the ways of the Mafia, less emotional about the wanton disregard for human life so often exhibited by his buddies, and even by his father. Although he had never pulled the trigger himself, Gregory had been witness to dozens of murders. He knew what to expect; he also knew that the time had come for him to get blood on his own hands. Scholnick was a rat anyway, which made him contemptible rather than pitiable. Gregory figured he'd have no problem doing the deed, especially since it would help his father.

A few days later, Gregory and Joe Brewster arrived at Scholnick's apartment building in a car driven by Carmine Sessa. They waited in the lobby, watching carefully at the passersby, trying to spot Dr. Scholnick. Finally, there appeared in the lobby a middle-aged man who resembled the photo they had studied. Joe Brewster stepped up to the man and smiled respectfully.

"Are you Dr. Scholnick?"

The doctor nodded and continued walking toward the bank of elevators.

Joe Brewster engaged Scholnick in conversation while Gregory walked behind them and shot the doctor in the back of the head. As the doctor slumped to the floor, Gregory pumped another bullet into his skull, just to be sure.

Joe Brewster and Gregory walked briskly out of the building and into the waiting car. The three wiseguys then drove into Manhattan and discarded the murder weapon in a sewer drain before proceeding to a neighborhood bar, where Joe and Carmine congratulated Gregory and bought him a round of drinks. Gregory called his father and told him the job had been done. On the other end of the line, Greg Scarpa Sr. smiled, his heart filling with paternal pride.

Killing is not such an easy or forgettable thing, however — not even for a career mobster. Gregory was living alone when he got home that evening, drunk and high on cocaine, he collapsed into bed. But he couldn't sleep. The room swirled and his heart began to race. Gruesome images of the late Dr. Scholnick flickered across the back of his eyes, like an internal movie — blood-spattered scenes of an execution, in all its horrific detail. He saw the doctor fall, a crimson geyser gushing from his head. He felt the gun's report against his hand, smelled the cordite and the blood and the stink of a man's bodily functions letting go. Suddenly Gregory was out of bed, lurching and stumbling toward the bathroom. He fell on the floor, dropped his head against the toilet seat, and vomited.

After he emptied his stomach, Gregory crawled back into bed, mumbling to himself about what a lucky guy he was. Like his father, Gregory had a license to kill, and it came with the blessing and backing (not to mention the formidable protection) of the FBI.

The next morning, when Gregory arrived at Wimpy Boys, the guys in the crew treated him differently. There were knowing winks, the odd pat on the back, an occasional congratulatory embrace. No one spoke explicitly about the execution of Dr. Scholnick, but clearly it was a subject of great interest. Through this single, violent deed, Gregory had crossed a threshold. In the eyes of his friends and colleagues, he commanded greater respect and admiration; he was one of them now. The cost, of course, was a piece of his soul — after that night, Gregory never blanched nor fell sick at the thought of taking a human life. With each subsequent killing (and there were many), the act became easier, less personal. A glass or two of whiskey and a couple snorts of coke were all the anesthetic Gregory needed to get the job done.

Shortly after the execution of Dr. Scholnick, Gregory was officially inducted into La Cosa Nostra in a ritual that had been handed down for ages. Formally attired in his finest suit, the son of Greg Scarpa was taken to an underground garage and offered a seat at a large table, along with several other Mafia inductees. As the bosses looked on proudly, the rookies joined hands and recited vows of loyalty. A drop of blood was drawn with a needle from each man's trigger finger (signifying membership for life — "blood in, blood out"). Then there were handshakes and hugs, and a party that went on all night, replete with steak and shrimp, top-shelf liquor, and a bevy of high-priced prostitutes. For Gregory Scarpa Jr., there would be no turning back.

So skilled was Gregory that within a year he became a capo with his own crew. In effect, this placed him higher in the pecking order than his own father. Lou Diamond, as Greg Sr.'s attorney, spent many nights with both father and son, and recalls at least one occasion when Gregory attempted to pull rank on his dad. It happened at Wimpy Boys. In response to a request from Greg Scarpa Sr. to retrieve a car, Gregory retorted sharply, "Get it yourself. I outrank you now."

When questioned about the incident, Gregory shakes his head in disbelief.

"I must have been kidding," he says. "I

never would have spoken that way to my father. Although it's true that I was a capo and Dad was just a 'soldier,' my father was meaner than anyone I've ever met. I always knew that if I disrespected him in any way, or crossed him in any way, no matter how long it took him, he would have found a way to make sure I would one day be found dead."

This seems not an unreasonable assessment; moreover, given Scarpa's link to the FBI, Gregory's death might well have gone virtually unnoticed, or at least unsolved. Hunter Scholnick, now a Manhattan attorney, was away at college when his father was killed, but had seen him a few days earlier during Thanksgiving break. The younger Scholnick recalls that his father had expressed confidence that his earnings would soon increase to prior levels, and that life would improve.

"I'm finally going to get my money back," he told his son.

Several months later, as the investigation into his father's death stalled, detectives informed Hunter that they were unlikely to solve the case.

"They had hit a wall," he says. Detectives also strongly suggested that the Scholnick family not try to retrieve the doctor's business from Dajani, advice the family accepted.

"That's what they said to us," Hunter recalls. " 'Don't do it. You don't want to get involved. It's probably what got your father killed.' In retrospect, they may have been right."

16
CRAZY LOVE

A solid earner who never missed an opportunity to make a buck — illicit or otherwise — Gregory was slightly ahead of the curve when it came to the digital gaming revolution that would eventually grip America's youth. With his father's approval, Gregory transformed a front room at Wimpy Boys into a video arcade for kids from the neighborhood. (Meanwhile, of course, he and the rest of the Scarpa crew continued to operate a criminal enterprise in the rear of the club.) The arcade included such cutting-edge attractions as Pac-Man, Space Invaders, and Frogger, along with pinball machines (for nostalgia's sake) and other kid-friendly games. Soon the arcade was bustling with activity: Kids would get out of school in the afternoon and rush right over, unwittingly dropping money from their allowances or part-time jobs into the coffers of the Scarpa crew.

Among the regulars was a charming, doe-eyed, sixteen-year-old girl named Maria, who quickly captured the attention of the arcade's owner. Gregory had known Maria's mother, Alice, who once had been married to a Colombo family mobster named Ernie. Well liked by his peers, Ernie had suffered a fatal heart attack one afternoon while sitting in a parked car with his daughter, Maria. Unbeknownst to Maria (or anyone else, for that matter), Ernie had long been dealing with health problems. As he felt the telltale signs of angina, Ernie had pulled the car off to the side of the road and began struggling to retrieve nitroglycerin pills from his shirt pocket. But the pain was incapacitating, and soon he lost consciousness. He died in the car, with the unopened pills in his pocket.

Ernie's death had a profound impact on Maria, not least because she held herself at least partially accountable. Gregory was deeply attracted to Maria, despite her age, and soon struck up a friendship. He told the girl that he had been a close friend of Ernie's, and that if she ever needed anything, all she had to do was ask. Soon, Maria and her friends were playing the machines daily; Gregory fueled their fun with an endless supply of quarters.

"Maria was so beautiful," Gregory recalls. "And yet she had a certain sadness about her."

Although Gregory took financial care of Diane and Lilly, the mothers of his three children, and had a stable of girlfriends, there was no woman with whom he was in love. Now what began as a platonic, almost brotherly infatuation morphed into something else entirely around the time of Maria's seventeenth birthday, when Gregory received a phone call from one of his younger crew members. The kid, a teenager, was with a bunch of friends, hanging out at a club. They wanted Gregory to join them. At first, Gregory demurred. But then he heard Maria in the background, pleading with him to come out. And his knees weakened.

"Over the next few weeks," remembers Gregory, "we were together every night," a development that deeply disturbed Maria's mother. This was no great shock to Gregory. For one thing, he was much older than Maria; for another, he was, well, a gangster. "Alice had been married and divorced from a goodfella, so that was the last thing she wanted for her daughter," Gregory says. "I didn't blame her."

Unfortunately, for Gregory, there were

potentially lethal consequences to the manner in which Alice voiced her displeasure. She complained to the Colombo family bosses about Gregory dating Ernie's seventeen-year-old daughter. The next day Gregory received the unpleasant news from his captain, Anthony "Scappy" Scarpati: "Stay away from Maria."

But Gregory could no more avoid Maria than he could stop breathing; life without her had become unimaginable. With seemingly callous disregard for mob protocol, Maria and Gregory continued to "date." Most of their encounters took place at a Holiday Inn on Staten Island, which fell under the protective umbrella of the Scarpa crew. If the hotel had any problems with guests or contractors, Gregory would solve the problem. In exchange, Gregory was entitled to an endless supply of free rooms, with room service and champagne.

It was, of course, impossible for the affair to go undetected for long, and eventually word got back to Maria's godfather, a wise-guy nicknamed Black Sam. For the second time a beef was registered against the actions of Gregory Scarpa Jr. regarding his relationship with Maria. This was no minor transgression. Among the unwritten rules in the Mafia, this is one of the oldest: "You are never told twice." Under normal circumstances, Gregory would have been dead within a matter of days; however, this was one occasion when family ties proved to be lifesaving. Out of respect for (and perhaps fear of) Greg Scarpa Sr., the bosses gave Gregory a pass. But there were limits to their tolerance. Greg Sr. was told that his son's life would be spared — so long as the father agreed to clean up the mess that the kid's personal life had become.

Greg Sr. followed through on his promise, meeting with Gregory and informing him, in no uncertain terms, that he would give up Maria. Business depended on it. The family depended on it. His *life* depended on it. To Gregory, however, a life without Maria was not a life worth living. So he did the unthinkable: He went behind his father's back and arranged a meeting with the acting bosses of the Colombo family; Gennaro "Jerry Lang" Langella and Donnie "Shanks" Montelabano. Gregory went to them, hat in hand, heart on his sleeve, and begged for their understanding. He loved Maria and had only the most honorable intentions toward her. Swearing that he would marry her, Gregory talked as fast as he could, the words tumbling forth as the wiseguys listened intently.

When he was done, Gregory sat for a moment, his heart still racing. (*The things a man will do for love,* he thought.) With a wave of their hands, the bosses dismissed him while they conferred on the matter. After a time, Gregory was called back into the room and presented with a verdict: The family would permit him to continue the relationship with Maria, on the condition that he agree to marry her.

"I swear it," Gregory said, "on my life."

Langella nodded, as if to say, *Good thing, because it is your life we're talking about here.* When he finally spoke, however, this is what Langella said: "In the meantime, no sex."

Gregory's jaw dropped; his shoulders sagged. Montelabano took one look at the kid and laughed.

"Jerry, if we tell him he can't have sex with this girl, it would be the same as sitting across the table of the guy that put you in jail and you had a gun but were told you can't use it."

Langella smiled. "Okay, just don't get her pregnant."

Young and rebellious, and seeking freedom from her family as much as anything else, Maria moved in with Gregory. He bought her a Chrysler convertible and a four-carat diamond ring. They drank a lot and began doing cocaine together. Aside from the occasional bracing preexecution snort (the hit before the hit, as it were), Gregory was something of a neophyte when it came to drugs. But his girlfriend was more experienced.

"Maria was like a wild mare," recalls Gregory. "But it turned out that instead of taming her, I joined her. [The partying] was a bit too much for me. Still, I couldn't give her up. I believed that if I married her, things would slow down, and we could start a family of our own."

For a while Gregory owned a nightclub in Staten Island known as On the Rocks; Maria, of course, was a regular, dancing and partying till closing time (usually 4:00 A.M.). After hours, a second party would begin, this one involving only Maria and Gregory. They'd continue drinking, do a few lines of cocaine, then go home and have sex until one or both partners passed out. Greg Sr. began to worry about his son, who would disappear for days on end, lost in a fog of alcohol, sex, and drugs.

Through the eyes of a father (concerned for his son) and a mobster (concerned about business), Greg Sr. viewed Maria as a terrible influence on Gregory; his opinion was shared by Linda. Nevertheless, against the wishes of just about everyone in his circle, Gregory married Maria in a quiet ceremony at Staten Island City Hall. Predictably the marriage quickly showed signs of fraying. When Maria became pregnant, Gregory begged her to stop drinking and to get off drugs. A halfhearted attempt failed, and Maria continued to use both alcohol and cocaine throughout her pregnancy.

Remarkably, Maria gave birth to a healthy baby girl (also named Maria), and for a while she seemed happy and content in her new role as a mother. But she proved to be an impatient, distant parent. Whether suffering from a prolonged bout of postpartum depression, or burned out from years of abusing drugs and alcohol, Maria became distant and withdrawn. She slept nearly all the time, rising from her bed only to eat or go to the bathroom. She paid little attention to the baby, which naturally provoked enormous tension between her and her husband. Then exhaustion gave way to restlessness and insomnia. Maria paced the house day and night, mumbling to herself, ignoring her husband and her child. Disagreements between Gregory and Maria escalated dramatically, into full-blown battles, until finally Gregory could take it no longer and ordered Maria and the baby out of the house. He drove them to the home of Maria's mother, figuring perhaps Alice was better equipped to handle the problem.

The next morning Gregory learned that Maria had been admitted to Coney Island Hospital after suffering what appeared to be some sort of emotional breakdown. Doctors refused to let her go home until she underwent a complete physical and mental evaluation. When Gregory learned that Maria was being held against her will, he rushed to the hospital and angrily told the admitting nurse that he was picking up his wife. The nurse's response was hardly sympathetic: She called security. Within minutes, Gregory was surrounded by a half-dozen guards armed with batons, telling him to vacate the premises.

Of course, Gregory Scarpa Jr. was not so easily dissuaded. He walked outside and immediately put in a call to a few of the Scarpa crew heavyweights, summoning them to the hospital. They showed up en masse, nearly a dozen strong, and entered the hospital alongside their boss. As they approached the security guards, Gregory calmly stepped forward. He didn't want trouble; he simply wanted to take Maria home. And no one would stand in his way.

"I'm going to find my wife," he said. "And if any of you try to stop me, my guys are going to hurt you real bad." The guards — who were neither trained law enforcement officials nor sufficiently well paid to risk their lives — quickly let him pass.

Gregory walked through the hospital, looking in every room and calling Maria's name. He finally found her alone, strapped to a bed and crying hysterically. Gregory cut off the straps, took her into his arms, and raced down the hospital corridor toward the front door. As his crew stood watch, keeping patients and personnel at bay, Gregory placed Maria in the backseat of a car. Together, they drove off, stopping only at his mother-in-law's house to pick up the baby.

As Gregory quickly discovered, however, there were some things that one could not fix through sheer force of will. Within a matter of days Maria had slid back into a state of depression. Helpless to "fix" his wife, and overwhelmed by the task of caring for his baby daughter, Gregory sought help from Maria's doctor, who convinced him that she needed long-term professional care; in the short term, however, she needed to be hospitalized. So Gregory dropped the baby off with Maria's mother, and then took Maria, screaming and flailing every inch of the way, back to the hospital.

For the next two and a half months Gregory dutifully visited Maria in the hospital, holding her hand and accompanying her as she lurched about the building like a zombie. Heavily medicated and uncommunicative, Maria seemed a mere shell of the vibrant young woman Gregory had married, and he wondered if she would ever recover. Sometimes, when he left for the night, Maria would stir from her trance just long enough to cry and hold him and beg him to take her home. Gregory would apologize, give her a kiss, and then drive home, his eyes brimming with tears as he thought of the hell that his life had become.

To a point, Gregory's bosses and crew members were sympathetic to his plight, but business was business, and as a capo he could only be absent so long. Not knowing where else to turn for assistance with his infant daughter (Maria's mother had a full-time job and was thus unavailable), Gregory turned to his ex-wife. Now happily married to a New York City fireman, Diane agreed to care for the baby. Surprised at her generosity, and his good fortune, Gregory offered to pay all expenses for little Maria and his two older girls — and he threw in a little something for Diane, as well.

Six months later, weaned from drugs and seemingly recovered from her bout of depression, Maria was released from the hospital; she and the baby returned to Gregory's home, and the three of them enjoyed a period of comfort and security they had not previously known. For a while, at least, life was good; anything seemed possible.

17
THE DEATH OF DONNIE SOMMA

By early 1985 federal law enforcement officials had begun to suspect that a crew run by Greg Scarpa Sr. was involved in a fairly extensive credit card scam. On this occasion, however, it was not the FBI that went after Scarpa — rather, it was the United States Secret Service. Acting upon a series of tips, the agency decided to set up a sting involving an undercover officer who, during a meeting at Wimpy Boys, sold more than three hundred blank (counterfeit) credit cards to Scarpa. Arrested and indicted by the Brooklyn Organized Crime Strike Force, Scarpa entered a plea of guilty.

Prior to sentencing, in July 1986, Judge Leo Glasser received a letter from the strike force detailing Scarpa's criminal history and his penchant for violence. Glasser was strongly urged to hand down the maximum sentence allowed by law; at the very least, the letter noted, Scarpa should face a severe fine (one that would cripple his business enterprise) and do time behind bars. But Lin DeVecchio came to Scarpa's rescue, submitting a memo to the court detailing the informant's contributions to the FBI; largely due to the influence of Agent DeVecchio, Scarpa drew a virtual slap on the wrist: a $10,000 fine and five years probation. He remained a free man.

If there was a drawback to DeVecchio's interference, it was merely this: The sentence was so light that it raised suspicion not merely in law enforcement circles, but among Scarpa's own crew. How, they wondered, could the guy possibly have beaten such a serious rap? They understood, of course, that Scarpa curried favor with the cops, but they had no inkling as to the depth of his involvement or betrayal. Instead, it was assumed that Scarpa, like many wiseguys before him, simply paid off law enforcement officials when necessary to keep himself and his crew out of trouble, and to deflect undue interest.

But this case was different. It involved the Secret Service, and as such one needed more than the usual amount of Teflon to keep the charges from sticking. And so Scarpa's fellow mobsters began to think the unthinkable: Perhaps — just possibly —

Greg Scarpa Sr. was a rat.

Their concerns were allayed one evening at Wimpy Boys, when Scarpa drew a gun on Dominick "Donnie" Somma. Greg Sr. had been planning to murder Donnie for some time — ever since a well-planned bank job that he and his crew had carried out over a three-day holiday. The burglars had dismantled the alarms and the crew members were working as quickly and quietly as possible. Outside, on the street, Donnie Somma and Gregory Scarpa Jr. were at opposite corners from the bank, communicating via walkie-talkie and watching for any heat (this could include uniformed officers, plainclothes detectives, or even innocent bystanders who had the misfortune of stumbling onto the scene). If either man saw anyone approaching the bank, he was expected to alert the crew; all work would stop temporarily until the person had passed by. Meanwhile, DeVecchio and Greg Sr. circled the surrounding streets in separate cars, prepared to alert the crew of any law enforcement in the vicinity.

The heist was going as planned when, suddenly, a truck bearing the logo of a cleaning company pulled up in front of a nearby bank. But instead of entering that bank, the uniformed cleaner walked into the bank that

Scarpa's crew was burglarizing. The startled crew members ran out the door and escaped, but they were both perplexed and angered that neither Donnie nor Gregory had warned them about the cleaner. Was it possible that they hadn't seen the man? Or his truck? It seemed unlikely.

For whatever reason, the blame was pinned on Donnie, who quickly passed the buck to Gregory. Instead of attempting to resolve the situation within the crew, Donnie put in a beef with Greg Sr.'s captain, Anthony Scarpati. Scappy, of course, was a close friend of Scarpa's and saw nothing to be gained by getting involved in this dispute; he told Donnie to calm down and forget about the whole matter. It would soon blow over.

Scarpati then told Greg Sr. what Donnie had done. Greg Sr. was enraged that Donnie Somma had put a beef out on his son. To disrespect Gregory was tantamount to disrespecting Greg Sr. And such an act was not undertaken lightly, for the end result might well be murder. This was precisely what Greg Sr. had in mind; Somma, however, was a made man, and thus could not be killed without the consent of the family's boss. These things took time. More often than not, as days bled into weeks, weeks into months, the grievance lessened in severity, and perhaps even dissolved — and the head of the family would not have to rule on the killing of a made man.

But Greg Scarpa Sr. was a patient and unforgiving man. He bided his time as the months passed. Finally, Scarpati told Greg Sr. that Donnie had been involved in a drug deal with the Gambino family — without seeking permission from the Colombo bosses. This alone was enough to get Donnie whacked. (In fact, it was a far more egregious offense than putting in a beef against Gregory Scarpa.) Carmine Persico, the Colombo family boss, told Scarpati that he wanted Donnie killed. And who better to carry out this task than Greg Scarpa Sr.?

According to Gregory, a few days after Greg Sr. was let off with probation on the credit card conviction, he was hanging out at Wimpy Boys, in the back office, with John Sap, Carmine Sessa, Joe Brewster, and a couple of young shooters named Mario and Billy. Sitting behind his desk, Greg Sr. calmly telephoned Donnie Somma and asked him to come over to Wimpy Boys right away — another bank job had come across the table, and they wanted to discuss the details. After hanging up the phone, Scarpa turned to Mario and Billy and told

215

them to clear out the arcade at the front of the club.

"I don't want any kids around," he said.

Fifteen minutes later Donnie Somma walked into an empty Wimpy Boys and headed for Scarpa's office. When Donnie walked into the back room, the guys greeted him warmly, as if nothing out of the ordinary was about to happen. Greg Sr. invited Donnie to sit across from him. Small talk ensued (which was typical before getting down to business), the whole gang chatting and telling jokes, stepping on one another's punch lines. As the noise increased, Greg Sr. casually reached into the bottom drawer of his desk, withdrew a handgun, pointed it at Donnie's head, and pulled the trigger. Donnie Somma tipped backward in his chair and slumped to the floor. Unmoved, and with the cool detachment of a man simply completing an assignment, Greg Sr. pushed back from his desk, stood up, walked over to the fallen form of the unfortunate and arrogant Donnie Somma, and shot him in the head once more.

A cleanup naturally ensued. Greg Sr. told the guys to pull up the area rug covering much of the office floor, and to wrap Donnie Somma inside it. They stuffed him into the trunk of a stolen car, drove to Staten Island,

and dumped him on the side of a service road.

By morning, the blood had been wiped from the office walls and a new rug had been installed. It was a fine rug, though Scarpa found it less attractive than the previous model. That rug had been his favorite, and he missed it now, sitting at his desk, looking out at the room. But he took comfort in knowing that at least it had been put to good use.

18
BAD BLOOD

If Greg Scarpa Sr. appeared on the surface to be a man unburdened by ethical dilemmas, perhaps the reality of his life was somewhat more complicated. Consider, for example, his medical history, which included ongoing gastrointestinal maladies, the culmination of which occurred in the summer of 1986, while Scarpa was awaiting resolution on the credit card case. The cool, soulless killer had developed bleeding ulcers and was admitted to Victory Memorial, a small private hospital in Brooklyn's Bay Ridge neighborhood. There physicians observed him for several days before deciding that the ulcers were likely the result of an aspirin habit Scarpa had developed to self-medicate for chronic back pain. Whether it was exacerbated by the stress of escalating legal woes and the moral baggage that comes with being a murderer is anyone's guess; certainly Scarpa himself never admitted to any such issues.

Regardless, when medication failed to stop the bleeding, doctors told Linda that Greg Sr. would require a series of blood transfusions. Linda knew this would be a problem. Greg Sr. was at once naturally suspicious and racist to the core: He would reject the idea of accepting blood from anyone he didn't know, especially a person of color. Too, there was the threat of contaminated blood. Hospital staff and other patients advised Linda to seek donations from relatives. Even though the hospital supposedly screened all donations, the process was far from flawless, and there was always a chance that donated blood could contain HIV, hepatitis, or some other infection. Linda dutifully instructed Larry Mazza to recruit friends and family members to make blood donations. Within a few hours more than two dozen volunteers had lined up to give blood for Greg Sr. Among these was a twenty-nine-year-old crew member and devout bodybuilder named Paul Mele.

Mele's impressive physique could be attributed not only to rigorous daily workouts at a Brooklyn gym, but to the anabolic steroids that were part of his "nutritional" regimen. Mele and his buddies routinely shared performance-enhancing drugs, as well as the needles required to inject them. For some time that summer, Mele had complained to friends and crew members of a steady, low fever; Scarpa had been concerned about Mele; for such a big, strong kid, he always seemed to be suffering from one malady or another.

"You should get that taken care of," Scarpa told Mele, shortly before falling ill himself.

Facing life-threatening internal bleeding, Greg Sr. was rushed into emergency surgery at Victory Memorial. With Scarpa's personal physician unavailable, the procedure was overseen by a resident, Dr. Angelito Sebollena. Afterward, the patient spiked a raging fever; he lapsed in and out of consciousness. When Scarpa began hemorrhaging blood in the postoperative ward, Linda panicked and ordered him transferred to Manhattan's Mt. Sinai Hospital; there he underwent a second surgical procedure to repair his herniated stomach.

Scarpa remained hospitalized at Mt. Sinai for six weeks, finally earning a discharge on October 21, 1986. He exited the hospital a shell of his former self, having withered from a muscular 230 pounds to a skeletal 150 pounds. To repair his bleeding ulcers, doctors at Mt. Sanai had been forced to remove a portion of Greg's stomach, so now he required pancreatic enzyme pills to help digest his food; with the assistance of a walker, he moved painfully and slowly, each step as tentative as a toddler's.

With Greg Sr. home, friends and associates stopped by to pay their respects; the guests included Paul Mele, who was still running the same low fever. A few weeks later Greg Sr. and Linda were shocked to discover that Mele had died after checking into Lutheran Medical Center. The cause of death, they learned, was pneumonia. In reality, though, Mele had died of AIDS, which had severely compromised his immune system. It was presumed that he had contracted the disease from a contaminated needle.

Not long after that, Scarpa received a call from his personal physician. The doctor had some very bad news. Greg Sr. had apparently contracted the HIV virus from a blood transfusion at Victory Memorial. Shocked and depressed, Scarpa sought second and third opinions. His blood was checked and rechecked. Each time the diagnosis was grim: positive for HIV. As Linda drove him home from a lab one day, Greg Sr. accepted his fate. He began to cry, something Linda had never witnessed.

"I have it," he sobbed. "The virus. The AIDS thing."

Scarpa filed a lawsuit against Dr. Sebollena and Victory Memorial for exposing him to AIDS.

Linda and Greg Sr. decided to keep the exact nature of his illness a secret. If anyone (even Greg Sr.'s closest friends and family members) asked, they were told some type of fabrication. Greg Sr. was sick, they said. If more information was requested, Linda would say he had "cancer," but she never specified the type of cancer, never discussed treatment options. There was, until the very end, an air of mystery surrounding the health of Greg Scarpa Sr.

Although Greg Sr. grew steadily thinner, he showed little other evidence of illness. Slowly, he regained strength, and for a time medication seemed to halt the progress of the disease. He still went to Wimpy Boys every day, still joked with the crew and plotted new scams and schemes.

There were, however, practical considerations stemming from Scarpa's health issues, most notably a cash flow problem. He turned to his son to bring in more money. Gregory, of course, didn't hesitate to help his dad. Together they decided to enter the most lucrative (and dangerous) of illicit enterprises: the trafficking of narcotics. As with many old-school mafioso, Greg Sr. had long avoided this enterprise, but now he had no choice. There was too much money to be made — and Scarpa needed cash. He made Gregory take a vow of professionalism: "Deal, but do not use." Gregory agreed, although he had been smoking weed and snorting coke for years, which Greg Sr. realized but declined to acknowledge.

With the financial backing of his father (who received the lion's share of the profits), Gregory set up a marijuana operation out of the College of Staten Island. It was a simple business with an eager clientele. Gregory employed a half-dozen college kids, who hawked small bags of pot while standing along the side of a road heading into the campus. Word of the enterprise quickly spread, and sometimes traffic would back up for nearly a mile as the runners moved from car to car.

Before long the Scarpas had a thriving and lucrative business at the College of Staten Island. But Gregory's crew was violent and ambitious — and soon they began expanding their territory. Dealers who sold marijuana and other drugs in areas that Gregory considered his turf, (including the College of Staten Island), were required to make substantial payoffs (as much as $1,000 a day) or risk serious physical harm.

With cash flowing freely, Greg Sr. suggested that Linda take a trip to Florida and invest in a second home; eventually, he hoped, they would retire together, so that Greg could spend his last days in warmth and comfort, accompanied by the one great love of his life. Knowing how sick he was, Linda hesitated to leave his side, but Greg Sr. insisted. So Linda traveled to Singer Island, Florida, and found a beautiful condo on the beach. The price: $125,000. It seemed to her an exorbitant amount of money for a luxury neither of them really needed, and she called Greg Sr. to tell him as much.

"My love, do you like it?" he asked her.

Linda could not deny that indeed she did like it. Very much.

"Well, make sure you take it," he said.

Linda returned to Brooklyn, picked up $125,000 (in cash, of course) from Greg Sr., and flew back down to Florida to close the deal.

The condo on Singer Island was popular with the entire Scarpa family. But no one enjoyed it more than Greg Sr. He loved taking long walks on the beach with Linda, and wading into the surf, looking out at the vast blue ocean. One day he and Joey were standing in the water, talking the way father and sons do, when suddenly Greg Sr. lost his balance. He fell into the waves and rolled about helplessly, unable to regain his footing. Joey lifted his father into his arms and just stood there, crying, knowing how weak Greg Sr. was, and yet he was still trying to do the things he loved. Joey walked Greg Sr. back to the beach and made him sit down.

"I'm okay, Joey. Don't worry about me," said Greg Sr., rubbing Joey's head lovingly.

It was a scene that broke Linda's heart, for she knew that Greg Sr. was growing weaker, and that soon he would be gone. And yet it seemed as though he wanted to use whatever power he had left to make his family happy. When Larry Mazza visited Greg Sr. and Linda on Singer Island, they all went to the beach, had lunch, and then drank and partied. Greg Sr. smiled when he saw Linda and Larry together, for he knew that Mazza provided something that he no longer could. By necessity, his relationship with Linda was devoid of sexual intimacy (although they loved each other more than ever), and Larry had become Linda's only sexual partner. At home alone, late at night, whether in Brooklyn or on Singer Island,

Greg Sr. and Linda would lie in bed together, talking, holding hands, and sometimes crying themselves to sleep.

19
WHERE HAVE YOU GONE, JOE BREWSTER?

Greg Scarpa Sr. and Joe Brewster were the very best of friends — as close as two made men could be. Scarpa was godfather to Brewster's oldest son; over the years, Greg Sr. and Linda had spent hundreds of evenings with Joe and his wife. They were a foursome regularly spotted on the New York nightclub circuit. Sometimes they went to Jilly's, an Italian restaurant in Manhattan notable in part because it was a favorite hangout of Frank Sinatra (who was friendly with the owner, Jilly Rizzo). Sinatra often dined at Jilly's when he was in New York, and it wasn't unusual for Scarpa and Brewster to be seen at the legendary singer's table.

It was a pet peeve of Scarpa's, however, that Sinatra, one of the wealthiest and most famous performers in the world, seemed to be rather tight with a buck. Indeed, more often than not, it was Scarpa who picked up the check when he dined with Sinatra. Having grown weary of the chairman's stinginess, Scarpa one night turned to Joe Brewster and said, "Let's leave while Sinatra is still sitting there."

Brewster's eyes bulged out of his head. "What? Are you kidding?"

"No, let's stick him with the check," Scarpa said.

They exited the restaurant slyly, leaving Sinatra with the bill; it was a story they never tired of relating, and that never failed to provoke a torrent of laughter.

But in later years there developed a crack in the friendship between Joe Brewster and Scarpa. It began in 1987, with an intervention of sorts on the part of agent Lin De-Vecchio, who confronted Scarpa with news that the mobster found almost incomprehensible. Joe Brewster, according to DeVecchio, had developed a bit of a drug habit, and this, perhaps, was clouding his judgment. How else to explain the robberies Brewster had pulled off on his own, without the knowledge of his friend and boss? How else to explain the rumors that DeVecchio had heard, rumors of Joe Brewster's impending sit-down with the cops, during which he planned to divulge all kinds of information that would prove detrimental to the Scarpa business (which included De-Vecchio, of course). It was DeVecchio's considered opinion, according to Greg Jr. and Linda Schiro, that Joe Brewster had become dangerous and unworthy of trust; he had to be eliminated. As quickly as possible.

The next day Scarpa invited his old friend over for breakfast. They chatted over pancakes and coffee, just as they had so many times in the past; as if nothing had changed. Then Scarpa gave Joe an assignment — a murder, to be carried out immediately. In the past Joe Brewster would have taken this news with nothing more than a nod of acknowledgment; this time, though, he blanched. Joe Brewster stopped eating and fell silent.

"What's wrong?" Scarpa asked.

The words fell out of Joe Brewster amid a flood of emotion. He told Greg Sr. and Linda that he had fallen in love with a beautiful young woman, a born-again Christian; together they were on some sort of spiritual journey.

A hard-nosed killer, Joe Brewster did not cry easily. In fact, that morning Greg Sr. and Linda saw Joe cry for the very first time. "I love you, Greg, and I'm sorry to let you down," he said. "But I just can't kill anyone anymore."

Greg Sr. stood up from the table and put his arms around his old friend. "Don't worry about anything, Joe. If that's how you feel, I understand."

The two men hugged. Joe Brewster, who had been terrified of Scarpa's reaction, breathed a heavy sigh of relief and returned to his pancakes.

Later that day Greg Sr. met privately with Gregory; the two had a sad and solemn discussion about the fate of their beloved buddy, Joe Brewster. There were no options, they agreed. Poor Joe had become unreliable. His head was spinning from this new relationship; he had drug and money problems. A man like that, they knew, was capable of almost anything. He could get himself killed or arrested; he might turn to the cops for protection or some pathetic attempt at redemption. Regardless, Joe Brewster had become more trouble than he was worth. The years of friendship, the loyalty he had displayed in the past — none of that mattered now. Joe Brewster had to go.

Scarpa determined that the execution — cleared through the family boss, Carmine Persico — should be carried out by Gregory. This naturally came as a shock to the son. While Gregory agreed with his father's grim assessment of the situation, he had no interest in completing the job himself; nor did he think it was necessary. The last person in the world he wanted to murder was Joe Brewster, who was nearly as close to Gregory as he was to Greg Scarpa Sr. Joe was one of the few people Gregory could talk to about his problems. He loved Joe Brewster, recent transgressions notwithstanding.

From that day on, Joe Brewster was doomed, although you wouldn't have known it from the warmth and friendliness exhibited by the Scarpas. From the outside it seemed as though nothing had changed. But, shortly thereafter, the body of Joseph "Joe Brewster" DeDomenico was found in the backseat of a stolen white 1982 Buick Regal, parked on Seventy-second Street, between Twentieth and Twenty-first Avenues in Brooklyn, with its motor and air conditioner still running. It was not known whether he was killed on the spot or driven there after being shot. He carried $340.50 in cash, and was still wearing a watch. Joe Brewster had been shot four times: in the right temple; through one eye, and in the mouth and chest. It was referred to by local media outlets as a "gangland-style execution."

Greg Sr. suffered over the death of his best friend, but blamed him for signing his own death warrant. "That fucking guy," he told Linda late on the night of the murder. "I don't know why he had to do this. Joe was such a great guy. I loved that guy."

Gregory also loved Joe, and after his murder, something inside Gregory began to change. For the first time he thought about getting away from his father, escaping the life he had been born into — a life of murder and madness. The only life he had ever known. He fantasized about running away and starting all over again. But how? Where would he go? Gregory knew that he was doomed, caught in the middle between the Mafia and the FBI, between his father and the cops.

20
SINS OF THE FATHER

In October 1987, acting on advice from Agent DeVecchio, Greg Scarpa Sr. ordered his son to shut down the crew's Staten Island narcotics business. The reason: Federal law enforcement officers, led by Assistant U.S. Attorney Valerie Caproni, were about to cast a net over the entire operation. To convince his son of the severity of the threat, Scarpa showed Gregory a handwritten list (provided by DeVecchio) bearing the names of Scarpa crew members about to be indicted for drug trafficking. Gregory was sufficiently impressed; however, something about the list seemed unusual. While it included the names of criminals who were very close to Greg Sr., and younger crew members who were friends of Gregory's — as well as young women who were merely acquaintances of his wife, Maria — it lacked two very prominent names: Greg Scarpa Sr. and Gregory

Scarpa Jr.

By way of explanation, Greg Sr. said that the investigation was far from complete. De-Vecchio was working around-the-clock to prevent Scarpa from being indicted, but there were no guarantees.

"If nothing can be done," said Greg Sr., his voice suddenly hoarse and cracking, "I'll probably end up dying very soon. If I go to prison with AIDS, there's no way I would get the care that I'm now getting from my private doctors."

On the verge of tears, Scarpa suddenly looked frail and frightened to his son. And then he divulged the truth: This was a major investigation, and there was no way that De-Vecchio could protect both father and son. One of them was going to jail.

"They only need one of our names," Greg Sr. explained. And then he paused. The tears came to his eyes. "How would you feel if your name was put on the list instead of mine? Would you be able to do a little time until Dello and I pull the right strings and get you out?"

Do time? Gregory felt kicked in the stomach. This was the last thing he expected from his father; moreover, since his life was finally going well, heading to prison was hardly high on his agenda. He loved his wife and adored his baby girl, and his other kids were also young and vulnerable. They needed him.

Although his father was the operation's boss, and thus the person who should have taken the hit from prosecutors, Gregory paused for only a split second before issuing the only possible response: "Sure, Dad."

He put his arms around his father, held him tight, and felt the old man's bones practically sticking through his clothes. "If that's what it will take to keep you living as comfortably as you are now, I'll do whatever I have to do."

Greg Sr. nodded and embraced his son. "I knew you wouldn't let me down."

A few days later Greg Sr. told Gregory that DeVecchio had met with Valerie Caproni and informed her of Scarpa Sr.'s status as a top echelon informant and his decades of work with the bureau. DeVecchio then twisted the truth a bit, suggesting that Gregory (not Greg Sr.) managed the day-to-day operation of the narcotics business, and thus was the person who should face indictment. Caproni needed scant convincing, especially when presented with evidence of Gregory's brutality: A rival drug dealer, who had been beaten badly with baseball bats by a couple of Gregory's crew, had talked, helping to build the DEA's case.

A revised list of names, agreed upon by Caproni and DeVecchio, was presented to Scarpa. There would be no more discussion, no more dealing. Greg Sr. agreed, and immediately called his son. When Gregory arrived, his father was sitting dejectedly on the couch with Linda by his side. Greg Sr. showed his son the revised list; at the very top was the name of Gregory Scarpa Jr.

"Dad became very emotional," recalls Gregory. "He told me that I was being indicted as the head of the drug crew, instead of him. Suddenly, he left the room, too overcome to speak. I'd never seen him that disturbed. While I was alone in the living room with Linda, she told me that my dad was so miserable about my taking his place on the indictment that he had placed a gun behind the couch, and was talking about committing suicide."

Gregory wasn't about to let that happen. A deal was a deal, and now it was the son's responsibility to make the father feel at peace.

"When Dad returned, I put him at ease as best I could by telling him not to worry about it, and that I'd be able to handle it," Gregory says. "I never thought I'd still be in prison twenty years later."

There was, however, one other possibility, and according to Gregory it was suggested by Lin DeVecchio, of all people. Rather than turning himself in, or waiting for the inevitable bust, Gregory could simply disappear. It happened all the time in the world of the Mafia: Mobsters who recognized the certainty of an arrest and jail time went on the lam. It wasn't the best of lives — hiding out, avoiding friends and perhaps even family members — but it was preferable to prison. DeVecchio's only caveat was this: If Gregory were to run, he'd have to do it alone; if other crew members fled, the feds would understand that there was a breach in the information channel (the indictment, after all, had been sealed), and then there would be hell to pay for everyone.

"Anyway," Greg Sr. said, "I need those guys around to get all the business in order so that the guys who aren't going to be busted can pick up the slack."

Not to worry, DeVecchio said. It would be at least a month before the pinch. "Enough time for you to straighten out your affairs."

Father and son met at the Scarpa farm in New Jersey to review their ledgers before Gregory went on the lam. Afterward, as they did approximately once each month, Gregory drove his father through the countryside, along undulating two-lane county roads, to a secluded spot, where DeVecchio would be waiting in a rented car. To avoid suspicion, DeVecchio rented a different car each time they met; on this particular day he was sitting in a dark blue Plymouth.

Gregory says that, as usual, he waited in his car while Greg Sr. got into DeVecchio's car and handed the agent an envelope stuffed with cash; the two men then talked for about twenty minutes. Afterward, Greg Sr. showed his son a piece of paper that he said DeVecchio had given him; on the paper was the name "Catanzano." Cosmo Catanzano was a college kid who was facing indictment along with Gregory. According to DeVecchio, DEA officers believed that Cosmo was frightened and easily exploited; in other words, he was a prime candidate to rat out anyone and everyone — including both of the Scarpa men.

There was little time to pause for reflection, or even to properly plan a course of action; the DEA arrests were imminent. Greg Sr. wanted Catanzano murdered and buried quickly. Two crew men dug a grave for him in a secluded spot off Staten Island's Arthur Kill Road, and a contract was placed on his head. But Catanzano was fortunate: The cops got to him before the mob could complete its work, and the arrest saved his life. Interestingly, though, DeVecchio's information, at least in this instance, turned out to be erroneous. Catanzano never cooperated with the investigation.

One week before government agents arrested seven Scarpa crew members, Gregory left Brooklyn with Maria and their baby daughter. Greg Sr. had arranged for the family to hide out in a quiet, secluded chalet on Lake Naomi, Pennsylvania, deep in the Pocono Mountains. Greg Sr. had strongly advised his son against traveling with his wife and daughter, but Gregory had refused to leave them behind. In part, Greg Sr.'s concern stemmed from personal animosity toward Maria, stemming from her drug use and emotional problems, but also because he knew that a mobster on the run couldn't afford to be bogged down by family baggage. It was simply too risky.

Life on the lam turned out to be reasonably comfortable, thanks largely to weekly cash deliveries of roughly $2,000. As often as he could, Gregory met with his father to discuss business (including updates on the indictments of other Scarpa crew members). Sometimes his three older children would travel to the Poconos and they'd all spend a few weeks together, hanging out at the pool, playing tennis, watching television.

Greg Sr. reassured his son that DeVecchio (who of course knew exactly where Gregory was hiding) was working fervently on his case, and had everything under control. The plan was supposedly this: DeVecchio would quietly monitor the DEA investigation and determine the merits of the case. This would help the Scarpas build a defense and determine when it was appropriate for Gregory to return home.

In August, Greg Sr. instructed Gregory to bring Maria and the baby to Connie's house for a big Sunday dinner. Greg Sr. said that he would bring the rest of Gregory's children. This wasn't unusual. Since going on the lam eleven months before, Gregory had often driven to his mom's house for Sunday dinner, staying with Maria and the baby at a nearby hotel and driving back to Pennsylvania in the morning.

The family had a wonderful time that Sunday. Connie prepared a lavish spread, including all of her children's favorite dishes and desserts. As the day came to a close and Gregory began discussing where to spend the night, Greg Sr. offered a suggestion: a nearby Best Western Hotel. Fine, Gregory said, nodding in approval. There were hugs and kisses all around as Gregory prepared to leave with Maria and the baby. Shortly afterward, without telling anyone where he was going, Greg Sr. also left the house.

Several hours passed before Greg Sr. returned — with Maria and the baby in tow. He had disturbing news for the family: Gregory had been arrested. The feds had been waiting for him at the hotel. According to Scarpa, a man named "Cocoa" had ratted out Gregory.

Most of Gregory's family now believes that Greg Sr. did the unimaginable — the ultimate act of betrayal — and turned in his own son. However, an opposing (and less biased) viewpoint is offered by Jerry Capeci, a reporter, columnist, and author who has covered organized crime for more than three decades.

"It wasn't Greg Scarpa who dropped the dime on his son," says Capeci. "Two decades ago, when Ms. Caproni was an assistant U.S. attorney in Brooklyn, she was so frustrated by the FBI's do-nothing approach in finding Gregory, who'd been indicted in November 1987, that she decided to call in the U.S. Marshals Service to track him down."

Nine months later, deputy U.S. marshals located Gregory Scarpa Jr. at the Best

241

Western Hotel in Lakewood, New Jersey, contacted the DEA, and together they arrested him. According to Capeci, "Gregory and Maria had used that hotel before, as well as others in the area. It was right off an exit of a main drag. They had distributed photos of Maria, not Gregory, to a bunch of hotels and motels in the area. They knew Gregory and Maria were together, so they focused their inquiry on her, not him. She was spotted by a hotel employee, who scored some brownie points with the feds by calling them to say she was there. The rest is history."

When FBI officials read in the New York *Daily News* about Gregory's arrest at the hands of deputy U.S. marshals and DEA agents, they responded with neither graciousness nor admiration, but rather with something approaching jealousy. There were, for example, no congratulatory letters sent to either agency. Instead, the FBI commissioned an inquiry to determine why the U.S. Marshals' office had notified the DEA about the impending arrest, but, curiously, had neglected to inform the FBI.

Capeci, who has been writing about the Scarpas for years, says, "Trust me. Everything the family members say may be true, but it wasn't his old man or DeVecchio who turned Gregory Scarpa in. There's no way they would have done it without Lin and Greg taking credit for it with the bureau."

Greg Sr. tugged at whatever strings he could in an attempt to ensure that Gregory would be incarcerated at the federal penitentiary in Lewisburg, Pennsylvania, so that he would be close to his wife and children. The U.S. attorney's office, however, had a different plan: Gregory would be sent as far away as possible, to a prison in San Diego. Greg Sr. hired Joe Benfante, a well-known mob lawyer, to represent Gregory. Benfante was paid by, and took his orders from, the father, not the son, an arrangement that would come to have more than passing significance as the case against Gregory Scarpa Jr. developed.

21
RICO Act

On January 27, 1988, the U.S. attorney's office filed an indictment charging Gregory and eight codefendants with various violations of federal criminal laws. Count one alleged that Gregory conducted an enterprise in violation of the Racketeer Influenced and Corrupt Organizations (RICO) Act: Its activities included the killing of Albert Nacha in December 1985; conspiracy to distribute marijuana; conspiracy to affect commerce by extortion; and conspiracy to extort property, as well as other racketeering acts.

While awaiting trial, Gregory was visited in jail by Maria, who complained that Greg Sr. had suspended all payments to her and to the mothers of his other children. Gregory was outraged. He had always supported his ex-wives and children, even when he didn't live with them, and he presumed that his father understood and approved of this arrangement. Gregory, after all, was taking the rap for his dad; the least Greg Sr. could do in return was ensure that the son's family was cared for.

At once perturbed and perplexed, Gregory called his brother Frankie and asked him to arrange a meeting with Greg Sr. When Frankie and Greg Sr. arrived, things quickly heated up between father and son.

"I was very angry," recalls Gregory. "My father absolutely refused to send any of my money to my wife and daughter, and to my other children, so I finally told him that I was through with the mob and that it had brought me nothing but misery."

This, of course, was precisely the sort of scenario Greg Sr. (and countless mob bosses before him) had dreaded: an angry, bitter member of the crew stewing behind bars, longing to hold his wife and children — and perhaps willing to do almost anything to shorten his bid. That the aggrieved happened to be a family member — a son, no less! — only complicated matters further. Still, protocol dictated a certain response, and Scarpa did not hesitate to issue the expected proclamation. On the way home from jail, Greg Sr. told Frankie to spread the word: If any crew member discussed any activities or the exchange of money with

Gregory, he would be killed. There would be no exceptions, no debate.

On subsequent visits, even when Greg Sr. was accompanied by Larry Mazza or other members of the crew, he never again discussed mob business with Gregory. Clearly, he no longer tusted his own son.

When Gregory went on trial, his own father stacked the deck against him. According to Gregory's older sister, Debbie, Joe Benfante would leave court every evening and dutifully visit the home of Greg Scarpa Sr. There they would rehash the day's proceedings; more important, Benfante would receive his marching orders from the old man. According to Debbie, the conversations didn't bode well for her brother, as Gregory, rather than Greg Sr., was portrayed as the crew's boss. Debbie desperately wanted to know why her father was betraying her brother, but she was too frightened to ask.

"The man was the master of the unpredictable, and knew absolutely no bounds of fear," Benfante says of Greg Sr. "He abided by no moral codes; he made his own rules."

In February 1988, Gregory Scarpa Jr., then thirty-eight years of age, was convicted of substantive RICO and other charges; as his father had predicted (and with the help of Lin DeVecchio), he was sent to Lewisburg, Pennsylvania, to begin serving a twenty-year sentence.

Lewisburg is a federal penitentiary located on twenty-four acres in rural central Pennsylvania, about three hours west of New York City. Like many "fresh fish" (new convicts), Gregory found it nearly impossible to accept that Lewisburg's dank, depressing, maximum-security area of the prison would be his home for at least the next twelve years (the time typically served on a twenty-year sentence). But he tried to be strong; he tried to make the best of an intolerable situation.

"In those days, the prison was very lenient with phone calls," recalls Gregory. "I was able to call home three times a day, every other day, to talk to my two Marias."

Sadly, with Gregory absent, the adult Maria resumed her old habits, and quickly developed an escalating drug habit that threatened not only her own health, but that of her daughter. Gregory begged her to give up the dope for the sake of their child, but Maria just cried and threatened to kill herself if she couldn't be with Gregory. Sometimes he would receive long, downtrodden poems written by Maria, verse so sad that it left him depressed and vulner-

247

able. Gregory begged her to stop; if she couldn't be positive and cheerful in her correspondence, then he preferred no correspondence at all. The poems, he explained, broke his spirit. But they just kept coming.

"She didn't understand that she was making me walk around with a heavy heart," Gregory says. "Or maybe she was putting pressure on me in the hopes that I would really go out of control and escape and come home."

Gregory remembers one particularly moving poem, entitled "Daddy's Little Girl." It describes the little girl's loving relationship with her father — their laughter and playful affection for each other. "Her daddy was her everything and her living teddy bear." Maria's own difficulties in witnessing her daughter's pain, and concerns about how Gregory's absence is affecting the child, are evident. She finds it hard to answer the question "When is my daddy coming home?" Gregory's wife describes her empathy for their child, and she ends the poem with a kind of prayer that father and child will someday be together again.

"Even now, eighteen years later, I can't read that poem all the way through, because it's so real to me," recalls Gregory. "My baby girl, Maria, and I were so close, and now I only speak to her through letters. I know how much I let her down, and yet I know she loves me as much as I love her."

With Gregory in prison, Sunday dinners at Connie's house became joyless affairs, especially for Connie and Frankie. They'd sit at the table and stare mournfully at the seat he had occupied, and they'd tried to imagine what it would be like for that seat to be empty for the next twelve years — or twenty years. It was unfathomable. Greg Sr. was persistent in his attempts to deflect the sadness, and to spin matters in a more positive direction. There was no way Gregory would serve his full sentence, he promised. Be patient, he urged. It will all work out.

Whether Scarpa truly believed his own words or was merely slinging a line of bullshit to keep family members off his back is a question that has never been answered. Certainly his words of encouragement were welcomed by the family. Hope, after all, was all they had.

Other than Maria, Frankie was probably the most devastated by Gregory's incarceration. The baby of the family, Frank was now married and living the straight life; with his brother Buddy he had worked for years in the horse business. Neither one had ever wanted to work for their father. Unlike Gregory, Frank had known his whole life that his father was a gangster. And a rather perverse one, at that.

"I remember how I would sit on his lap right after he would come home from killing somebody, and he would tell me how he did it," Frankie recalls. "The first time was when I was about four years old. I remember it was a very foggy night. I heard him open the front door and come up the stairs and go around the corner, and I looked out and saw that he had blood all over him. He walked right past me. I followed him to the bathroom, and he's washing the blood off, and then he walked downstairs. I followed him downstairs, and I sat on his lap, and I asked him what happened. He said, 'I just had to go kill someone.'

"He told me that he put the gun behind the guy's ear and killed him. And that wasn't the first time. He told me three or four times during my childhood how he killed people. I used to have nightmares about it. He programmed me to believe that *we* were the good guys, and *they* were the bad guys."

What Frankie did not know, and never suspected (at least not until many years later), was that his father was an FBI informant. That would have been unthinkable.

"We were always raised to believe that informants were no good," Frankie says. "Anyone who dealt with the police was no good. If you're a rat, you get killed."

Interestingly enough, Greg Sr. had been ambivalent about Frankie joining the business. Whereas he'd always hoped that Gregory would follow in his bloody footsteps, for some reason Greg Sr. viewed Frankie differently. "The good son," he called him (as if Gregory, for all his devotion to the old man, was something less than good), and the understanding was that life would be different for Frankie. Like his siblings, though, Frankie both respected and feared his father, and indeed would have done anything the old man requested. With Gregory behind bars, Greg Sr. was no longer ambivalent about Frankie's future; nor was he particularly concerned about protecting him from the family business. One day he asked Frankie to handle some cash for him. It was a simple job, one with few risks, and one that would put a good deal of cash in the young man's pocket.

Frankie hesitated. He wasn't so sure.

"Please," Scarpa said, shamelessly playing the paternal card. "You're the only person I can trust."

So Frankie went to work for his father. In the beginning his role was minimal and white collar. He handled the books, helped with cash flow, offered advice. Once indoctrinated, though, Frankie was an easy mark for Greg Sr. What was a little more mud when one's hands were already dirty? Pretty soon Frankie was running his own narcotics operation, making great piles of cash, and occasionally succumbing to the dealer's ever present temptation: dipping into his own supply.

"He would give me kilos of marijuana and cocaine to sell," Frankie says of his father. "I had my own crew of guys. Dad used to call us the Jersey Gang. And I was using drugs myself, as we all were. There was just so much around, and the price was right."

22
WHO KILLED
PATRICK PORCO?

Although Joey Schiro adored his father and wanted nothing more than to make him proud (preferably by succeeding in the family business), he was burdened by two things: an innate sensitivity and a fierce desire to be his own man.

Like most fathers, Greg Sr. found the challenge of dealing with a teenage boy to be endlessly frustrating and oftentimes exhausting. He didn't like the way Joey cut his hair, or the clothes he wore. More disturbingly, he disapproved of Joey's choice of friends. This was not a small matter to a man like Greg Scarpa Sr., for whom loyalty, camaraderie, and trust were essential character traits. In part to protect his son, and in part to help him learn the ropes, Greg Sr. encouraged Joey to hang out with his crew. Joey, of course, wanted to be with kids his own age, boys who shared his taste in music, clothes, and girls.

Joey's best buddy was a young man named Patrick Porco. The two spent vast amounts of time together, and indeed were nearly as close as brothers. (Porco even had the approval of Greg Sr. and Linda, who came to think of the kid as another son.) Among the hobbies that bonded the boys was recreational drug usage; in the beginning they sold marijuana to Bensonhurst stoners to fund their own habits, but soon the operation expanded to include cocaine. Linda knew that Joey was selling pot but not coke. Greg Sr. knew about the cocaine but didn't tell Linda, because he didn't want her to worry; he did enough of that for both of them. In fact, Greg Sr. fretted endlessly about Joey, certain that the kid's careless, wandering ways were going to get him killed. Scarpa would stay up into the early hours of the morning, waiting for Joey to come home. He didn't confront the kid or challenge him on his behavior; that would have been hypocritical. He simply wanted to know that his little boy had arrived safely. When the car would pull into the driveway, Greg Sr. would roll over in bed and fall asleep.

Linda was less forgiving of her son's wayward behavior. One day, while cleaning his room, she turned over Joey's mattress and found hundreds of small plastic bags filled with white powder. She became hysterical and called Greg Sr. into the room: "What is this? What is our son doing?"

Effortlessly, calmly — as only a seasoned liar could — Greg Sr. pulled Linda close and told her not to worry. He knew all about the cocaine. Joey had explained everything. He wasn't selling, and he wasn't using. He was merely holding the drugs for a friend.

On Halloween night 1989, Joey Schiro and Patrick Porco, along with two of their buddies, Ray Aviles and Craig Sobel, became involved in an egg-throwing incident with another group of young men that somehow turned lethal. The two factions were arguing near Our Lady of Guadalupe Church on Fifteenth Avenue in Bensonhurst. Two shotgun blasts were fired from Ray's car; one of the shots struck seventeen-year-old Dominick Masseria, who later died from his wounds.

On May 27, 1990, Linda claims that De-Vecchio called Scarpa at home and asked him to call back from a pay phone, to ensure privacy and confidentiality. Linda drove Greg Sr. to a phone booth near Fort Hamilton Parkway and Tenth Avenue, and stayed in the car while Scarpa called. It was a relatively brief conversation, after which Scarpa returned to the car and said to Linda, with more than a trace of exasperation in his voice, "I can't believe this fucking kid. Patrick is going to rat on Joey. We've got to do something about this."

In Mafia parlance, "doing something" usually meant eliminating the problem. If Porco were to be silenced, then the case against Joey Schiro would likely unravel. Initially (and logically), another crew member was assigned the contract on Patrick Porco, to deflect suspicion away from Joey, who stood to benefit the most from Porco's death, and who surely would be considered a prime suspect in his murder. Fate, however, intervened, in the form of car problems experienced by the assigned killer; rather than wait another day (and risk having Porco feed information to the cops), Greg Sr. decided that it might be most efficient to have Joey commit the murder himself.

Understandably reluctant to kill his best friend, Joey at first expressed trepidation: He had a hard time believing Patrick would rat him out; and even if Patrick were to commit such an act of betrayal, Joey couldn't imagine putting a gun to the head of his lifelong buddy. And yet — an order was an order. Especially when it came from your father. Joey had no choice but to accept the contract. Joey and his cousin, John Sinagra, picked up Patrick and drove to McDonald Avenue in Sheepshead Bay, where they are alleged to have killed him. They then dumped Porco's body on another street.

At home, afterward, Joey Schiro locked himself in his bedroom and cried for days on end. Greg Sr. urged his son to attend Patrick's wake, but he refused, so Linda went alone. When Patrick's mother, Carol, spotted Linda, she began crying hysterically.

"Joey couldn't come," Linda told her as the two women hugged tightly and sobbed. "He's just too upset."

Perhaps this was true — maybe Joey was too upset to go to Patrick's wake; then again, Lori Porco Wagner, Patrick's sister, recalls that on the evening of her brother's death, she went looking for answers from Patrick's best friend. She found Joey Schiro alright, but he wasn't holed up in his room, sobbing over the death of Patrick Porco; instead, Lori found Joey happily sharing a meal with his cronies and fellow crew members at Romano's Restaurant.

Lori recalls the feeling of anger and astonishment that washed over her as she looked at Joey Schiro, whom she now recognized as a cold-hearted killer. "I just said to him, 'You killed my brother. You're sitting here having dinner, and my brother is dead.' "

Joey simply continued eating. He never said a word to her.

John Novoa, who had reportedly been partners with Joey Schiro in a drug enterprise, said that he had encountered Joey and Sinagra in a corner store in Bensonhurst shortly after Porco's murder. Novoa, who later testified as part of a cooperation agreement with the prosecution, claimed that Sinagra was playing a video game while Joey was "pacing up and down the store, looking outside. They were panicking all over the place, and Joey was just screaming that he wanted to get out of there." According to Novoa, the two boys acknowledged having "clipped Pat. They thought he was a rat."

Later, Novoa said that he later heard separate and competing accounts of the murder from the killers. Sinagra had told him that Joey had been driving; from the front passenger seat, Sinagra had "spun around and shot Pat. Pat was pleading for his life, and he shot him in the mouth." A couple of years later, however, Novoa recalled that Joey Schiro insisted that he, and not Sinagra, had been the triggerman.

Indeed, their stories dovetailed in only one ghoulish aspect: Disposing of the body had been more difficult than they'd anticipated.

"Patrick Porco's foot got stuck on the seat belt," Novoa testified. "And they were pulling and pulling and they couldn't get him out."

23

THE COLOMBO
CRIME FAMILY WAR

When Greg Scarpa Sr. communicated with his incarcerated son, the conversations tended to be light, upbeat. They talked about family and friends, and the likelihood that Gregory would soon be a free man. Each of them — father and son — refused to wallow in self-pity, or to traffic in relentless negativity. There was, after all, no point in that. During one memorable visit to Lewisburg in 1990, however, Greg Sr. seemed unusually stressed. The reason, he said, had less to do with his physical maladies than a rumor that had been circulating back home.

"Dad was very disturbed," recalls Gregory. "He told me he had some problems in Brooklyn. A story was in the newspapers saying he might be an informant, and he wanted to make sure that I would be alright in prison with this information coming out in the papers."

Gregory told his father not to worry — that he was quite capable of taking care of himself — and everything would be just fine. This, of course, was a lie.

"We both knew that when the news about his being an informant hit Lewisburg, I was as good as dead," Gregory says.

Primarily responsible for fueling the rumors was a mob associate named Tommy Ocera. Greg Sr. dealt with Ocera's loose lips by placing a contract on his head. But that was merely a piece of a far more elaborate and Machiavellian scheme devised by Greg Sr. He also planned to create enormous dissension in the Colombo organization, and in the process eliminate his enemies and eventually take over as the family boss.

The Colombo crime family had been in disarray for some time, ever since its boss, the aging Thomas DiBella, had stepped down in the late 1980s. DiBella's logical successor, Carmine "Junior" Persico, the family's most powerful capo, had been sent to prison for life in 1989, leaving an empty seat at the head of the family table. But he remained the head of the family even while in prison, and named Victor Orena as his temporary replacement, pending the release from prison of his son, Alphonse. Once in power, however, Orena was reluctant to give up the throne, and when Carmine Persico attempted to anoint his son as the family's leader, Orena challenged him.

Orena asked the commission, still the governing body of the Mafia in the United States, to declare him the boss, and to eliminate the Persico element. The Gambino boss, John Gotti, supported Orena, but the commission's sitting bosses declined to appoint Orena, and the Colombo family was divided. Orena loyalists included high-ranking captain William "Wild Bill" Cutolo, Salvatore "Big Sal" Miciotta, and Armando "Chips" DiCostanzo. They all stood to gain if Orena became boss and controlled the money-making crews loyal to Persico.

Persico loyalists included Larry Mazza, Carmine Sessa, and Johnny Pate, among others, most notably Greg Scarpa Sr. At the funeral of Johnny Sap in 1991, Greg Sr. and Linda ran into Victor Orena. This, of course, was neither the time nor the place for a discussion of business; nevertheless, Orena approached Scarpa — and asked for his support in the family dispute. Greg Sr. looked at Orena and responded with three simple words: "Go fuck yourself!"

When Little Linda was eighteen, she'd met and married a young man in the construction business. She was soon pregnant with her son, Freddy. Unfortunately, the marriage was short-lived and Little Linda and her toddler son moved back in with her parents. On November 18, 1991, three of Greg Sr.'s crew came to the Scarpa home to pick him up and drive him to Wimpy Boys. Little Linda and Freddy were also leaving the house, so Greg Sr. carried his grandson to Little Linda's car before leaving with his associates. As the two cars backed out of the driveway, a large truck suddenly barreled down the one-way street and came to a halt, effectively blocking all traffic; immediately behind the truck was a van. As Greg Sr. looked on in horror, a half-dozen men, all wearing black ski masks, jumped out of the van and began shooting at the two cars, riddling Linda's car with bullets and shattering the windows.

Somehow, both Little Linda and Freddy escaped harm. Nor was anyone in the other vehicle hurt. For Greg Sr., however, relief quickly turned to rage; he vowed vengeance against Victor Oreno and his supporters, rallying soldiers loyal to Persico and declaring outright war on the Orena faction.

Greg Sr. took no chances with his family's safety. Although Linda stayed with him, Greg Sr. sent his other children and grandchildren to live with relatives (although Joey returned home almost daily to check on his father). Throughout what came to be known as the Colombo War, Greg Sr. could be seen driving with his troops along Brooklyn's Avenue U, scouting social clubs and bars known to be frequented by the Orena faction. Larry Mazza remembers the day in December 1991 that he, Greg Sr., and a few other heavily armed representatives of the Scarpa crew spotted a rival wiseguy named Vinnie Fusaro hanging Christmas lights in front of his girlfriend's house.

At Scarpa's direction, the driver slowed the car down so that they could verify the target's identity, and maintain an element of surprise. It was late afternoon; the streets were clogged with traffic. The timing and circumstances could not have been worse for conducting a hit. Escape routes would be blocked; witnesses would be numerous. Nevertheless, Greg Sr. grabbed his rifle and rolled down the window. He fired three shots, all of which hit their target. The man fell to the ground and died in a tangle of Christmas lights, the irony of which seemed lost on Scarpa.

As the car sped away, weaving through traffic, Greg Sr. smiled, saying, "I love the smell of gunpowder."

During the seven months of the Colombo War, FBI agent Lin DeVecchio frequently contacted Greg Scarpa Sr. FBI documents showed that the two men rarely went more than a week to ten days without speaking by phone or meeting in person. Indeed, according to prosecutors, DeVecchio was actively involved, if only from a distance, often supplying Scarpa with pertinent information about the Oreno faction. Once, when Scarpa was unable to locate Big Sal Miciotta, DeVecchio provided him with a home address, despite knowing full well that Greg Sr.'s intent was murder. Somehow, Miciotta escaped with his life. Aware that Greg Sr. was under surveillance by federal and local law enforcement agencies, DeVecchio provided his informant with a radio scanner and private frequency code, so that the mobster could monitor communications between surveillance teams, and thus remain one step ahead of the authorities; this, quite literally, allowed Scarpa to get away with murder.

In January 1992, Greg Sr. and Larry Mazza gunned down Nicholas "Nicky Black" Grancio, a feared Orena capo, as he was leaving his Gravesend, Brooklyn, social club. According to later testimony by Larry Mazza, "Greg and I tailed Grancio in a stolen car, and then pulled up alongside him." After Scarpa wounded Grancio with a handgun, Mazza completed the job with a shotgun blast to the head. The Grancio hit was a major turning point in the war and a major victory for the Persico faction, Greg Sr., and, by extension, the FBI.

Greg Sr. believed that if Orena was murdered or arrested, Persico loyalists would emerge victorious. Scarpa personally had attempted to kill Orena several times, without success; after Nicky Grancio was murdered, however, Orena and his men went into hiding ("hit the mattresses") in remote safe houses. Their fear of the Grim Reaper, as Scarpa had come to be known, was palpable and legitimate.

Escaping from Scarpa and his crew was no mean feat, especially since DeVecchio was allegedly providing much more than tacit approval of the hunt. DeVecchio at one point provided Greg Sr. with an address where Orena was thought to be hiding; on June 20, 1991, a five-man hit team — led by consigliere Carmine Sessa; capo John Pate; and mobster Robert "Bobby Zam" Zambardi — converged on Orena's Long Island home, only to discover that he wasn't there. The crew spent the better part of the night driving through surrounding neighborhoods, searching for Orena. They were about to give up when Orena coincidentally pulled up alongside their car at a stoplight. Recognizing the occupants as members of Scarpa's crew, Orena wisely sped off, avoiding what surely would have been a fatal confrontation.

Throughout the Colombo War, DeVecchio acted as supervisor of the FBI's C-10 squad, which had been assigned to investigate the Colombo and Bonanno crime families. Among DeVecchio's subordinates was Special Agent Christopher Favo, the case agent in charge of the FBI's investigation into the Colombo War. In December 1991 and January 1992, Agent Favo learned that Big Sal Miciotta and Joel "Joe Waverly" Cacace, two Orena mobsters, were establishing hit teams; presumably, Greg Scarpa would be a prime target. Favo dutifully notified DeVecchio, who promptly informed Greg Sr.

Cacace struck first, in January 1992, by initiating a shoot-out with Greg Sr. as the two sat in adjacent automobiles. Cacace shattered the windshield of Scarpa's car; Greg Sr., whose TEC-9 had misfired, sped off with glass fragments in his hair, a reminder of just how close he had come to getting killed. Ultimately, however, the duel belonged to Scarpa, who, on February 26, shot Cacace in the stomach, wounding him seriously (Cacace recovered from his wounds; in 2004 he was convicted on charges related to the murder of the father of a federal prosecutor; he remains incarcerated to this day).

By the middle of 1992, Greg Sr. had killed two rebels, wounded a third, and accidentally shot and killed Thomas Amato, a Genovese family associate (who was blamed for his own death, primarily because he was at a hostile Colombo hangout at the time). The Colombo War was a tonic for the ailing Greg Sr., who seemed to draw strength from his involvement. His men began calling him, "General Schwarzkopf," after the Desert Storm hero. Greg Sr. would murder a rival, return home, and stand in the living room giving Linda a thumbs-up sign. Imitating Ian Fleming's famous James Bond character, he'd exclaim, "Scarpa! Greg Scarpa! Brooklyn's 007!"

24
THE BULLET HE COULDN'T DUCK

Although DeVecchio maintained that Greg Scarpa Sr. was not an active participant in the war, younger agents (like Favo) were growing alarmed by the mobster's success and apparent indestructibility. In 1980 the Department of Justice had issued detailed ethical and legal guidelines regarding the handling of informants. If an informant was suspected of involvement in any "serious act of violence," the supervisor in charge was required to consider closing him and targeting him for arrest.

The operative word, of course, is "consider." While the guidelines urged agents to seek the moral high ground, it left matters open to individual interpretation. DeVecchio was understandably reluctant to close a top echelon informant, particularly someone who had helped make his career, but that reluctance put him at odds with some of his own agents.

Because criminal informants are frequently essential components of the judicial process (in short, they help prosecutors make their cases), the courts have long upheld the legality of using them. However, because informants, almost by definition, are practicing criminals, they must be handled with extreme sensitivity and caution, so that, in the words of the Justice Department guidelines, "the government itself does not become a violator of the law." As the Colombo War escalated, younger agents became acutely sensitive to this potential abuse of power by older, more established agents. The FBI had become a different place than the organization De-Vecchio had joined many years earlier; sometimes, though, he seemed almost oblivious to the transformation.

When a loan shark named Carmine Imbriale was arrested by the Brooklyn district attorney's office, he quickly offered useful information about Greg Scarpa Sr. in exchange for consideration of lesser charges and a shorter prison sentence. According to Imbriale, at a dinner the previous evening, Greg Sr. had proposed a toast and bragged about shooting Cacace. The DA's office alerted Agent Favo, who reported the information up the chain of command, to De-

Vecchio. According to Agent Favo, DeVecchio later received a phone call from Greg Sr., and during the course of their conversation, DeVecchio informed Scarpa that Imbriale was in custody, adding, "I don't know what he's saying about you." It was Favo's contention that DeVecchio was leaking the information to not only protect Scarpa, but perhaps to encourage a hit. Indeed, not long after that, Greg Sr. talked about killing Imbriale.

Deeply concerned that a suspect's life had been placed in danger, Favo says he persuaded DeVecchio to call Greg Sr. the following day and warn the mobster that if any harm came to Imbriale, Scarpa would be considered a prime suspect. DeVecchio, however, denies making such a phone call. That Greg Sr. had boasted about shooting someone was not sufficient evidence to warrant his arrest; however, it should have led the FBI to consider closing his file. Yet DeVecchio declined to do so.

Around this same time, DeVecchio's immediate supervisor, Donald V. North, the assistant special agent in Charge of the FBI's New York Criminal Division, became uneasy about the activities of Greg Sr., particularly as they related to the Colombo War. On March 3, 1992, Scarpa was closed as an informant after North "found credible allegations that Scarpa was involved in planning violent criminal activity." DeVecchio was ordered to cease all contact with his informant.

However, in subsequent informal conversations with North, DeVecchio appeared "adamant" that Scarpa was not involved in violent activity. Thus, in early April 1992, DeVecchio initiated the process of having Scarpa reinstated as a top echelon informant; remarkably, the FBI granted him authority to reopen Scarpa on April 8, 1992, pending completion of a suitability inquiry. On April 22, 1992, DeVecchio notified FBI headquarters that such an inquiry had been conducted, and that Scarpa was deemed suitable. DeVecchio attributed the murder conspiracy charge against Scarpa to rampant "paranoia" among Colombo family members; their accusations and concerns, DeVecchio determined, were largely baseless, and had been exacerbated by the war.

According to Linda Schiro, during a May 15, 1992, meeting at the Scarpa home, Greg Sr. told DeVecchio that he wanted to kill an Orena supporter named Lorenzo "Larry" Lampasi. Greg Sr. solicited DeVecchio's assistance in this endeavor, requesting the usual pertinent information: home address, workday routine, etc. DeVecchio, according to Linda, said he would supply the information.

Allegedly, because law enforcement agencies had conducted physical surveillance on Lampasi's Brooklyn home, they knew that he left for work at approximately 4:00 A.M. Each morning Lampasi unlocked his gate, backed his car onto the street, paused momentarily to exit the car and close and lock the gate, and then drove off. It was a routine he performed with mind-numbing reliability. A few days later, as Lampasi walked to his car in the early morning darkness, three members of the Persico faction — Greg Sr., Larry Mazza, and Jimmy Del-Masto — were waiting for him. As always, Lampasi backed his car into the street; just as reliably, he put the car in park, opened the driver's side door, exited, and walked to the front gate. But he never made it. As Lampasi stepped away from his car, Greg Sr. shot him with a rifle. As Lampasi fell to the sidewalk, DelMasto, the driver, started to pull away. But Greg Sr. instructed him to stop.

"He wasn't sure [Lampasi] was dead," recalls Larry Mazza.

Greg Sr. and Mazza got out and fired

again. As Lampasi lay on his side, bleeding profusely, he looked up at his assailants.

"What did I do?" he asked.

There was no reply, just another shot from Mazza; this one hit Lampasi in the back. The shooters then returned to the car and drove off.

When Agent Favo reported the Lampasi killing to DeVecchio, he was shocked at De-Vecchio's reaction: "We're gonna win this thing," the agent shouted, slapping his hand on the desk for emphasis. (This scene would later be reenacted, for dramatic purposes, in a pivotal episode of the acclaimed HBO series about the New Jersey mob, *The Sopranos*.) Agent Favo quickly reminded DeVecchio that the FBI had no rooting interest in the Colombo War. The stunning outburst, in Favo's estimation, betrayed just how far over the edge DeVecchio had gone.

"He seemed like he didn't know we were the FBI or that Scarpa was not on our side," Favo later testified at a Colombo racketeering trial. "It was like a line had been blurred, over who we were and what this is. I thought there was something wrong. He was compromised. He had lost track of who he was."

In July 1992, the FBI, led by DeVecchio, arrested Victor Orena at his girlfriend's Long Island home, effectively signaling an end to the Colombo War. And what a bloody fray it had been. Ten people had been killed, including an unfortunate customer accidentally shot at a Brooklyn bagel shop. Ten other people had been wounded, including a fifteen-year-old innocent bystander. The most violent participant in the war (by a wide margin) was Greg Scarpa Sr., who had murdered four men and wounded two others. Despite his relatively advanced age and weakened condition, he had hunted down and shot most of the soldiers who had died or were wounded on the Brooklyn streets.

Surviving capos, along with rank-and-file "soldiers," were rounded up and herded into holding cells, and charged with participating in the war — all except Greg Scarpa Sr., whose license to kill apparently was still valid. Even after several of Scarpa's men predictably flipped and began cooperating with the FBI, naming Scarpa as the shooter in nearly all of the killings attributed to the Persico faction, DeVecchio continued to protect his "girlfriend."

By this point several members of DeVecchio's C-10 squad — most notably Agent Favo; Agent Jeffrey Tomlinson; and Agent Raymond Andjich — had grown deeply suspicious that their boss had provided confidential law enforcement information to Greg Scarpa Sr. During the Colombo War, Agent Favo had secretly planted surveillance microphones in the home and car of a man named Joseph "Joey Brains" Ambrosino, a member of the Scarpa crew. The bugs connected Greg Sr. to the murder of Nicholas Grancio, and to the shooting of Joel Cacace. They also learned that Wild Bill Cutolo had been the target of an aborted hit by Greg Sr.

In March 1992, the Brooklyn district attorney's office had obtained a warrant for Scarpa's arrest on a gun possession charge after two officers saw him drop a gun from his car window; it would be several months, however, before Scarpa would have to answer the charges. Between March and August 1992, Scarpa kept a low profile, although he and DeVecchio met or spoke on the phone on at least seven separate occasions. Despite having ample opportunity, DeVecchio allegedly declined to execute the warrant for Scarpa's arrest; nor did he alert the DA's office of Scarpa's whereabouts. Each of these was a clear violation of FBI protocol and guidelines, if not an outright criminal act.

Lacking any respect for or trust in his superior, Chris Favo decided to go over De-

Vecchio's head. He obtained a warrant from the United States District Court for the Eastern District of New York (EDNY) to arrest Greg Scarpa Sr. for conspiracy to commit murder.

And then he waited.

Favo's persistence and patience paid off.

In August 1992, Scarpa (showing remarkably poor judgment, no doubt born of greed) surfaced long enough to testify at his $1.5 million negligence and malpractice suit against Victory Memorial Hospital. Visibly frail and aged, with hollow cheeks and sunken eyes, Scarpa made for a superb and sympathetic witness on his own behalf. One juror, apparently willing to overlook Scarpa's legal and moral transgressions, later described Greg Sr. as a "noble man." Other jurors said they were prepared to award him millions of dollars. The day after his testimony, though, a cash settlement of $350,000 was offered. Scarpa, too exhausted to continue the trial, accepted the terms of the deal. The next day, Linda Schiro and Larry Mazza picked up $350,000 at the bank — in cash — and dumped it into canvas bags.

Greg Sr. was so proud of his victory that ego got the best of him. He arranged a press conference that was covered with great interest by the local media in New York, and soon Greg Scarpa's angular, withered face was flashing across television screens throughout the city.

"I was not made aware of the tests they have perfected to find the AIDS virus in the blood," he said slowly. "If I had been aware, I would never have accepted that blood. It would have been easier to just take a jump off the Verrazano Bridge. This turned out to be one bullet I just couldn't duck."

25
ONE-EYED GREG

Against his better judgment, Greg Scarpa decided to appear at an arraignment on the gun possession charge. Lin DeVecchio had advised Scarpa to show up for the hearing, saying it was merely a formality, and that the agent would take care of everything. Greg Sr. was somewhat skeptical; he was also tired of running and hiding.

As Greg Sr. and Linda waited for the hearing to begin, they noticed FBI agents in the back of the courtroom. Greg Sr. had Linda call DeVecchio to find out what was going on. DeVecchio seemed surprised to hear about the agents and promised to learn more and call back.

Greg Sr. was arraigned on the gun charge and bail was set. As he left the courtroom, however, FBI agents intercepted him and informed the mobster that he was under arrest. Linda screamed at the agents as they placed him in handcuffs and read him his rights. When Linda informed the agents that Scarpa was scheduled to visit his physician that day for blood work and other tests related to his ongoing battle with AIDS, the agents were not unmoved. They agreed to take him to his doctor before going on to the Metropolitan Correction Center (MCC) in Lower Manhattan, where he would be held. At MCC, Greg Sr. spoke on the phone several times with DeVecchio. But that night DeVecchio called Linda to tell her that Greg Sr. should avoid communication from MCC because all phone calls were recorded and monitored.

Behind bars, Scarpa's condition naturally deteriorated. He grew thinner, weaker. Dementia, a common occurrence in AIDS patients, came and went. When it was in full bloom, Greg Sr. would call Linda continually, reminding her of exactly what sandwiches and booze to bring him in prison. Linda cut the sandwiches into small pieces and hid the liquor in baggies, or slipped little bottles into the waist of her pants; sometimes she emptied bags of potato chips and refilled them with contraband. Greg Sr. passed the food and drinks around to the guys he knew at MCC: Robert "Bobby Zam" Zambardi, Joseph "JoJo" Russo, and others. They had all been arrested before Scarpa.

Sometimes Scarpa's requests bordered on the ridiculous — he'd ask Linda to bring him a porterhouse steak, for example. When Linda showed up without the aforementioned item (which, of course, was impossible to sneak in), Greg Sr. would throw a temper tantrum in the visiting room, jumping up and down, stomping his feet, and screaming at the woman he loved. But Linda was neither offended nor hurt; she understood what Greg Sr. was going through. And, on some level, she knew that the man she loved was gone, replaced by the ghostly figure in front of her now.

After serving a combined eight months at MCC and Rikers Island, Scarpa was transferred to a prison hospital in Pittsburgh. Linda flew down to visit him, only to find Greg Sr. in isolation. When he was brought out, Linda nearly fainted at the sight of him. Greg Sr. could hardly walk; he had long hair and a beard; his fingernails were untrimmed and encrusted with dirt. With tears in her eyes, Linda stepped forward and took Greg Sr. into her arms.

"What are you doing to him?" Linda yelled at a guard. "Look at him. Get me a scissor and a razor. I'll cut his hair and shave him."

The guard declined Linda's request, saying that a barber would take care of Scarpa. Linda sat with Greg Sr. for some time, talking to him, encouraging him, trying to be strong. When the visitation period ended, she kissed him and left. Sitting on the steps outside the prison, feeling utterly helpless, Linda cried until the tears would no longer come.

At home in New York, with the assistance of Scarpa's attorney and physician, Linda worked hard to secure a reduction in Greg Sr.'s sentence. Her argument: Because of the serious nature of his illness, Greg Sr. should be a candidate for house arrest; this was the only way to ensure that he would receive proper and adequate medical care. Eventually Linda stood before Judge Jack Weinstein and took full responsibility for Greg Sr., promising the judge that no crew member would be allowed in the house. At the end of September the magistrate released Greg Sr. to home detention to await trial. Greg Sr. was required to wear an ankle bracelet attached to an electronic device; if he tried to leave the house, the device would instantly relay an alarm to federal probation officers.

At the time, both Little Linda and Joey,

having left their mates, were living at home. Linda got the technicians to attach the alarm device to furniture near the backyard so Greg Sr. could go outside and play with his grandchildren, and enjoy some fresh air once in a while, without tripping the alarm. And, of course, business went on as usual, with visitors sneaking across a neighbor's lawn and entering the house through a back door.

The benefits of house arrest (a proper diet and the love and support of his family) had an immediate impact on Scarpa's health. He gained weight, and his appearance improved dramatically. Beneath the surface, though, Scarpa continued to deteriorate, as the dementia steadily progressed. Sometimes he would forget completely where he was, confusing his own living room with the back office at Wimpy Boys, or the backyard with the New Jersey farm. Although Linda warned visiting wiseguys of Scarpa's failing mental health, he continued to exert considerable influence over family business — often to his detriment, and certainly to the detriment of his crew.

Like many "successful" mobsters, Scarpa lived a life largely off the books. His home was a treasure trove of secret compartments and safe-deposit boxes, in which Greg Sr.

hid hundreds of thousands of dollars in cash. As his mental state worsened, so, too, did his judgment, and he began spending money like never before. There was the time, according to Linda, that Greg Sr. summoned Fat Larry Sessa to the house and handed him $80,000 in cash, along with a painfully naive set of instructions: "Buy some cocaine; sell it at a profit."

A younger, more vibrant (and more lucid) Greg Scarpa Sr. would never have done this.

In late December, Sessa had bought more than forty pounds of marijuana that he thought the crew could sell; however, the pot was of such poor quality that it was deemed unmarketable. So it sat in large garbage bags in a corner of Scarpa's living room for weeks on end, giving off a rank and powerful odor.

On the morning of December 28, 1992, up early as usual, Greg Sr. summoned Larry Mazza to the house.

"I'm gonna get Linda a Mercedes convertible and I'm gonna buy a BMW for Connie," Greg Sr. declared (by this point he had also become oddly committed to fostering a positive relationship between his wife and his longtime lover), as he removed $40,000 in cash from a false drawer in a bedroom dresser and handed it to Larry.

"Okay boss, no problem," said Larry.

Greg Sr. seemed especially happy that day. He had a couple of drinks in the afternoon and smoked some marijuana. Then Joey came home complaining that he and his good friend, Joe Randazzo, had gotten into a beef over a drug deal with two Bay Ridge brothers who were also dealers. Joey had grown by this time into a formidable young man with a bodybuilder's physique. But his facial features remained innocent and youthful, and often he wore a sad or pained expression. In all, he was a complicated package, and his parents worried about him constantly.

When Greg Sr. heard that his son had been disrespected, he flew into a rage; vowing to exact rage on the dealers, Scarpa pulled a puny .25-caliber pistol from a desk drawer, a gun so utterly lacking in firepower that it was almost laughable; it was, in other words, a gun that a competent Greg Sr. never would have taken into battle. Alarmed, Joey tried to calm his father. He made Greg Sr. promise not to do anything rash. (In reality, all Joey wanted was a show of muscle from his father to get face time with the dealers, who surely would recognize the old man and be appropriately impressed — and intimidated.)

Scare them, if you want, he said to his father. But please don't kill anyone.

The words fell on deaf ears. Greg Sr. rushed out the door, triggering the alarm on his bracelet. Ignoring the beeping sound, he jumped into Joey's red Ford Escort. With two unarmed boys (Joey and his buddy) as passengers, Greg Sr. drove around the neighborhood until he spotted the two dealers hanging out with some friends. As Joey had hoped, when the brothers saw his father, one started toward the car with his hand out, ready to shake the hand of the great mobster, Greg Scarpa Sr. But that man was gone, replaced by the shrunken, delusional gangster behind the wheel. As the dealer approached the Escort, Scarpa shot and wounded him. The dealer's friends reacted instantly, firing a volley of bullets into the car, hitting Greg Sr. and Joe Randazzo. Lost in the fog of battle, and certain that both his father and his friend had been killed, Joey Schiro panicked and ran away.

As it turned out, Greg Sr., who had been shot in the face, survived the attack, but with a badly damaged eye. Even in his weakened state, however, he remained a tough old bastard. As blood seeped out of his wounds and covered the side of his face, Scarpa turned the ignition key and drove off in the direction of home. Once safely parked in the driveway, he got out of the car (leaving the wounded Joe Randazzo behind), staggered into the house — and poured himself a Scotch. As Scarpa drained the glass, the phone began to ring. Greg Sr. answered it. On the other end of the line was his probation officer, calling to inquire about the triggering of Scarpa's ankle monitor.

Scarpa made up a story, something about the monitor getting wet while he was in the shower. Then he hung up the phone, just as Linda walked into the room and began to scream. What she saw was horrifying: a large, bloody gash where Greg Sr.'s eye was supposed to be; another hole near his nose — sort of a third nostril. Frantically looking for her son, Linda ran out to the car and discovered Randazzo, apparently bleeding to death in the backseat. She called Larry Mazza to take Greg Sr. to the hospital, and then summoned an ambulance for Randazzo. As she waited for help to arrive, Linda felt her heart racing, the fear so palpable she thought she might lose consciousness. Where was Joey? Given the carnage before her, there was, it seemed, only one logical answer: He was dead.

A few minutes after Larry picked up Greg

Sr. and drove off to the hospital, Joey Schiro walked into the house. Visibly shaken, crying, his clothes matted with sweat, Joey was relieved, if not stunned, to discover that his father had survived the attack.

But there was no time to talk, or to share the details of what had happened. Linda suddenly realized that Greg Sr.'s tainted blood was everywhere: on the walls, the carpet, the furniture. There was a medical protocol for dealing with spills such as this — they had been given instructions by Scarpa's physician — but Linda could hardly think straight at the moment. Acting on instinct, she dashed into the kitchen and grabbed a bottle of Clorox and some towels. Wearing latex gloves, she furiously mopped up the blood as the cops pounded at her front door.

Linda sent Joey downstairs before allowing the police into her home. When she finally opened the door, Linda saw not just one cop, but a veritable phalanx of police cruisers and ambulances. A plainclothes detective and several uniformed officers started to push past Linda into the house. Two of the cops immediately caught sight of the large, green, pot-filled plastic bag, and gave Linda a quizzical look. Presuming that they smelled its contents (how could they not?), Linda went on the offensive.

"If you want to look around, come back with a warrant," she said.

The police backed off, vowing to return with the appropriate documentation.

After they left, Linda raced to the hospital, where she discovered federal marshals already camped out in the lobby. Other Scarpa family members, including Connie, had begun to arrive; Greg Sr., they were informed, had already been taken into surgery. Hours later, when Linda was finally allowed to see Greg Sr. in a room surrounded by uniformed police and federal marshals, she found him sitting up in bed, the left side of his head swathed in bandages. She began to cry as she held his hand.

"Don't worry about it, sweetheart," Scarpa said with a smile. "You know what you do? You just call me 'One-Eyed-Greg.' "

26
DEMENTIA

In the days that followed the shooting, the Schiro home fell into a persistent state of depression. Joe Randazzo had succumbed to his wounds, leaving his best friend, Joey Schiro, sick with guilt.

"I thought Daddy was going there to let the guy apologize," he cried to his mother. Linda tried to explain that Greg Sr. was not his old self (nor in his right mind), but nothing she said could ease Joey's pain.

Not that Linda didn't have discomfort of her own. For more than thirty years she had believed Greg Sr. virtually invincible; time and circumstance, however, had taken their toll, and now the tough old mobster was back behind bars, gravely ill, and unlikely ever to see the outside world again. For all practical purposes, Linda had lost him; and she could have lost Joey, as well. Unable to stop these thoughts, Linda wandered about the house, sleep coming only with the help of medication. But this was merely a temporary respite, and it did nothing to shake Linda from her depression. She was falling apart.

On May 6, 1993, Greg Scarpa Sr. pled guilty to three counts of murder and conspiracy to murder several others. He faced life imprisonment without parole. Ravaged by disease and rapidly deteriorating, Scarpa was a pitiable sight, his new glass eye staring blindly around the courtroom, taking in everything and seeing nothing at all. On the misdemeanor gun charge, Greg also pled guilty, and his attorney requested a one-year penalty, to be served at the medical facility for prisoners with AIDS on Rikers Island. The request was granted, and the date for sentencing on the federal charges was adjourned to December.

With AIDS-related dementia, Greg Sr. spent money wildly, asking Linda to send money orders to people he barely knew (or did not know at all). He instructed her to give $2,000 to a nurse who brought him candy and cigarettes, as well as sweat suits and sneakers for other inmates. On one visit he told Linda that a doctor would soon come to the house to pick up $3,000 in cash. The doctor would then draw blood from inmates who were even sicker than

Scarpa and substitute Greg Sr.'s name on the vial. The thinking was this: If Greg was deemed sufficiently ill, he might be granted early (compassionate) release. But the prison learned of the illicit scheme and the doctor quickly disappeared from Rikers.

In October, Scarpa met with prosecutors at the United States attorney's office in Brooklyn; in establishing ground rules for the meeting, Scarpa had asked his new attorney, Steven Kartagener, a former prosecutor, to make sure that Lin DeVecchio would be in attendance. It was Scarpa's plan to offer his services as a cooperating government witness — again, with the hope of obtaining an early release. To sell the deal, Scarpa turned to his old friend, DeVecchio, for support.

As Kartagener recalls, "Greg said, 'I've always been helpful to the government in the past,' isn't that right, Mr. DeVecchio?"

"Yes. That's true," replied DeVecchio.

Unmoved, the prosecutors refused Scarpa's offer.

On December 15, 1993, Greg Scarpa Sr. stood before Judge Weinstein for sentencing. The judge asked Greg Sr. if he had anything to say. No, Scarpa replied, adding, "other than I expect to go home."

"You're not going home," Judge Weinstein

said. "You're going to prison."

Judge Weinstein sentenced Scarpa to a relatively lenient term of ten years in prison, which permitted him to be sent to the federal hospital facility in Rochester, Minnesota. (The judge also levied a fine of $200,000.) It was presumed, of course, that Scarpa would be dead long before the completion of his sentence.

They settled into a routine, with Linda dutifully and lovingly flying to Rochester each Friday morning and flying home on Monday. She and Greg Sr. sat in the visiting room together, with Linda fetching food and coffee from prison vending machines. If it was a nice day, they walked outside. On these occasions Linda made sure to hold his arm tightly, to keep him from slipping and falling. By now Linda had taken to protecting and caring for him, a development that surely would have saddened and confounded Greg Sr. had he been lucid enough to understand. Sometimes, of course, the dementia would lift just enough to give Linda a glimpse of the man she had met so many years earlier. And other times Greg Sr. would just sit and stare, or cry because he felt guilty about the things he had done in his life — not the killing or the stealing, mind you, but the failure to carve out enough quality time with his younger children.

As Greg Sr.'s condition worsened he was precluded from entering the prison visiting room, so Linda went to his hospital room, where she would find him lying in bed, staring morosely at the ceiling. When he saw Linda, Greg Sr.'s spirits would invariably lift; he would smile and wave, and she would help him out of bed and into a wheelchair. Accompanied by guards, they would go outside for a walk; they'd smoke cigarettes and talk about anything and everything. Greg Sr. asked about the grandchildren and why Joey never came to visit. Linda found it easy to lie to Greg Sr. by this time — it just seemed to make more sense than hurting his feelings — so she would make up some story about Joey having a cold or the flu or being busy with work, instead of telling him the truth, that Joey couldn't bear seeing his father this way.

On pleasant days, Greg Sr. put his face up to the sun and said, "I feel like we're in Florida." Then, after a time, he would add, "I should never have gotten involved in the war. It was a big mistake."

Soon, Greg Sr. was confined to his bed. The scabrous sores indicative of late-stage

AIDS covered his body — even his mouth and throat were infected, making it difficult for him to eat solid food or even drink water. Linda wasn't permitted to bring food in, so she paid a guard to buy fresh oranges. She then squeezed them by hand and held the glass up to Greg Sr.'s mouth as he sipped. She combed his hair, bathed him, and attempted to lift him so that he could sit in a wheelchair and go outside. On the best of days, with the help of hospital attendants, she was able to get him out of bed and into a chair, so that they could go outside and hold hands in the sunlight, one more time.

The federal government had been attempting to make a case against Carmine Persico's son, capo Alphonse "Little Allie Boy" Persico, believing that Persico had willfully initiated the Colombo War because he wanted to appoint his son the boss of what remained of the Colombo family. A few weeks before his death, Greg Sr. dictated a final revelation, an explosive document that wrecked the feds' case against Alphonse Persico. His deathbed affidavit absolved Persico of any participation in the Colombo War.

"Rival hoods shot at me while I was in the

car with my daughter Linda and two-year-old grandchild," the affidavit read. "I was so upset over this that my only intention was to retaliate. I had no instructions to retaliate from anyone, especially Allie Persico. I did not need anybody's permission to act. Allie Persico had nothing to do with any of these events."

It's worth noting that Greg Scarpa Sr. offered no such document in support or defense of his own son, Gregory Scarpa, Jr.

27
THE LAST DAYS OF
THE GRIM REAPER

Greg Sr. desperately wanted to come home to die. Linda had petitioned the court successfully to grant his wish, but as he was about to leave the facility, the prosecutor told the judge that Greg Sr. was still dangerous, that if he left the prison and killed someone, the judge would have Greg Sr.'s actions on his conscience. The order was rescinded.

The last time Linda Schiro saw Greg Scarpa Sr. was at his sixty-sixth birthday party, held at the prison hospital. A small group of nurses joined Linda in serenading the dying mobster with a chorus of "Happy Birthday."

"I love you, baby," Greg Sr. said to Linda.

"I love you, too."

Linda pushed Greg Sr.'s wheelchair outside, and together they sat quietly, holding hands, until he grew too tired to stay awake. As Linda helped him back into bed, she noticed tears falling from his good eye. Sobbing, he said, "I'm so sorry for what I did to you. I'm so very sorry."

"All you've done is love me and make me happy," Linda said. Greg Sr. squeezed her hand and continued crying. "Greg, I love you. You are going to get out of here. We're going back home together."

They both knew she was lying.

Soon afterward the prison doctor called Linda to inform her that Greg Sr.'s condition had worsened. What action, if any, did she want them to take? Knowing that Greg Sr. would not want his life extended through the use of artificial means, she denied authorization of life-support technology. The following night, on June 4, 1994, Linda received a phone call from the prison chaplain; Greg Scarpa Sr. had died.

They put him in a cheap black suit and sent him back to New York in a tin box. By the time he was buried, Scarpa had been outfitted in one of his favorite suits; he was laid to rest in an expensive coffin with his name engraved in gold on the side. When Linda looked into Greg Sr.'s coffin, she felt nothing so much as relief: His suffering had ended, and so had hers. She couldn't help but notice the undertaker's craftsmanship; Greg Sr. looked so much better than he had the last time they had seen each other, when she'd said good-bye at the prison hospital. Linda knelt by the side of the coffin and leaned in, kissing Scarpa's cold face and lips for the final time.

"I will love you forever," she whispered.

"Bless the body of Gregory," prayed the Catholic priest over the polished-oak coffin at Saint Bernadette's church in Bensonhurst. Few people gathered on that warm day to mark the passing of Gregory Scarpa Sr. Linda and Connie were both there, along with their sons and daughters. But there were no friends or former cronies. The six pallbearers who carried Scarpa's casket had been hired for the day. Not that much effort was required; the weight was predominantly the casket. Scarpa weighed just fifty-six pounds at the time of his death.

A single crime reporter stood in the back of the church; across the street, two FBI agents took pictures. DeVecchio had told Linda that he wanted to attend the funeral but didn't think it would be good idea. He offered his condolences and told her to call him if she ever needed anything.

In a state of shock, Linda tried to cope. For more than thirty years she had been the "wife" of Greg Scarpa Sr., living inside the mob, under his protection; she knew no other life. She began self-medicating. Then, suddenly, residual payments from the shy-locking enterprise of Greg Sr. simply dried up. At first, Linda wasn't sure what had happened, but soon she discovered that Al-lie Persico had cut her off. Enraged, Linda reminded Persico of Scarpa's loyalty — how Greg Sr. had signed an affidavit that helped earn Persico his release from prison. This money, Linda argued, was her insurance policy. It was Greg's business, and now it belonged to his "widow."

But Persico was unmoved. Greg Sr. was dead, and that was that. Linda Schiro would receive nothing from the Colombo family.

Linda was lonely. A few months after Greg's death, she received a call from Lin DeVecchio. She was glad to hear from him and invited him to the Long Beach condo she had bought after selling the Brooklyn house and Florida condo. He had been such a part of their life for so long, always fixing everything for them, and now he was one of the few remaining links to the life she had known with Greg Sr. They shared a few drinks, swapped stories about the old days, and then Linda began to cry. DeVecchio instinctively took her into his arms to comfort her. He had always been attracted to Linda, for years wondering what it would be like to make love to her. In truth, Linda had wondered about him, too. In a way, De-Vecchio was not so different from Greg Sr. They were both big, brash men who refused to play by the rules.

According to John Connolly, a highly respected journalist specializing in the coverage of organized crime, a sexual relationship quickly developed between DeVecchio and Linda Schiro.

"That night, after more than a few drinks, Linda and DeVecchio made love," said Connolly, who interviewed Linda for a book project (the book never materialized). "It wasn't the best sex Linda ever had, and it wasn't the worst."

From then on, DeVecchio would come by as often as he could. The liaison, built more upon mutual dependency than anything else, suited them both. Linda shared with DeVecchio concerns about her financial situation, and DeVecchio mentioned the possibility of her working for the FBI. Just as Greg Sr. had done, Linda could funnel information to the government and earn money as well. At first Linda hestitated. But DeVecchio was clever and manipulative — he reminded Linda that the Colombo family (in particular, Allie Persico) had done her no favors of late; indeed, they had betrayed her. Wouldn't it be nice to exact some amount of revenge? Linda smiled. She had to admit that he was right. She wanted them all to burn in hell.

And so, according to Andy Kurins, a former FBI agent and DeVecchio's longtime pal, "a few weeks later, Linda became an informant for the FBI."

28

INTERNAL INVESTIGATION

In January 1994, Chris Favo and Jeffrey Tomlinson, along with other FBI agents who had worked under Lin DeVecchio, voiced their concerns about their supervisor to the New York bureau office. The decision to step forward was not made lightly — indeed, more than a year passed between the end of the Colombo War and the beginning of an internal FBI investigation. Initially, Favo was commended for his action and assured of confidentiality; two weeks later, however, an FBI official exposed Favo as a whistle-blower, telling the agent that he personally believed in DeVecchio's innocence. Favo soon realized that informing the bureau about DeVecchio's behavior was a mistake that would haunt him for his entire FBI career.

Due to Favo's and Tomlinson's concerns, the FBI did open a formal internal investigation into DeVecchio's performance. However, because then AUSA Valerie Caproni was worried about the investigation's potentially adverse impact on her upcoming trial, involving Anthony "Chuckie" Russo and several codefendants in a major Colombo War prosecution, she asked the agent investigating DeVecchio not to interview any mobsters expected to testify.

In 1994, Brooklyn federal prosecutors tried Alphonse Persico as the leader of the Colombo War, despite his incarceration. The state's witnesses included Big Sal Miciotta and Larry Mazza, who had helped Greg Scarpa Sr. commit murders during the war. Persico's lawyer reminded the court that two days before his death Greg Sr. had sworn that he, not Persico, had instigated the war. Based in no small part on Scarpa's testimony, Persico walked out of court a free man.

While the internal investigation proceeded slowly and quietly, DeVecchio was neither discharged nor put on administrative leave, but simply transferred to another supervisory position, as the FBI's drug enforcement coordinator for the entire northeastern United States, a position he continued to hold even after informing the bureau in a sworn statement that he was unwilling to take a voluntary polygraph test.

In the meantime, Valerie Caproni continued to prosecute several Colombo crime family members, including Anthony Russo. Any investigation of DeVecchio's conduct with a key Mafia figure threatened to scuttle Caproni's cases, so she continued to request that the Justice Department delay the investigation. In addition, when U.S. District judge Charles Sifton received a request for copies of all government documents related to DeVecchio and Scarpa, Caproni allegedly withheld vital information: an FBI 302 form in which a key Scarpa associate, Larry Mazza, stated that DeVecchio had regularly provided confidential information to Scarpa Sr. Part of that information related to DeVecchio providing Scarpa with the addresses of people who would then be murdered.

In addition to withholding evidence and impeding a legally required investigation of criminal misconduct by a supervising FBI agent, Caproni allegedly instructed the FBI's Office of Professional Responsibility (OPR) investigators not to conduct any interviews of the defendants in the upcoming Mafia trials. The purpose of the ban was to prevent the surfacing of additional evidence that demonstrated the criminal relationship of a key FBI agent with Colombo capo Gregory Scarpa Sr.

That summer, when the DeVecchio investigation was publicly revealed, Colombo War trial defendants formulated a "comrade in arms" defense, which theorized that through DeVecchio the FBI had actually given Greg Sr. information to help Greg Sr. win the Colombo family war. In essence, it argued, DeVecchio (and, by extension, the FBI) had been an active participant in the war.

At one trial Favo testified that he was convinced DeVecchio had leaked Scarpa information illegally. Colombo capo Carmine Sessa told the court he also knew that DeVecchio was giving information to Scarpa. FBI agent Howard Leadbetter testified that he and agents Chris Favo and Jeffrey Tomlinson had reported to their superiors that DeVecchio had tried to obstruct a probe of Greg Scarpa Sr.

The comrade-in-arms theory had an impact on jurors. Of the nine Colombo War trials, two were presided over by judges who permitted evidence regarding the DeVecchio-Scarpa relationship; in these proceedings, all fourteen defendants were acquitted. Additionally, defendants convicted before the DeVecchio investigation became public made motions for new trials.

Victor Orena, the former acting head of

the Colombo family who had spent much of the war hiding from Greg Sr., had been convicted of conspiracy to murder and sentenced to life imprisonment. While seeking a new trial for his client, Orena attorney Gerald Shargel leaked information to the *New York Post;* on May 15, 1996, the newspaper published a story saying that, despite the internal investigation, and his own FBI agents' testimony that DeVecchio had given secret information to the mob, he still had access to classified documents. When Shargel cross-examined DeVecchio during Orena's appeal hearing, the FBI agent repeatedly invoked his right under the Fifth Amendment to avoid self-incrimination.

In April 1996 — two years into the FBI's investigation of DeVecchio — James Kallstrom, then special agent in charge of the New York FBI office, sent a memo to FBI director Louis J. Freeh, indicating there was "insufficient evidence" to prosecute DeVecchio; moreover, failure to resolve the matter was having a "serious negative impact on the government's prosecution" of several Mafia cases. The investigation of Lin DeVecchio ended abruptly with a two-sentence letter, stating that prosecution of DeVecchio was "not warranted."

After thirty-three years of service, DeVecchio retired from the FBI with a full pension. At a party held for him in Manhattan, speeches were made and a retired agent broke down in sobs, declaring, "Lin DeVecchio is not corrupt. Lin DeVecchio did what he believed was right!"

DeVecchio has steadfastly maintained his innocence, claiming that in his dealings with Greg Sr. he was acting under "express authority" conferred on him in his capacity as an FBI supervisory special agent.

29
THE SINS OF THE SON

A few months after the death of his father, Joey Schiro left his wife, Maria, and daughter, Linda Maria, in Staten Island, where they lived, to take up residence in his mother's Long Beach condo. Joey had long been overweight, but depression, triggered by his father's passing and the emptiness of his personal life, had left him withered and gaunt.

Linda, perhaps selfishly, enjoyed having her baby in the house. She doted on him, washing and ironing his clothes and cooking so many of his favorite foods that he called her Mama Leone (after the famous Italian restaurant). Linda gave him money to help support his family, and even bought him video games. (It is worth noting that Joey Schiro was twenty-five years old at the time of this regression.)

Linda naturally wanted to spend every minute with her son; when Joey, who was

still a small-time neighborhood drug ped-
dler, would get beeped for a drug deal, he
would say, "Come on, Ma. Take a ride." And
Linda would join him as he met with cus-
tomers. Linda's chief regret in this arrangement was that she lacked the financial
wherewithal to rescue Joey from the danger
of seedy street-level crime. Had the Persicos
not cut her off, she could have protected
Joey, made sure that he didn't have to sell
drugs. Then, she thought, he would be safe.

Inevitably, Joey ran into trouble, as he
always did. Along with two friends, Jay and
Vincent Rizzuto Jr., he had robbed a small
amount of pot from two other dealers;
regrettably, their victim turned out to be
connected to a highly placed mafioso named
Fabiano. Despite Linda's protestations, Joey
naively believed that the matter could be
handled peacefully, through a meeting arranged by Vinny's father, Vincent "Vinny
Oil" Rizzuto Sr., who knew Fabiano.

At the meeting Joey and Vinny were instructed to compensate the dealer for the
pot they had stolen. They politely agreed to
the terms, and everyone shook hands.

Case closed.

But when Joey excitedly told his mother
about the meeting, Linda became hysterical. "Joey, please, don't believe him," she

310

pleaded. "They don't let you off that easily. I've been in this life over thirty years. I know how they work."

Joey threw an arm around Linda. "Ma, you don't know what you're talking about. It's okay. Don't worry."

After spending the next weekend in Staten Island with his young daughter, Joey phoned his mother to say that he was meeting Jay and Vinny that afternoon, but would be free to have dinner with her that evening. Linda was to beep him so they could make plans. Linda begged Joey not to go with Vinny, but again he dismissed her concerns with a laugh, then hung up the phone.

Linda visited her sister, Maryanne, who lived in Brooklyn, for a few hours before paging Joey. She continued to call, but he never answered or called back. At 7:00 P.M., Linda drove back to Long Island, figuring Joey would call her there. From the Belt Parkway, Linda saw police swarming around a car at the Sheepshead Bay exit; she assumed it was just another traffic accident.

By nine o'clock Linda had become so frightened and nervous that she took two Ativans to calm down. When the phone rang, she jumped on it. On the other end was her daughter (and Joey's sister), Little Linda. She was weeping.

"Ma, I want you to know that Joey is with Daddy."

A feeling of dread came over Linda. "What do you mean?" she cried. "Daddy is dead."

Suddenly, Linda understood. "Oh, my God," she screamed. She hung up the phone, grabbed her Ativan bottle, and swallowed the remaining twenty-five pills. Within the hour police and paramedics were at Linda's home, breaking down the door with an axe.

Linda has little recollection of this event; it was, in fact, one of two emotional breakdowns sandwiched around the funeral of her son, the second of which resulted in her admission to a hospital psychiatric ward for observation, treatment, and counseling. For the first time in thirty years, Linda, who had passively accepted the necessity of murder in the mob, now understood the suffering that so many others had endured. She felt pain so enormous and overpowering that she lost her will to live.

Discharged from the hospital into her sister's care, Linda remained severely depressed. She kept in touch with detectives working on Joey's case. She joined a support group, Parents of Murdered Children. Inconsolable and irrational, Linda saw several doctors in an attempt to acquire prescriptions for pain medication.

Knowing that she still had a family to care for, Linda sold her home on Long Island and used the money to support her daughter, daughter-in-law, and two grandchildren. She bought a small house on Staten Island, where she lived with her daughter, Little Linda, and her grandson, Freddy. With no use for material possessions (and no money to buy them, anyway), she divided her time between her family and various support groups, therapy, and church. She appeared on the television show *America's Most Wanted,* and pleaded for someone to help find her son's killer and bring him to justice.

Linda later discovered that the flashing lights she had passed on the way home that night in Sheepshead Bay had actually belonged to police investigating the death of Joey Schiro, who had been shot twice in the back of the head by Vinny Rizzuto. Joey's other friend, Jay, had also been wounded, but he'd managed to escape and flag down a passing police car. Friends waiting in another car had helped Rizzuto escape, and he'd been on the lam ever since.

After three years on the run, Rizzuto was captured. Linda read about it in the newspaper after a detective had called to tell her the news. Although she'd thought about this moment nearly every day, the news left her feeling oddly sad and hollow; rather than bringing some sense of closure, the news of Rizzuto's arrest rekindled the memory of Joey's death so vividly that Linda again had an emotional breakdown; and, once again, she landed in a psychiatric ward.

On a bitterly cold February day in 2000, the surviving family of Joey Schiro gathered in the courtroom of Brooklyn federal judge Edward Korman for Vinny Rizzuto's sentencing. On one side of the courtroom were the Rizzuto family women; on the other side, the Scarpa/Schiro women. There were no males representing either family — not surprising, really, since most were either dead or incarcerated.

Linda Schiro, Little Linda, Maria, and Linda Marie each asked permission to address the judge to condemn Rizzuto and to express their pain and loss.

Linda spoke first. "My son, Joey, stands beside me today as he always does," she said, tears streaming down her cheeks. "You can't see him now, Vinny, but you saw him the night he was killed and sitting alone in a car to die by himself. Because of you, Vinny, his life is over. When Joey was killed, so was my body and my mind. My family's lives have changed so dramatically, and we ask you why. You took away a father, a brother, a husband, and my son. He was ripped from my life and left to die, and I was given no chance to say good-bye."

Maria was next, tearfully describing how her husband had spent all his free time with their daughter, "loving her, playing, teaching her to talk and walk." She then recounted his last day with her and their daughter, nervously dabbing her eyes with a wad of tissues while holding up a poster-size photograph of her late husband, with an image of their daughter superimposed over him.

"The day before he was murdered, it was St. Joseph's Day, and we all spent the day together," said Maria. "That would be the last time our daughter would ever sleep in her father's arms. The next morning, after breakfast, Linda Marie cried, 'Daddy, don't leave, Daddy, don't go.' Those were the last kisses, hugs, promises, and smiles she saw. My daughter is always crying and asking why that bad man killed her daddy. 'Why did he take my daddy? Everybody at school has their daddy, but I don't.' I am here to beg for the maximum sentencing of Vincent Rizzuto for taking my husband, and a father who can never be replaced to his little girl."

Maria then said that her daughter, who had been clutching a pink diary, wanted to address the court. "Tell him. Tell him how you feel," Maria urged Linda Marie. "Tell him what you wanted to tell him. You'll never have this chance again. Tell him. He's a good man. What he does is put bad people in jail. Go ahead."

Overwhelmed by the attention and the intensity of her surroundings, the little girl naturally was unable to speak. Judge Korman kindly asked if she wanted him to read her diary. After she nodded, he came off the bench and took it from her outstretched hand, reading several passages before passing it back to her.

Judge Korman then turned his attention to the convicted killer. "Did you want to speak, Mr. Rizzuto?"

Rizutto nodded.

"May I address the court without a child in the courtroom? Is that possible?" he asked, shifting anxiously on his feet.

Judge Korman said that he could not exclude the girl. Rizzuto explained he didn't want to speak badly about Joey Schiro in front of his daughter. This had less than the desired effect on the proceedings.

"Did you care about the child when you killed her daddy?" yelled Maria.

"Did you care about your victims' families?" retorted Rizzuto, as his attorney and the courtroom deputy tried to calm him. "Why is she saying something to me?" said Rizzuto, motioning to Linda. "Her husband killed, like, thousands of people. Her son killed four people. The man killed people for $10 bags on the street, killed someone in the front of a school with a shotgun."

Rizzuto stopped his tirade long enough to allow Linda Marie to be led from the courtroom; then he resumed without missing a beat. He ripped into the prosecutors for reneging on a promise of an eighteen-year sentence, saying that they had coerced him into pleading guilty, and made him take twenty-four years by threatening to prosecute his father. He said the government had ignored several murders by the Scarpas because Greg Sr. was a top echelon informant.

"The government gave Joey, the Scarpas, a pass to commit several crimes against innocent people," he said.

But, as Judge Korman noted, the Scarpas were not on trial in that courtroom. Rizzuto did in fact kill Joey Schiro, a former friend and partner in crime; both Joey and Greg Scarpa Sr. were now dead. And Rizzuto was still alive.

"You think I want to take twenty-four years?" said Rizzuto. "My kids are going to be my age when I get out. What kind of life is that? I wish I would have died. That's it. I wish it would have been me."

As Linda and her family left the sentencing, the mood was akin to a funeral. Linda could not stop crying. She resented the fact that Rizzuto had received a sentence of twenty-four years in prison. It was, in her opinion, insufficient compensation for the murder of her son. If it had been up to Linda, Rizzuto would have been executed on the spot.

30

THE MOBSTER AND
THE TERRORIST

In death, Greg Scarpa Sr. became larger than life. The story of his dual role as an FBI informant and Mafia kingpin was the stuff of legend, and the New York media predictably gobbled and regurgitated every morsel. If they helped sell newspapers and increase television ad revenue, the stories also had the rather obvious effect of making life miserable (and dangerous) for Gregory Scarpa Jr.

Faced with irrefutable evidence that Greg Sr. had been among the most prodigious and high-ranking rats the underworld had ever known, the heads of the Mafia had no choice but to retaliate — with whatever tools were at their disposal. If for no other reason than to save face, they had to show strength and unity on this particular issue. To that end, a contract was placed on the head of Gregory Scarpa Jr.

For his safety, Gregory was transferred

from Lewisburg to the federal prison in Leavenworth, Kansas, an all-male, high-security facility known, rather prosaically, as the "Hot House," because it was notoriously hot throughout the year. But the move hardly deflected all danger. When Lucchese family boss Vittorio "Vic" Amuso, serving a life sentence there, called Greg Sr. a "rat," Gregory beat him up in the prison yard while hundreds of inmates looked on.

In 1995 Gregory was transferred to MCC in Manhattan, an administrative facility housing both male and female prisoners who were waiting to appear before the New York federal courts. Although in solitary confinement, Gregory was relieved to be back in New York, if only for a short time, because it meant he could see his children: Kori, Diane, Gregory III, and little Maria, his baby girl. Gregory heard that his wife, Maria, had relapsed into drug use, and he worried incessantly about the care of his children. Of course, in his heart, he knew that he had only himself to blame for being absent from their lives.

Gregory soon learned that Eastern District of New York assistant United States attorney Valerie Caproni was indicting him, his brother Frank, and fifteen other mob members on new, superseding Racketeer Influenced and Corrupt Organizations (RICO) charges, including illegal gambling, tax fraud, and five murders. If convicted, Gregory was looking at a strong possibility of spending the rest of his life in prison. The charges stemmed from the testimony of other indicted Mafia members, including Larry Mazza, Greg Sr.'s protégé and Linda's former lover, who had cooperated with the government for a greatly reduced sentence.

In the cell next to Gregory was Ramzi Yousef, a Kuwaiti citizen born to a Pakistani father and a Palestinian mother; he was also the nephew of Khalid Sheikh Mohammed, a senior Al-Qaeda official. Yousef was at MCC awaiting trial for his role in the 1993 World Trade Center bombing and the 1995 Philippines Bojinka bombing plot against U.S. airlines.

After meeting Ahmad Mohammad Ajaj at a terrorist training camp on the Afghanistan-Pakistan border in spring 1992, Yousef and Ajaj had conspired to bomb the World Trade Center. That September they flew from Baghdad to New York, where immigration inspectors at John F. Kennedy International Airport (JFK) had discovered in Ajaj's luggage a "terrorist kit," including fake passports, bomb recipes, six manuals for creating explosive devices, and how-to videotapes on advanced weaponry. Ajaj was arrested and served six months in jail on a visa violation. After his release, Judge Reena Raggi ordered Ajaj's manuals returned to him.

Although initially detained, Yousef had been allowed to enter the United States, where he quickly contacted Islamic extremists in New York and New Jersey to obtain supplies and recruits. He rented a Jersey City, New Jersey, apartment, which doubled as a headquarters and a facility for manufacturing bombs and other explosive devices.

On February 26, 1993, on the second anniversary of the Iraqi army's withdrawal from Kuwait, Yousef had parked a bomb-laden van in the parking garage below the World Trade Center and set the bomb's timer. Just after noon, the bomb exploded, killing six people, injuring more than one thousand others, and causing property damage in excess of $500 million. Hours later, Yousef fled the United States; he was indicted, in absentia, for the bombing. In 1994, in Manila, Philippines, Yousef devised the Bojinka plot (a precursor to 9/11 and the attacks on the World Trade Center and the Pentagon), in which five terrorists would board twelve U.S. airliners serving Southeast Asia, assemble bombs onboard, and then exit the planes during a stopover before the bombs detonated en route to U.S. cities.

Testing a bomb in a Manila movie theater, Yousef injured several patrons. Ten days later, while in flight, Yousef placed under his seat a Casio watch wired to a nitrocellulose package, which would serve as a trigger that would ignite the center-wing fuel tank and blast apart the Boeing 747. After he exited at a stopover, the bomb exploded as anticipated — in the air — killing a Japanese passenger, injuring several others, and blowing a massive hole in the plane. The damage was severe, though not as severe as Yousef had intended: The bomb had been just a bit too far from the center-wing fuel tank to destroy the entire plane.

In January 1995, two weeks before the Bojinka plot was to be carried out, Yousef was mixing liquid explosives designed to pass through airport metal detectors when he accidentally started a fire and was compelled to flee his apartment. Upon arrival, fire department officials and police discovered chemicals, bomb components, and a laptop computer. The last of these was perhaps the most valuable piece of evidence, since it contained numerous files depicting, in great detail, plans for constructing bombs and destroying commercial airplanes. Yousef fled the country but was later arrested at an Al-Qaeda safe house in Islamabad, Pakistan, and extradited to the United States. In February 1996, a grand jury filed a twenty-count superseding indictment against Yousef; he awaited trial in a cell at MCC, right next door to Gregory Scarpa Jr.

From the time he was a small boy, Gregory had heard stories and warnings about sinister men who perpetrated unspeakable acts of violence upon the innocent; "terrorists," they were called, and while Gregory had no idea what that word really meant, the descriptions of torture and mayhem instilled within him both a fear and hatred of terrorists. He vividly recalled July 21, 1972 — Bloody Friday, it was called — when the Irish Republican Army detonated a series of bombs that killed 9 people and injured 130 more. Later that summer Palestinian terrorists killed 11 Israeli athletes and coaches at the Olympic village in Munich, Germany. As Gregory grew up and took his place in the family business, his fear of terrorists naturally diminished; however, his hatred intensified. Like most mobsters, Gregory saw a clear distinction between the violence that punctuated his life and the violence that fueled terrorism. The mobster would argue that he killed only when left with no other option; he was intent only on protecting his family and his business interests. Typically, when someone was whacked by the Mafia, it wasn't exactly a shock. Chances are that person was engaged in activity that generously could be described as "risky." The terrorist, in contrast, preyed upon the innocent. Fear was the terrorist's ally, anarchy his goal. Gregory had long made a vow to himself: *If given an opportunity to fight terrorism* (and this could be construed as merely killing a terrorist), *he would not hesitate to act.*

Gregory decided to solicit intelligence from Yousef for the government in exchange for a reduced sentence under Rule 5K1.1 of the U.S. federal sentencing guidelines, wherein the government states that the defendant has provided substantial assistance in the investigation or prosecution of another person who has committed an offense. He felt confident in his ability to gather information, as he had done it for his father for years. With no way to know if his terrorism intelligence would be worthwhile, the U.S. attorney's office wanted him to plead guilty to the five murders and other charges in return for serving seventeen more years; Gregory rejected this deal, hoping that his terrorism intelligence would shorten his sentence greatly. It was, in essence, a giant roll of the dice.

Concerned that Gregory might have to disclose information that could harm his defense in his upcoming trial, Gregory's court-appointed lawyer, Larry Silverman, wanted Gregory to talk only to Southern District of New York (SDNY) prosecutors. Under this arrangement, only AUSA Valerie Caproni (who had agreed not to take part in prosecuting Gregory), would be privy to his information. In this way she could offer an unbiased evaluation of whatever intelligence he acquired.

Charming and charismatic despite his time behind bars (much of which was spent in relative isolation), Gregory quickly won the confidence of Yousef, who wrongly assumed that as a Mafia leader and convicted criminal, Gregory hated the U.S. government and American society as much as he did. Yousef exchanged cryptic, heavily coded notes (known as "kites" in prison parlance) with Gregory; Gregory would then pass the kites on to another Al-Qaeda terrorist and Bojinka codefendant, Abdul Hakim Murad, who was housed in another adjoining cell. (It was almost a perverse prison joke: Gregory Scarpa Jr., who carried an intense hatred of terrorists, had become the meat in a terrorist sandwich.) Before forwarding the messages, however, Gregory photographed the kites (which included recipes for making homemade bombs), using a miniature spy camera provided by the FBI.

Gregory and his attorney met with AUSA Caproni and AUSA Patrick Fitzgerald, then assistant U.S. attorney in the U.S. attorney's office for the Southern District of New York and chief of the Organized Crime-Terrorism Unit. (Fitzgerald later was the special counsel charged with investigating the government's leak of undercover CIA agent Valerie Plame's identity, which resulted in the perjury conviction of Vice President Dick Cheney's chief of staff, I. Lewis "Scooter" Libby.) Gregory's intelligence report was stunning. It even included information regarding the presence of an Al-Qaeda cell operating in New York City; a connection between Al-Qaeda and the Khobar Towers bombing; the location in Qatar of Yousef's uncle, Khalid Sheikh Mohammed; Osama bin Laden's plot to hijack a plane to free blind Sheikh Omar Abdel Rahman; plots to kidnap and kill judges and prosecutors; the names of countries, such as England, that terrorists would use as conduits to enter the United States; the testing of U.S. security procedures; detailed diagrams of the Casio watch bomb; instructions for smuggling explosives, chemicals, and detonators onto airlines; schematics for onboard bomb assembly; and plans to blow up a Boeing 747 airliner.

Yousef told Gregory that a terrorist attack on a plane during his Bojinka trial would surely prejudice the jurors against him, allowing Yousef to request a mistrial and forcing Judge Kevin Duffy to start over with a new jury.

Almost by definition, any relationship between a terrorist and a mobster is one built on a foundation of half truths or outright lies — indeed, this can be said of most prison relationships. But embellishment or false proclamations of innocence were more than mere bluster on Gregory's part; he lied to Yousef with a purpose and a plan: to entrap the terrorist, which would have the twin benefits of helping U.S. security efforts and enhancing Gregory's bid for an early release.

Among the tidbits of misinformation Gregory shared with Yousef: There existed within the Mafia a militia wing that could smuggle into prison a cellular phone for secret phone calls. That Yousef fell so completely and guilelessly for such a tale is surprising, but he did. James Kallstrom, the FBI special agent in charge (SAC) of the New York office, arranged to have Yousef's "secret" calls monitored by the FBI's Arabic translators. Yousef called his uncle, Khalid Sheikh Mohammed, and other operatives outside the United States who were trying to obtain passports that would allow coconspirators into the United States; they also openly discussed attacks on U.S. passenger jets.

On March 5, 1996, Yousef told Gregory that Al-Qaeda had already positioned "four terrorists . . . here in the United States" who were awaiting orders from bin Laden to poison New York City's drinking water, attack government installations, or take down a plane. Gregory arranged for his "associates" (in reality, undercover FBI agents) to meet the four terrorists; however, the meeting never took place because the FBI refused Yousef's demand for a payment of $3,000 to broker the deal.

Yousef spoke in bold, self-aggrandizing terms, proclaiming that he and his fellow Al-Qaeda operatives would "bring New York to its knees" by, among other methods, blowing up the World Trade Center with American-owned "flying massive bombs." When Gregory related this startling news to the FBI, it was met with a predictable degree of skepticism. Gregory recalls AU-SAs Fitzgerald and Michael J. Garcia laughing at Yousef's half-baked plot. The idea that American planes might one day crash into the World Trade Center with full loads of jet fuel, thus acting like "flying massive bombs," was nothing short of unfathomable. In hindsight, of course, any such threat should have been taken seriously; but in the mid-1990s? Who would have guessed that a small band of Islamic fundamentalists, armed only with box cutters, could commandeer four American jets and create the most devastating terrorist attack in U.S. history?

By the spring of 1996, convinced that the government was basically dismissing the information he'd obtained from Yousef, Gregory contemplated ending his cooperation.

From Abdul Hakim Murad, Gregory learned that loyalists to Khalid Sheikh Mohammad were devising a plot to blow up a U.S. airliner; however, because he believed that his trial was proceeding in a positive manner, Yousef encouraged a delay in the execution of the plan. Again, Gregory relayed this news to the FBI. Later, however, when Yousef became convinced that the government was trying to sabotage his case, he told Gregory of an impending plot to bring down an American jetliner. The cause of the crash, according to Yousef, would be a small explosion (a "bomb trigger") near the center-wing fuel tank. According to Yousef, the plane was scheduled to be brought down the very next day, on the thirty-fifth anniversary of Iraq's Liberation Day. Gregory relayed all of this information to the FBI from his cell at MCC.

At 8:31 P.M., on July 17, 1996, a few minutes after takeoff, TWA Flight number 800 from JFK to Paris blew apart at thirteen thousand feet, smashing into the Atlantic Ocean off Long Island, New York, and killing 230 people.

The following morning Yousef's counsel asked Judge Duffy for a mistrial, citing the "unfortunate confluence of circumstances" in the downing of a 747 and its similarity to the Bojinka charges. Judge Duffy, a tough Irishman, denied the motion, saying that although the TWA 800 disaster was a "tragedy," it had "nothing to do with this case."

Assistant FBI director James Kallstrom, who was investigating the crash, told Gregory's attorney that his information was of "utmost importance"; at the appropriate time, Kallstrom said, the government would "do the right thing" for Gregory. Within days of the crash, however, AUSA Caproni transferred responsibility for the investigation from the National Transportation Safety Board (NTSB) to the FBI — this, despite the fact that the FBI had not even declared TWA Flight 800 a crime scene.

Although extensive explosive residues were found at the crash site and in the wreckage of the plane itself — including Yousef's personal favorites, nitroglycerine, research development explosive (RDX), and pentaerythritol tetranitrate (PETN) — the FBI appeared reluctant to link Al-Qaeda or any other terrorist organization to the crash. The residues, according to a bureau report, had instead resulted from a faulty dog-training exercise in St. Louis five weeks earlier. However, Herman Burnett, the St. Louis police officer who performed the dog-training exercise, said that his test "was not conducted on the 747 that became TWA 800." NTSB investigators eventually concluded that a "mechanical malfunction" caused the center-wing fuel tank to explode after arcing wires ignited leaking fuel vapors. Surprisingly, in the wake of such a catastrophic failure, not a single Boeing 747 was grounded to check for similar mechanical malfunctions.

On November 12, 1997, Kallstrom informed the families of Flight 800 victims that the FBI had found no evidence of a crime and was suspending its investigation of the accident. Kallstrom then wrote a letter to the head of the NTSB prior to its public hearing on Flight 800 in December 1997, demanding that the board not discuss eyewitness reports, explosives, residue trails, or any other "details of the criminal investigation" until the NTSB had "definitively determined an accidental cause for the crash."

Gregory's intelligence left government officials with a dilemma: If they took seriously his information regarding Yousef (and as yet, they had not — at least not publicly), they also would have to concede a degree of credibility regarding information about his father's relationship with Lin DeVecchio. Why? Because Gregory had shared explicit information regarding DeVecchio's corrupt alliance with Greg Scarpa Sr. No fewer than seventy-five trials had resulted from the Colombo War, and all relied to an extent on DeVecchio's testimony. Increasingly, however, defense attorneys had begun constructing their arguments around the questionable nature of the DeVecchio-Scarpa relationship; as a result, a federal judge already had dismissed charges against fourteen defendants in the Colombo War; if it could be demonstrated that there existed between DeVecchio and Greg Scarpa Sr. an unethical or illegal arrangement, then the sixty-one remaining cases would all be in jeopardy.

On May 5, 1997, following a meeting with the FBI to review and evaluate Gregory's information, AUSAs Caproni and Fitzgerald terminated the intelligence operation between Gregory Scarpa Jr. and Ramzi Yousef. It was their determination that Gregory would receive no credit for spying on Yousef; his intelligence was deemed a "hoax and scam."

In early 1998, defense attorney Silverman learned that AUSA Caproni would join the team prosecuting Gregory, and asked the judge to disqualify her on the grounds that she was privy to privileged information regarding his terrorism intelligence; this, Silverman argued, could compromise Gregory's defense. The judge declined his motion.

Within the next year Ramzi Yousef was tried for his role in both the 1993 World Trade Center bombing and the 1995 Bojinka bombing plot; along with his codefendants, Yousef was found guilty on all counts.

By claiming that TWA Flight 800 was caused by a mechanical malfunction, however, the government significantly raised the bar for the prosecution of future terrorist acts, which would now have to be so disastrous that the suppressing of criminal evidence would be impossible. Khalid Sheikh Mohammad, who was implicated in the TWA Flight 800 bombing but was never pursued or arrested, went on to become the mastermind of the 9/11 attacks.

Meanwhile, having rejected a plea bargain of seventeen years because he felt that his information regarding Yousef was of far greater value, Gregory Scarpa Jr. found himself at the center of a trial that had the potential to keep him in prison for the rest of his life. He had gambled . . . and now it appeared as though he had sustained a rather spectacular loss.

31
THE SON GOES DOWN

After several delays, the trial of Gregory Scarpa Jr. moved forward in 1998, in Brooklyn's federal court. In his opening statement Larry Silverman set the tone for the defense, arguing passionately that his client was paying a severe price for sins committed by his father; moreover, Silverman argued, former Scarpa crew members (some of whom were Gregory's friends), knowing that that they could not buy their way out of jail by testifying against a dead man, had agreed as a compromise to assist the prosecution in its pursuit of Gregory Scarpa Jr.

Greg Scarpa Sr., Silverman said, "was vicious, treacherous, deceitful, manipulative, and known by his crew as the Grim Reaper, the Mad Hatter, and Hannibal Lecter." Greg Sr. was "the one calling the shots, not his son, Gregory Jr."

In her opening remarks, AUSA Sung-Hee Suh countered that Gregory Scarpa Jr. was an eager and active participant in the Scarpa family business; indeed, the son was a prolific criminal and killer who wanted nothing more than to follow in his father's bloody footsteps. The prosecution's first witness, Scarpa crew member William Meli, implicated both Scarpas in several killings, adding that after a 1981 murder, Gregory had been so close to his victim that he had to change his clothes "because they were full of blood."

As the trial progressed, Gregory realized that he had only one hope for presenting to the jury a more well-balanced version of the story: He would have to testify on his own behalf. On the witness stand, Gregory swore that his father had committed the five murders with which he had been charged. Then Gregory testified about his father's corrupt twelve-year relationship with FBI agent Lindley DeVecchio. Valerie Caproni, Patrick Fitzgerald, and others who knew of the Scarpa-DeVecchio relationship were silent as Gregory spun a riveting tale of murder, deception, and greed. But they offered no counterargument, preferring instead to allow the inherent implausibility of his testimony to hang in the air. DeVecchio, testifying under a grant of immunity from the prosecution, denied any wrongdoing.

Silverman wanted to call two witnesses who could corroborate Gregory's testimony about DeVecchio: Linda Schiro and Gregory's mother, Connie. But neither was willing to take the stand. Both women now claim that their reticence was intended neither as a lack of support for Gregory nor a signal that they had nothing to offer in the way of corroborating evidence. Rather, each says she was vigorously threatened with the prospect of criminal prosecution if she took the witness stand. It is unclear what charges Linda Schiro or Connie Scarpa might have faced, but given their involvement with the Scarpa men, and the likelihood that they possessed knowledge of criminal activity, the possibilities are endless; thus, the threat was hardly idle. Regardless, their unwillingness to testify helped ensure that Gregory Scarpa Jr. would be found guilty, and that the alleged complicity of DeVecchio would go unpunished.

"They're trying to make my son pay for his father's sins," said Connie, outside the courtroom, "and it's not right."

Gregory, of course, testified about his government informant work regarding Ramzi Yousef, freely acknowledging that he had hoped to help the FBI fight international terrorism while also earning a reduction in his sentence. As they had during Gregory's testimony regarding DeVecchio, Valerie Caproni and her prosecution team remained silent. They neither refuted nor even addressed Gregory's testimony. Instead, in their summation, prosecutors told the jury that they had no idea what Gregory was talking about when he claimed to have helped the government gain information regarding Yousef's terrorist plans. Feigning ignorance, they suggested that Gregory had concocted this fantastic tale simply to gain sympathy and, perhaps, freedom. In the media Gregory was portrayed, at best, as a self-aggrandizing opportunist; at worst, he was a murderous liar. Regardless, the coverage placed both Gregory and his family in considerable danger.

"It was all over the media," recalls Gregory. "This made me very nervous, because Yousef possessed the address of many members of my family, which he had his associates find. Without any care or help from the government, my family, who were just getting by financially, made it their business to relocate."

After a lengthy trial, the jury deliberated for three days before acquitting Gregory of the five murders; however, he was found guilty of racketeering and separate counts of loan sharking, bookmaking, and tax fraud. Before sentencing on January 9, 1999, Silverman reached out once more to the prosecution, and asked for leniency. In a letter to AUSA Fitzgerald, Silverman wrote of Gregory's courageous work in gathering intelligence from Ramzi Yousef: "There ought to be little dispute as to the facts of his cooperation, and these facts ought to be made known to the trial judge, Judge Raggi." Silverman added that because there could be "security reasons for with-holding disclosure, it may be appropriate for you to set forth the details, significance, and uses of his cooperation in a sealed, in-camera submission to Judge Raggi."

Silverman never received a response from AUSA Fitzgerald.

At a sentencing hearing in May 1999, Judge Reena Raggi, declaring that much of his testimony was perjury, said that Gregory was "from start to the last, a criminal."

In a last-gasp attempt to convince the court that there were mitigating circum-stances (in the form of Gregory's spying on Ramzi Yousef), Silverman asked the judge to consider Gregory's cooperation with the government before handing down his sen-tence.

"We strongly believe that he prevented

serious harm to people, both government officials and others," Silverman said.

In keeping with the skepticism encountered by the defense, the judge dismissed Gregory's spying as insignificant at best, and more likely part of a scam. She similarly dismissed Gregory's testimony about De-Vecchio. Judge Raggi sentenced Gregory to twenty years for racketeering, ten years for the three loan-sharking convictions, five years for bookmaking, and five years for tax fraud. Four decades in all — to be served consecutively. Additionally, she ordered that the forty years be tacked onto his 1988 sentence for a racketeering conviction that would have ended in 2000. The net effect, of course, was that Gregory Scarpa Jr. would, in all likelihood, be spending the rest of his life in prison.

Although Gregory had obtained plans from Yousef for several terrorist acts that Gregory had conveyed to his FBI contacts, the FBI and other Department of Justice (DOJ) personnel declined to act on the information. As a result — directly or indirectly — several significant and perhaps preventable terrorist actions occurred.

TWA Flight 800 was downed on July 17, 1996, with considerable evidence of terrorist involvement, a month after Yousef had warned of similar attacks. And, of course, four U.S. airliners were hijacked on September 11, 2001. In all cases, Gregory's attempts to encourage the FBI to act on reasonable evidence and information were unsuccessful.

If there was fallout from what, in retrospect, could certainly be considered negligence on the part of federal law enforcement officials, it wasn't readily apparent. For example, AUSA Valerie Caproni, lead prosecutor in the case against Gregory Scarpa Jr., having labeled the information that he obtained from Yousef as a hoax, helped (perhaps unwittingly) enable the events of 9/11 and bombings at U.S. embassies. In 1998, the DOJ elevated her to the position of chief of the Criminal Division in New York. Caproni later identified the convicting of Gregory Scarpa Jr. as one of the proudest accomplishments of her career.

Regarding intelligence gleaned through Scarpa's interactions with Ramzi Yousef, Patrick Fitzgerald, in a sealed affidavit dated June 25, 1999, allegedly wrote that a follow-up investigation "appeared to corroborate Scarpa's information." Incredibly, this document has never been unsealed, and Fitzgerald has thus far refused to publicly comment on the case.

Meanwhile, Gregory Scarpa Jr., who turned down a plea bargain of seventeen years because he believed in the inherent fairness of the U.S. judicial system, got forty years in virtual solitary confinement in the administrative maximum security penitentiary in Florence, Colorado, where conditions have been called "brutal beyond compare."

32
THE TOMB

Gregory was flown to Colorado and then driven to the six hundred-acre federal correctional complex in Florence. Completed in 1994, the prison is a sprawling facility housing a broad spectrum of inmates in a variety of circumstances — from a minimum-security camp for insider traders and small-time pot dealers to a concrete fortress built to be the most secure supermax prison in the country: the U.S. Penitentiary Florence Administrative Maximum (ADMAX).

The growing popularity of supermax prisons represents a profound reversal in America's perspective regarding the purpose of the criminal justice system. For most of the twentieth century, rehabilitation had been the primary goal; however, by 1980, frustrated by escalating violent crime and rising drug-related convictions, society generally supported a move toward a more punitive experience for convicts, including mandatory minimum sentences, removing exercise equipment from prisons, barring grants for inmates' higher education, and, finally, entire prisons devoted to housing the most dangerous criminals, usually in solitary confinement.

Built on the twin pillars of prolonged solitary confinement and extreme conditions, ADMAX embraces a system in which inmates rarely interact with or touch another human being. Theoretically (and ironically, given the type of inmate commonly found there), this makes Florence ADMAX one of the safest prisons in the country. Hard-core proponents of the supermax experience would add that solitary confinement and sensory deprivation naturally bring about "behavior modification," especially when prisoners are disabled through psychological and/or physical breakdown, including beatings, torture, and psychological abuse.

One could also argue that ADMAX is among the least humane of American penitentiaries. Prison psychology experts, like Dr. Craig Haney of the University of California at Santa Cruz, believe that long-term solitary confinement can have devastating effects. Faced with constant harassment, sensory deprivation, and isolation, some prisoners become enraged and aggressive, almost animalistic. Others retreat into themselves, sleep most of the day, and enter a private world of madness, screaming incessantly in their cells, and even covering themselves with their own feces. In other words, confinement under supermax conditions is likely to drive men mad, and encourage their violent tendencies, and thus legitimize their solitary confinement. As one federal judge noted, prolonged supermax confinement "may press the outer bounds of what most humans can psychologically tolerate."

This was where Gregory Scarpa Jr. was to live the rest of his life.

"At the prison," says Gregory, "I went through 'intake,' the abusive and humiliating experience of becoming a new inmate at a federal institution." Then, shackled and box-cuffed, he was led down a series of lengthy hallways until he saw a yard filled with steel cages where he would receive recreation for one hour each day; the remaining twenty-three hours he would be locked down in his cell. On weekends even that meager respite would be withheld; he would be locked in his cell for the entire day.

"It was inconceivable to me that I would

have to spend the rest of my life here," recalls Gregory. "Locked in this tiny cell, which resembled a tomb."

Shortly after his arrival, Gregory received from the prison's legal education department three large books devoted to the study of law. Gregory was surprised to receive this delivery, particularly since he hadn't requested the books; oddly, however, the delivery included a copy of a formal library request form, on which was printed Gregory's name and prison identification number. The back of the request form was covered with unintelligible letters — scribbling, it seemed to Gregory. Then Gregory noticed in the corner of his window that inmates in the outside cages were trying to get his attention. Pressing his face to the glass, Gregory saw, in separate cages not far in the distance, two of the most notorious federal prisoners in U.S. history: Terry Nichols, the Oklahoma City bomber, and Ramzi Yousef.

Yousef's eyes met Gregory's. With his hands, Yousef pantomimed the action of reading a book, flipping imaginary pages as Gregory looked on. The intent was clear: Yousef wanted Gregory to look inside the law volume that had recently been delivered. Gregory picked up the book and began fingering the pages. Tucked inside was a slip of paper covered with more scribbling, similar to that which had appeared on the back of the request form. No stranger to incarceration, Gregory recognized the paper for what it was: coded correspondence, a kite.

Gregory set about the task of decoding the note; its contents did not surprise Gregory. Yousef had heard disturbing rumors of Gregory spying on him and wanted Gregory to refute the rumors by incriminating himself, acknowledging that he had paid Yousef money to assist in various terrorist acts, including the downing of TWA Flight 800. Gregory, knowing that his life was in danger and feeling instinctively that he should try to maintain some sort of relationship with the terrorist, responded in exactly the manner Yousef requested. The coded letter was tucked inside the law books and returned to the prison library before ultimately making its way to Yousef.

After a few months, prison officials got wind of the correspondence between the terrorist and the mobster, and began quietly intercepting their kites. This wasn't unusual at ADMAX — prison officials often discovered unauthorized communication between inmates and acted accordingly. The inmates, in turn, searched for new vehicles with which to transport kites. Gregory wasn't surprised when, after a short period of silence, he started receiving items from the prison chapel and the laundry department, all containing messages from Yousef.

"One day I received a very disturbing kite," recalls Gregory, "in which Yousef told me that the legal issues that he'd been working on since New York had come to light in a great way, and that he would be getting released in early September 2001."

Having communicated with Yousef in a conspiratorial manner for a number of years, Gregory knew that this was code for there being a great possibility of an attack by Al-Qaeda on U.S. soil, and that the attack would include American-owned "flying massive bombs."

Deeply disturbed by this information, Gregory wrote the FBI two separate letters, each stating specifically that Yousef had leaked word of a terrorist attack scheduled for early September 2001. When he heard nothing, Gregory contacted the ADMAX special investigative supervisor (SIS), and relinquished the decoded kite to an SIS officer who, according to Scarpa, said he would take care of it. A few days later, another officer told Gregory that the FBI wanted to interview him, and would soon be paying a visit.

That meeting never took place.

On the morning of September 11, 2001, Gregory was watching television in his cell when the program was interrupted to present breaking news of an apparent terrorist attack. Gregory watched in horror as images of the burning World Trade Center towers flickered across the screen. As he thought of the coded messages he had received from Ramzi Yousef, and his failed attempts to convince the FBI that such an attack was imminent, Gregory felt sick to his stomach. Overwhelmed with sadness, he fell back on his bunk and began to cry.

In the wake of the tragedy of 9/11, Gregory was nearly consumed by rage and resentment. *Why,* he wondered, *had the FBI so completely ignored his warnings?* It wasn't as though Yousef was a benign figure howling at the wind. Indeed, he had been convicted of numerous heinous crimes and was known to be a high-ranking, intensely active, and well-connected terrorist. At the very least, it seemed, law enforcement officials had an obligation to investigate the information Gregory had shared. But they hadn't, leaving Scarpa "very angry with the government. Again I mentioned to the SIS officer and another officer that if the FBI would've come to see me, perhaps 9/11 might have been prevented."

The FBI clearly suspected some link between Yousef and 9/11, as evidenced by the fact that bureau agents eventually did come to ADMAX to interview him. But they never spoke with Gregory.

Most inmates at Florence ADMAX endure a lengthy three-part indoctrination program. They enter at Level I and are expected to proceed through Level II to Level III. Level I inmates have no privileges and are kept in their cells twenty-three hours a day for the first year, then slowly, gradually, they are socialized with other inmates and the staff. Prisoners at Level II are permitted television access, but programs are determined by the prison correction officers (COs). All prisoners who are at Levels I and II must wear handcuffs, belly chains, and leg shackles, and must be escorted by two guards whenever they leave their cells. In their last year, prisoners are allowed to leave their cells from 6:00 A.M. to 10:00 P.M. and eat meals in a shared dining room, rather than having food shoved through a slot in a steel cell door.

At Level III, prisoners have more personal freedom. They are allowed to traverse the fifty-foot walk to the shower, exercise room, or telephone without escort. However, the stakes are high: Any violation whatsoever during the program means participants revert to Level I, and twenty-three-hour lockdown.

After devoting several years to the successful completion of Levels I and II, Gregory advanced to Level III. He was assigned to the prison's I Unit, which had a gym and a yard for exercising, along with handball and basketball courts. I Unit was populated by a staggering array of dangerous criminals, twenty-five guys who would kill at the "drop of a dime," according to Gregory. Interestingly, however, violent episodes in I Unit were extraordinarily rare. The reason was simple: The slightest transgression would result in lockdown for the perpetrator. Thus, "everyone kept cool and respected one another," says Gregory.

Gregory was sufficiently well behaved that he secured a prison job working as a "rotunda orderly," near security headquarters (an area off-limits to all but a handful of inmates), which allowed for access to extra food, a refrigerator, and a microwave oven, as well as the opportunity to converse on occasion with attractive female corrections officers.

"During this time," Gregory recalls, "things were going great for me, given the unpleasant circumstances. But, of course, as I've learned in life, as soon as things are going well for me, everything turns to shit."

33
THE SCARPA
INTELLIGENCE

In March 2003, Gregory was delighted (and somewhat surprised) to receive a visit from Dr. Stephen P. Dresch and his colleague, Angela Clemente, a forty-year-old single mother of three who worked as a forensic intelligence analyst and freelance legal researcher. They wanted to interview Gregory about retired FBI agent R. Lindley De-Vecchio.

Dr. Dresch, widely regarded for his tireless work on behalf of those victimized by the government, had met Angela Clemente when he was investigating a suspicious plane crash that had resulted in the death of, among others, U.S. Commerce secretary Ron Brown. Ms. Clemente was investigating alleged systemic corruption in the U.S. attorney's offices in New York's Eastern and Southern districts, and in the FBI's New York office. Dr. Dresch and Clemente had joined forces and discovered evidence they claimed proved DeVecchio's involvement in murders committed by Greg Scarpa Sr. and his crew.

For six years, at their own expense, Clemente and Dr. Dresch traveled extensively around the United States, interviewing hundreds of people, including judges, lawmakers, witnesses, and mobsters. Among these was Gregory Scarpa Jr. In the course of an interview that stretched out over several hours, Gregory eagerly detailed for Dr. Dresch and Clemente not only his father's relationship with DeVecchio, but also the work Gregory had done for the government regarding Ramzi Yousef. He provided the researchers with Yousef's prison kites, along with copies of the FBI 302 memos, a standard form used to record received information relevant to an investigation, which seemed to support Gregory's contentions.

After analyzing the material, Dr. Dresch and Clemente concluded that "not only was the intelligence supplied to the government by Gregory Scarpa Jr. credible and highly accurate, but it was the single most significant Al-Qaeda intelligence in U.S. history, prior to 9/11."

In a confidential report titled "The Scarpa Intelligence on the Terrorist Threat: An

Evaluative Report," Angela Clemente wrote that "FBI Forms 302 documenting information provided by Scarpa in his role as an informant and Scarpa's contemporaneous handwritten notes call into serious question the government's claim that Scarpa, Yousef et al. were engaged in a conspiracy to deceive the government," adding that she had discovered "evidence that the government has continued to use the Scarpa intelligence in criminal trials and appeals."

She added, "Evidence of the validity and credibility of the Scarpa intelligence so compellingly refutes the government's spurious claim of a Scarpa-Yousef 'hoax' that an official reassessment, and retraction, of that claim is mandated, however uncomfortable the consequences for the government and its agents. In other words, had Gregory Scarpa's intelligence been followed up, there is a great chance that 9/11 might have been averted.

"On April 5, 2004," Clemente recalls, "I submitted the confidential report to the following persons and/or entities: the 9/11 Commission; Chief Counsel to the President Alberto Gonzales; National Security Adviser to the President Condoleezza Rice; and senior staff member Grant Nichols of the U.S House of Representatives Committee on Government Reform. Only Nichols responded."

In 2004, during the course of his DeVecchio investigation, Dr. Dresch discovered that Larry Mazza had entered the Witness Protection Program and was residing under an alias in a southern state. Mazza had testified against fellow mobsters in exchange for favorable consideration from prosecutors; he had recently been released from prison after serving ten years. Mazza agreed to speak with Dr. Dresch, with one caveat: If subpoenaed (unless it was before a televised congressional hearing), he would disavow his words. Dr. Dresch agreed to the terms, and the two began a lengthy interview, during which Mazza revealed a number of interesting things about the relationship between Greg Scarpa Sr. and Lin DeVecchio. For example, Mazza provided new and scandalous details about the murder of Nicholas "Nicky Black" Grancio.

Grancio, a Scarpa rival in the Colombo mob war, was under NYPD surveillance when, on January 7, 1992, DeVecchio, at Scarpa's urging, instructed police to interrupt their surveillance activities; no sooner had the cops left than a van pulled up and Greg Sr. shot Grancio in the head. Armed with Mazza's unsworn testimony regarding the Grancio murder and other illicit DeVecchio-Scarpa dealings, Dr. Dresch sent a report to the U.S. congressional committee on government reform.

Flora Edwards, the defense attorney for former acting Colombo family boss Victor Orena, then subpoenaed Dr. Dresch and Mazza to testify in Brooklyn federal court, at the appeal hearing of Orena and Pasquale Amato. Despite Mazza's "confession," they were convicted in the killing of Grancio.

Attorneys for Orena and Amato had argued that the trial defense had been hampered by the federal authorities' unwillingness to release files pertaining to the Scarpa-DeVecchio relationship. Much of that information had been made available to defense attorneys in three later Colombo War trials, in which the defendants were all acquitted and jurors had expressed shock and outrage over DeVecchio's actions.

Gregory testified via a video linkup from ADMAX, revealing, among other things, that he personally (on orders from his father) had skimmed money from the Scarpa numbers racket to "pay off" DeVecchio. He also testified that on several occasions he had provided DeVecchio with hotel rooms, sometimes stocked with champagne and, at least once, visited by prostitutes. He estimated that his father had also given De-Vecchio approximately $100,000 over the span of their relationship. Furthermore, he testified to several murders and attempted murders committed by his father during the Colombo War, all of which were facilitated by DeVecchio's involvement — generally, this meant that the FBI agent had provided Greg Sr. with the victims' home addresses and telephone numbers.

Gregory claimed that his father and De-Vecchio had planted a murder weapon at Orena's home to help frame Orena and Amato for the Grancio murder. Understanding all too well that his testimony would be met with skepticism, Gregory attested that he had not been coerced to appear on the video linkup; he further claimed that neither he nor his family had been promised anything in exchange for his testimony. Despite his antipathy to the Orena faction, Gregory had come forward because Orena was in jail for a murder that his father had committed. Gregory said he wanted to "clear my conscience."

Predictably, DeVecchio's attorney denounced Gregory's claims as "scandalous and ridiculous."

Dr. Dresch subsequently testified to his conversations with Mazza, who apparently had developed a form of sudden-onset amnesia when he took the stand. Although he recalled Greg Scarpa Sr. making several calls to his "girlfriend," Mazza did not specifically recall Scarpa Sr. phoning De-Vecchio about Grancio; neither could he say with any degree of certainty that surveillance on Grancio had been withdrawn (on DeVecchio's order) on the day of the murder. As his testimony dragged on, it became rather clear that Mazza could vividly remember only one thing: that he was on supervised release, and that he wasn't about to do or say anything that might result in being sent back to prison (and surely testifying against an allegedly corrupt FBI agent fell under that umbrella).

In his testimony, DeVecchio acknowledged accepting small, innocuous gifts from Greg Sr. These, according to DeVecchio, included Cabbage Patch dolls (which at the time were notoriously difficult to obtain) for his daughters, along with fine wines, pasta, and other homemade Italian dishes during the holidays. Hardly the stuff of scandal. When questioned about being arrested in 1975 for illegally trafficking guns in Maryland, De-Vecchio testified (somewhat unconvincingly, given his position as a federal law enforcement officer) that he was unaware that transporting guns across state lines and selling them without a license constituted illegal activity. (The FBI and Maryland authorities had chosen not to prosecute DeVecchio because his personnel file contained glowing performance reports signed by the late FBI director J. Edgar Hoover.)

More disturbing, for those who sought to discredit the charges against DeVecchio, was the agent's generally uncooperative demeanor. He steadfastly refused to undergo a polygraph test; repeatedly invoked his Fifth Amendment right against self-incrimination; and answered forty-four questions with the words "I don't recall."

Edwards chided the government for trying to impugn Gregory's testimony due to his record of "criminal conduct" when its "entire case against Orena and Amato" was built on the "testimony of individuals whose criminal history before, during, and after they testified as government witnesses is legendary." Unlike the government's witnesses, who hoped to gain favor through their testimony and cooperation, Edwards argued, Gregory's only incentive was "to lift the burden of his father's crimes from his conscience."

In the latest example of a pattern of disbelief when it came to the testimony of

Gregory Scarpa, Federal judge Jack Weinstein, the same judge who had sentenced
Greg Scarpa Sr. to ten years in prison,
denied Orena's and Amato's motions for a
new trial. Regarding Gregory Scarpa's
testimony he wrote:

Gregory Scarpa, Jr. testified that DeVecchio was paid some $100,000.00, fur-
nished with such "entertainment" as call
girls, champagne, and a hotel suite at
the Holiday Inn in Staten Island, and
provided an all-expense-paid trip to
Aspen, Colorado, for services he rendered to Scarpa and the mob, and that
for these and other benefits DeVecchio
started the Colombo war, helped Gregory Scarpa and his associates hunt down
and kill members of a competing faction
of the mob, and protected the Scarpas,
father and son, from the police. The
court finds this witness to be not credible. His source is also not credible on
these matters; the only substantial information Scarpa, Jr. had was furnished to
him orally by his parent. The son, if he
is credited at all, was told by his sire
(now dead) what DeVecchio was doing
for the mob and what the elder Scarpa
was doing for DeVecchio. The son ob-

served nothing that took on significance without the father's extra-judicial statements.

34
GREGORY SCARPA AND THE OKLAHOMA CITY BOMBER

Five quiet, uneventful years into his sentence at Florence ADMAX, Gregory Scarpa Jr. was recommended for state placement, which would have allowed him to be transferred to a federal prison closer to his family in New York. Gregory, of course, was buoyed by this development; he hadn't seen his children in nearly seven years, and the prospect of regular visits lifted his spirits to a level he hadn't known since long before his incarceration.

As quickly as his hopes were lifted, however, they were dashed, the result of a disciplinary action initiated by a guard with whom Gregory had an ongoing antagonistic relationship. Gregory angrily dismisses the disciplinary report as "bogus." Nevertheless, on September 31, 2004, rather than being moved to a facility in the Northeast, Gregory was transferred to the D Unit at

ADMAX and locked down for twenty-three hours a day. His immediate neighbors were Terry Nichols, Timothy McVeigh's partner in the Oklahoma City bombing, and a man named Emilio "Tito" Bravo.

Gregory previously had known Bravo as an almost pathological rat, a double-crosser who would say anything to anyone "for a ham-and-cheese sandwich." True to the mobster's credo, however, Gregory believed that a man was well advised to keep his friends close — and his enemies even closer. Gregory feigned friendship with the rat, never letting Bravo know how he actually felt about him.

The Oklahoma City bombing, on April 19, 1995, was, at the time, the deadliest act of terrorism on United States soil. The attack on the Alfred P. Murrah Federal Building, a government office complex located in downtown Oklahoma City, Oklahoma, claimed 168 lives and injured more than 800 people. Timothy McVeigh, a U.S. Army veteran and former security guard, and his accomplice, Terry Nichols, were both arrested shortly after the bombing and charged with multiple counts of first-degree murder. McVeigh, who acknowledged placing explosives at the site, was executed by lethal injection on June 11, 2001. Nichols was sentenced to life without parole at AD-MAX.

It had long been speculated by law enforcement officials and conspiracy theorists alike that explosives left over from the Oklahoma City bombing had yet to be recovered. Aware of the potential for exploiting his new room assignment, Gregory decided he would attempt to ingratiate himself with his neighbor, in the hope that Nichols would reveal the location of the explosives. Providing this information to the FBI, of course, might help Gregory earn a reduction in his sentence — at least, that was his hope. Given his (and the FBI's) track record in such matters, Gregory's optimism was naturally tempered. At the very least, he figured, the information might prevent the explosives from falling into the wrong hands and harming more innocent people. Unfortunately, Gregory would need someone to corroborate his story, and while Gregory didn't trust Bravo, in this narrowly defined, rigidly controlled setting, he had no one else to vouch for him.

Federal authorities had never obtained the identity of John Doe Number 1, a man reportedly seen in a truck with McVeigh on the morning of the Oklahoma City bombing; there remained a $2 million reward for information leading to his capture. If Gregory and Bravo could learn who else was involved in the bombing, they could become the cooperating witnesses needed to testify against the defendant, get a reduction in their sentences, and perhaps (although it seemed highly unlikely) receive the reward.

Equipped with soundproof cells and windows, and with bars strategically placed two feet behind the cell doors, the layout of D Unit made it extraordinarily challenging for inmates to exchange kites or any other items. But prison inmates are nothing if not resourceful. By literally blowing all excess water out of the drains in their sinks and showers, and then speaking into the dry pipes, Gregory Scarpa Jr., Terry Nichols, and Tito Bravo were able to engage in something approaching normal conversation. "It was like having our own private phone," says Gregory. Also, during the one hour each day when the inmates were permitted to leave their cells for exercise, they were placed in adjacent, ten-by-fifteen-foot cages that were close enough to allow for some verbal interaction.

Gregory spent several months developing a cordial relationship with Nichols, and eventually felt comfortable enough to inquire about explosives that supposedly had been hidden and were to be used for a second bombing. Gregory played with Nichols, manipulating him into believing that Gregory sympathized with his plight, and with the mission that had landed him in prison. When Gregory asked about the types of explosives Nichols had used, and what would be needed for another bombing, Nichols seemed disinterested, if not offended.

"I don't want to be involved in another attack," he told Gregory. "I've changed."

Formerly an atheist, Nichols explained to Gregory that since entering prison he had experienced a profound change of heart. He was now a Christian. And, according to Gregory, an opportunistic Christian at that. While awaiting sentencing Nichols had committed to memory the timing of the guards' rounds; whenever a corrections officer passed his cell, Nichols made sure that the officer was treated to the sight of the convicted killer with his nose buried in the Bible. Later, at his sentencing hearing, several guards testified on Nichols's behalf, saying that he had clearly turned his life over to God; genuine or not, Nichols's conversion helped save him from the death penalty.

Of course, if Nichols had been sincere in

his desire to atone for his sins, he might also have considered revealing to authorities the location of any remaining explosive material. As Gregory pointedly asked Nichols, "Why don't you tell the feds where the explosives are and make a deal for yourself?"

Nichols said that he did not trust his "lawyer, the ATF, or anyone in the government. And what am I going to do, tell on my brother?"

According to Nichols, his brother, James, was the only other person who knew where the explosives were located. Although he wasn't involved in the bombing, hatred for the U.S. government ran at least as deep in James as it did in Nichols and McVeigh. He had invited Nichols and McVeigh to anti-government patriot meetings, where they had heard absurd and riotous proclamations, including, most often, a desire to "avenge Waco."

"Waco," of course, referred to an April 19, 1993, incident near Waco, Texas, where seventy-six members of the Branch Davidians, a heavily armed, antigovernment group, were killed in a shoot-out with government agents. It was McVeigh's contention that the Oklahoma City bombing should occur precisely on the second anniversary of Waco, to more clearly illustrate the militia's hatred for the government, and to avenge the deaths of the Branch Davidians.

No fool, Terry Nichols wanted to negotiate something for himself while also removing the explosives from circulation. As the tenth anniversary of the Oklahoma City bombing drew near, he became increasingly nervous and agitated, for he knew that if there was to be a second bombing, it would likely occur on that date. Gregory and Bravo agreed to assist Nichols in his attempts to communicate this information to the FBI in a manner that would be deemed not only credible, but perhaps even worthy of consideration for a reduction in sentence; failing that, Nichols might seek a transfer to a more accommodating facility.

Nichols's strategy, however, was complicated by his extreme mistrust of the FBI. It was Nichols's desire that someone (or some entity) other than the FBI "discover" the hidden explosives. It was Nichols's contention that the FBI would almost certainly tamper with evidence to cover their alleged involvement in the Oklahoma City bombing plot. If the FBI was first on the scene, Nichols told Gregory, agents would surely erase the fingerprints of a man named Roger Moore, a gun dealer who Nichols believed was an FBI informant, and who, he claimed, had committed perjury while testifying against Nichols and McVeigh. Nichols said that his robbery of cash, guns, and bomb components from Moore's home was a setup to cover Moore's involvement in the plot. If he could implicate Moore, Nichols felt that he might get a new trial, or at least a deal. Nichols also wanted to expose the FBI's role in supplying Moore with the bomb components in what Nichols felt was a government sting gone wrong. He refused to reveal anything until Gregory assured him that the FBI wouldn't be able to "mess with the evidence."

To gain Nichols's confidence, Gregory told him about Angela Clemente, the forensics expert, who had her own lab and could dust for Moore's fingerprints before turning the explosives over to the FBI. This, of course, was a bold-faced lie. Intrigued, Nichols asked if Clemente could also erase the fingerprints of both him and his brother; stringing Nichols along like a consummate pro, Gregory assured Nichols that she could (and would).

In prison, of course, lying is hardly a capital offense. Indeed, the telling of tall tales is an accepted practice; thus, an inmate is wise to view virtually all communication

371

with a skeptical eye. Despite his best efforts
to gain Nichols's trust, Gregory was unable
to discern the location of the hidden explosives. So, rather than attempt to win the
bomber's favor by promising favorable treatment from the government, Scarpa Jr.
turned to a more reliable and time-honored
motivational tool: greed. He told Nichols
that, far from being a two-bit mobster,
Gregory was actually a Mafia kingpin, with
many millions of dollars hidden away. This
was also a lie, but to bolster the fantasy, he
provided Nichols with IRS documents
showing that he owed $11 million in taxes.
He then offered to pay Nichols for information about the explosives. They agreed that
Gregory's daughter Kori would personally
take the cash to a church that Nichols had
designated for a drop-off (the "church" was,
in reality, a front for a white supremacist
organization).

Sufficiently hooked, Nichols negotiated
with Gregory a payoff of $450,000. As a
sign of good faith, Nichols sent Gregory a
blueprint of bomb components; however,
he continued to withhold information about
their whereabouts. This, Nichols said, he
would provide only after meeting with
Angela Clemente. Furthermore, he demanded a written guarantee from Clemente

that no federal agency would be permitted to inspect the explosives until after she had completed her fingerprint and DNA examinations.

Knowing that he couldn't produce the real Angela Clemente with fake documents, Gregory filed an inmate request "cop-out" form and submitted it to a prison counselor, saying that he sought an immediate consultation with the FBI concerning a "national security emergency." The next day SIS officials summoned Gregory, and he told them about his ongoing negotiations with Terry Nichols. Inmates facing severe sentences (and this includes almost everyone at ADMAX) of course often fabricate stories to curry favor with prison officials, so Gregory's information was initially met with little more than a shrug of indifference: "We'll see what we can do."

On March 1, 2005, seven weeks before the tenth anniversary of the Oklahoma City bombing, Gregory, who had grown increasingly anxious about the possibility that Nichols's brother and his extremist buddies might be in the process of planning another terrorist attack, reached out to Clemente's associate, Dr. Stephen Dresch, for assistance. Upon hearing Gregory's story, Dresch contacted both the FBI and Massachusetts congressman William Delahunt, who was working with Dresch on another FBI-related matter. Gregory wrongly (and perhaps naïvely, given his history with the organization) presumed that the FBI would willingly furnish false documents to find such a valuable prize; federal authorities, after all, had been searching for the cache of hidden explosives for the previous decade. Gregory told Nichols that Clemente would soon have the documents.

Two days later Gregory was summoned to a meeting with an SIS officer and an FBI agent named Stern. Having been burned before, Gregory insisted on a written cooperation agreement.

Gregory showed Nichols's kites to Agent Stern and asked him to quickly provide Gregory with the false documents he would need to advance negotiations with Nichols. Agent Stern, according to Gregory, seemed reluctant; he told Gregory that supervisory approval would be required to obtain them, and that could take some time: he would work on it. Then he made copies of Nichols's kites (Gregory was later charged eleven dollars in photocopying fees).

In an attempt to gauge the veracity of Scarpa's tale, Agent Stern asked if he was willing to take a polygraph exam. If Scarpa were lying, the agent knew, he'd never agree to such a test.

Gregory's response: "Absolutely."

The next morning Gregory met with an SIS officer, Agent Stern, and another FBI agent who had flown in from Washington, D.C., to administer the polygraph exam. After answering his name and age, Gregory was asked, among other things, whether he had forged Nichols's kites or had told Nichols what to say. Gregory truthfully answered all the questions. Afterward, the agents left to make a phone call, which Gregory suspected was to Valerie Caproni. Five minutes later they returned and informed Gregory that he had "failed the test."

"Stop playing games!" Gregory demanded. "There's no way I could have failed."

He reminded the agents of what was at stake. If they would turn over the false documents, Gregory would provide them with a career-making prize: the exact location of explosives that had proved elusive for nearly a decade. As a compromise, the agents demanded a second polygraph exam, figuring that they had either misinterpreted (deliberately or otherwise) the first test. Knowing that he had nothing to lose, Gregory agreed.

On the second test, rather than providing verbal responses, Gregory was instructed to simply nod — affirmatively or negatively — to a series of questions. Following the examination the agents again left the room; upon returning they told Gregory that he had failed a second time. Gregory was offered a third test — this time the questions would be limited to a single subject, Ramzi Yousef, but Gregory angrily declined: "You're kidding, right? A third test? When you know I didn't lie on the first two?"

Following another brief interruption, during which the agents again left Gregory alone, the bargaining session came to an end. The agents told Gregory they were through with him, and instructed him never to call them again.

"So I guess you guys are going to just leave the explosives out there?" Gregory asked sarcastically.

The agent who had administered the lie detector test laughed. "They allegedly have been out there for ten years. Let them stay out there for another ten years." He laughed again, saying that Nichols was probably just trying to beat Gregory out of the $450,000.

Later, Dr. Dresch's polygraph expert claimed that the examination the FBI had

376

given Gregory had been "absurdly flawed."

Realizing that he wasn't going to get any help from the feds, Gregory decided to tell Nichols that he should simply trust that he had received the documents; Gregory would demonstrate his sincerity by immediately authorizing his daughter to give Nichols's "people" half of the $450,000. Having dangled the right carrot, Gregory soon heard from Nichols that the cache of explosives was hidden at a house in Herington, Kansas, where Nichols had been living at the time of the Oklahoma City bombing.

Bypassing the feds entirely, Gregory promptly called Dresch and Clemente. Gregory insisted that they come to see him as soon as possible. He did not explain the reason for the request; when asked whether he knew the location of the explosives, Gregory said that he did not. Later, he would explain, he had lied out of concern that the feds would raid his cell.

On March 10, during a seven-hour interview with Dr. Dresch and Clemente, Gregory produced Nichols's most revealing kite: a message containing a detailed description of materials used to manufacture the cache of missing explosives, including nitromethane, blasting caps, and an explosive component known as Kinepak. What the kite did not contain was the location of the explosives.

By now Dr. Dresch had become wary of the FBI, so he worked through an acquaintance at the federal Department of Homeland Security to improvise a cooperation arrangement with Gregory, who then provided Dr. Dresch with Nichols's former address and a detailed description of the cache's location under a crawl space. During the next two weeks, Clemente and Dr. Dresch shared Gregory's intelligence with several government agencies, including the National Security Council, Homeland Security, and the Joint Terrorism Task Force; no one acted on the information. Finally, they contacted Congressman Delahunt; on March 31, 2005, "prompted by a recent tip," the FBI called in the Topeka bomb squad, and with the surrounding three-block area cordoned off, they worked through the night and into the next day removing the cache of explosives. Several weeks later, the FBI reluctantly admitted that the tip had been provided by Gregory Scarpa Jr.

Looking to cut his own deal, Bravo subsequently was interviewed by the FBI, and he told investigators what they wanted to hear: Gregory was lying, and Bravo was the person most responsible for obtaining the explosives' location. Still hoping to collect the $2 million John Doe reward money, Bravo added that Nichols would cooperate with the FBI (which no one had anticipated, primarily because of Nichols's long-standing hatred for the U.S. government). Later, when Nichols was called before a grand jury and asked about others involved in the Oklahoma City bombing, he replied, "Now is not the time or place."

For Gregory Scarpa Jr., life did not improve. Dr. Dresch's Homeland Security contact failed to make good on his promise to deliver a cooperation agreement, leaving Gregory, once again, without a bargaining chip. Angela Clemente secured for him the services of a pro bono attorney to negotiate a cooperation agreement based on his intelligence, and to request a transfer (for both Gregory and Bravo) from ADMAX into the Witness Security Unit, a program established to provide protection and security for witnesses in official proceedings. However, this too failed to evolve in quite the way Gregory had hoped, thanks to a change of heart (publicly, anyway) by the FBI, which suddenly denied that Gregory had provided the tip that led to the recovery of the explosives. In short order, FBI officials told his attorney that Gregory was not credible, that the government would not negotiate a downward sentence for him, and that he would remain in ADMAX.

A known informant, of course, is the most vulnerable target in any lockup — from Rikers Island to ADMAX. In the wake of published newspaper accounts regarding his cooperation with federal law enforcement officers, Gregory began receiving death threats. Some were written, some verbal. Others were acted out in the manner common to such settings: Another inmate would catch Scarpa Jr.'s attention and draw a finger across his own throat. Regardless, the message was always the same: "You are a dead man."

Prison officials ignored the death threats and denied Gregory's requests to be moved to another prison. Instead, the government rewarded Gregory by placing him in even more stringent solitary confinement.

Prison officials publicly declared that Florence ADMAX was among the most secure prisons in the world; inmates had little movement, constant observation, and an almost intolerable level of isolation. One could debate endlessly whether they were being treated "humanely." Not debatable, according to prison officials, was the safety record of ADMAX. Inmate on inmate violence was so rare as to be inconsequential. Thus, Gregory had nothing to fear. And yet, it happened, sometimes in spectacular fashion. In April 2005, for example, Florence ADMAX inmate Manuel Torres died after an encounter with two other inmates. According to Fremont County coroner Dorothy Twellman, the sixty-four-year-old Torres was "viciously beaten for several minutes about the head, neck and chest." Despite FBI claims of an ongoing investigation, no suspects have been identified in Torres's murder.

35

THE PEOPLE AGAINST DEVECCHIO

In 2004, Lin DeVecchio sold his home in Dumont, New Jersey. After a virtual lifetime of residence in the Northeast's I-95 corridor, the retired FBI agent and his wife, Carolyn, moved to a gated community in Sarasota, Florida, where DeVecchio joined a motorcycle club and served on the board of the homeowner's association.

In the fall of 2005, Representative William Delahunt, a member of the House Judiciary Committee, was preparing for hearings investigating allegations against FBI agents involved in the handling of organized crime. During a three-hour meeting, Angela Clemente and Dr. Stephen Dresch presented to Representative Delahunt their findings regarding DeVecchio and Greg Scarpa Sr., and their possible involvement in several murders. Representative Delahunt referred Clemente and Dresch to the Kings County (Brooklyn) district attorney, Charles Hynes.

Six months later, on March 30, 2006, DA Hynes announced the arrest and indictment of R. Lindley DeVecchio on charges stemming from four Mafia-related murders that occurred between 1984 and 1992. Hynes made no effort to hide his shock and contempt at the evidence, saying, "This is the most stunning example of official corruption that I have ever seen." DeVecchio faced a maximum sentence of twenty-five years to life for each of the murders.

According to the indictment, on September 25, 1984, Mary Bari, the thirty-one-year-old girlfriend of Colombo consigliere Alphonse Persico (brother of then Colombo family boss Carmine Persico), was shot and killed in a Brooklyn social club by a group of men, including both Greg Scarpa Sr. (the triggerman) and Gregory Scarpa Jr. (who pinned Bari to the floor while his father dispatched the victim). DeVecchio had allegedly alerted Greg Sr. to the fact that Bari was communicating with federal law enforcement officers, and suggested to the mobster that she "be taken care of."

(Not that Scarpa expressed any great reluctance about completing the job; far from it. Indeed, the Bari hit provided a unique glimpse into Scarpa's macabre sense of humor. The next day Linda Schiro received a phone call from the wife of Carmine Sessa, a Colombo family soldier — and future consigliere — telling her that during the course of the post-hit cleanup, her little French poodle had wandered through the crime scene, carrying in its mouth an earring belonging to Mary Bari — with the ear still attached! Greg Scarpa Sr., she said, had reacted by calmly scratching the pooch on the back of his head, pulling the ear from its mouth, and then extracting the ring and tucking it into his pocket. Linda was appropriately appalled by this tale; only later that evening, when the mobsters and their girlfriends or wives gathered for dinner, did she discover that the story was a hoax. There had been no hungry dog, no severed ear. It was merely a joke dreamed up by Greg Sr., with Linda as the unwitting target.)

According to the indictment, on September 17, 1987, Greg Jr. and others killed Joseph "Joe Brewster" DeDomenico, a forty-five-year-old Colombo soldier. DeVecchio had urged the killing because DeDomenico had become a loose cannon, and needed to be silenced.

The indictment continued that, in May 1990, DeVecchio told Greg Sr. that Patrick Porco was communicating with 62nd Precinct detectives about the Halloween murder that Joey Schiro was involved in. To keep Porco quiet, Greg Sr. had him killed.

Finally, according to the indictment, DeVecchio helped enable the murder, on May 22, 1992, of Larry Lampasi by providing Scarpa with information about Lampasi's routine that he had gleaned from FBI surveillance.

Each of these murders took place during a period of time in which DeVecchio was supposed to be using Greg Scarpa Sr. as an FBI informant; according to the indictment, however, the roles had been reversed. It was Scarpa who was using DeVecchio. Indeed, it was Scarpa who was in charge of the relationship. The prosecutor, Deputy District Attorney Michael F. Vecchione, head of the Rackets Squad, promised an unbridled attack, vowing to bring in to court civilians, FBI agents, and members of Greg Sr.'s crew to prove the people's case against DeVecchio.

DeVecchio's lawyer, Douglas Grover, claimed the allegations were "nonsense," attributing much of the case's misinformation to Greg Sr.'s longtime mistress, Linda Schiro.

At his arraignment, DeVecchio pleaded not guilty to all charges. Joining him in a show of support were forty-five current and former FBI agents, including many of the most respected officers in recent FBI history. Together, they put forth a signed legal document that sought to have DeVecchio freed on his own recognizance while awaiting (and during) his trial. The former head of the FBI in New York, James Kallstrom, was quick to defend DeVecchio's handling of Greg Scarpa Sr., calling DeVecchio a "hard worker" who had risked his life going undercover to help infiltrate the Mafia and incarcerate many of its top players.

"Lin DeVecchio is not guilty and did not partake in what he's being charged with. It's as simple as that," said Kallstrom, who later served as a senior counterterrorism adviser to New York State Governor George Pataki.

FBI agents filled the courtroom to capacity during the proceedings, and also formed a legal defense fund for DeVecchio. Because current and former FBI employees who are sued or arrested can apply for coverage of their legal costs, the Department of Justice ruled that at least part of DeVecchio's legal defense would be paid for by taxpayers.

On August 30, 2007, DDA Vecchione sent a "Molineux letter" to DeVecchio's trial judge, the Honorable Gustin L. Reichbach, justice of the Supreme Court, King's County. A Molineux letter outlines a defendant's prior "bad acts and conduct" that, for a variety of reasons (such as being unrelated to the charges at hand, or having surpassed the statute of limitations) are not included in the indictment but are nonetheless relevant to a defendant's credibility. If DeVecchio were to testify on his own behalf, the prosecutor planned to cross-examine him regarding these acts, and to introduce evidence that would contradict the defendant's denials.

These numerous "bad acts" included the following: DeVecchio's illegal sale of firearms to undercover agents in 1976; his assistance to Greg Scarpa Sr. in numerous murders and attempted murders; his refusal to terminate Scarpa as an informant, despite the fact that the mobster, through his countless criminal acts (including burglary, loan sharking, gambling, extortion, and narcotics trafficking), had far surpassed the standard for disqualification; DeVecchio's concealing these crimes from his superiors, the U.S. attorney, and local law enforcement officials, while also attempting to interfere with Greg Sr.'s arrest; regularly accepting from Greg Sr. cash and gifts, including stolen jewelry, and keeping for himself $66,598 of FBI payments intended for Greg Sr. Finally, although he was ordered by his superiors, "under condition of insubordination," not to communicate with Linda Schiro during the FBI's internal investigation into his conduct, DeVecchio had instructed Linda (through a close confidante) to disclose nothing to the investigators. DeVecchio later telephoned Linda several times, and also went to her house, to verify that she had remained silent on the subject of DeVecchio's "business" partnership with Scarpa.

36
ASSAULT

On February 5, 2006, in a lengthy letter to U.S. representative Dana Rohrabacher, a Republican congressman, the dogged investigator Angela Clemente once more reiterated her concerns regarding the case of Gregory Scarpa Jr.: Particularly galling, she said, was the federal government's continued refusal to validate the intelligence unearthed by Scarpa. In essence, she accused the FBI of a massive cover-up.

Here, verbatim, is a portion of that letter:

Two of the highest profile terrorism cases that [have] ever occurred on U.S. soil had a significant element of Gregory Scarpa Jr's intelligence involved in [them] and instead of taking his information and processing through the proper channels as they legally should do they instead are continuing to cover it up and their reason appears to be that now it is not a matter of simply having the organized crime cases falling apart on them it is a matter of them having been given the information directly related to 9/11 and them totally dismissing it as a hoax and realizing after it happened that his information was indeed reliable. And then years later he gains additional information on the [Oklahoma City] bombing case and they again for a second time dismissed his information. This was an embarrassment to all concerned and an abrupt realization that he was AGAIN reliable and accurate and they once AGAIN failed our country. How many more times will they do this? How many more lives will be lost? **HOW WILL THIS COUNTRY FEEL TO SEE THE CORRESPONDENCE FROM ATTORNEY CHECKMAN WRITTEN TO ME STATING THAT THE EDNY** *[Eastern District of New York]* **AND FBI DO NOT WANT ANY INFORMATION FROM SCARPA JR BECAUSE THEY DON'T WANT TO SPEND THE TIME, EFFORT, OR MONEY ON THIS SERIOUS TERRORISM ISSUE THAT HAS REMAINING TERRORISTS AT LARGE?**

I also strongly suggest that this systemic problem be addressed through a formal congressional hearing. Do we have a war on terror or are we more worried about covering up our mistakes? Would the President like to see this documented action taken by the FBI and the U.S. Attorney's offices in New York concerning terrorism as recently as months ago?

Gregory Scarpa Jr. is a wealth of accurate and credible information that is fully documented and cannot be disputed because it has been documented in the government's FBI 302's, which I have in my possession. Scarpa Jr. remains a significant threat to the FBI, EDNY and SDNY *[Southern District of New York]* especially if he were to expose this information and be found credible it would prove to be "an agency reputation and credibility danger" as well as a possible career ender for many officials whose careers are based on their reputations staying intact and keeping the knowledge of their own direct PURPOSEFUL dismissal of his information and their <u>continuous</u> and twice repeated complacent and lethal actions from being exposed.

Again I strongly suggest that this be addressed in a congressional forum because it not only involves a very serious systemic problem but it also involves our war on terror and both domestic and foreign terrorists some of which remain at large. Currently civil suits are being filed against the FBI and others concerning this matter (multiple deaths), there is a Grand Jury session occurring against this FBI agent and others, and Greg Scarpa Jr. is tucked away with all the terrorists just waiting to strike him.

The disturbing consequences of continuing governmental prevarication include but is not limited to:

- Serious failures and defalcations within the offices of the U.S. Attorney's for the Southern and (especially) Eastern Districts of New York and the New York office of the FBI, and, indeed within the U.S. Department of Justice, remain unacknowledged and uncorrected, and is indeed ongoing.
- Persons responsible for the outrageous actions of the government with reference to the Scarpa terrorism intelligence have not only been undisciplined but, in fact, have been rewarded

with promotions to higher positions (e.g., the appointment of former EDNY AUSA Valerie Caproni to the position of General Counsel of the FBI). When gross misconduct is rewarded, such misconduct can only be expected to be perpetuated.

In short, it is imperative that the Scarpa intelligence be reviewed formally; identifying non-, mis- and malfeasance, and initiating appropriate disciplinary and corrective actions.

Respectfully Submitted,
Angela Clemente

Clemente was relentless in her pursuit of what she deemed to be the truth, and her dedication nearly got her killed. On June 17, 2006, she agreed to meet a source who had promised to deliver critical information related to the murders involving DeVecchio. The meeting, however, turned out to be a violent and nearly fatal ambush.

In describing the attack, an article in the *New York Post,* written by Alex Ginsberg, stated:

The gutsy single mom who helped prosecutors crack the case against accused

FBI mob mole Lindley DeVecchio was found choked and left for dead early yesterday in a remote section of Brooklyn. Cops, responding to a 911 call at 5:45 a.m., found Angela Clemente in the driver's seat of her car, its door open, her body sprawled half in and half out, near the Caesar's Bay strip mall in Bensonhurst.

Based on her account of events, investigators believe Clemente — a forensic-intelligence analyst volunteering her services to prosecutors — was set up by the would-be tipster, who lured her to the meeting with promises of information about two Long Island murders she believed were linked to the recently indicted DeVecchio and his underworld canary, the late mob boss Gregory Scarpa.

From her bed at Lutheran Hospital in Brooklyn, where she suffered a seizure yesterday while being treated for neck and body injuries, a groggy Clemente told investigators she had received several messages from her assailant before agreeing to the early morning meeting. Clemente's daughter told investigators her mom did not think the meeting was dangerous "because the guy had something to do with law enforcement."

Clemente, a 5-foot-4 divorced mother of three, spent 20 years testing blood and doing autopsies before becoming one of the country's top forensic-intelligence analysts. Prosecutors revealed Clemente made a phone call to a journalist about midnight, informing the reporter about the meeting. "If I'm not back by 6 a.m., call the Brooklyn prosecutors."

The journalist called the DA's office at 7 a.m. Prosecutors made calls and learned of the attack.

Clemente made contact with her anonymous tipster at 82nd Street and 13th Avenue in Bensonhurst, and they agreed to drive their cars nearby to the southern end of Bay Parkway, at Gravesend Bay. There, the bearded would-be informant got into her black Hyundai and started talking about the case. She told investigators he pretended he had information. And then, Clemente said, he asked her, "Are you going to continue on this case?" "Yes," she answered. With that, she told cops, he whacked her on the right side of her body with something hard, and then put his hands around her neck and started choking her. Apparently convinced he had killed her, he took off.

At 5:45 a.m. Clemente was spotted lying halfway out of her car door by a passing dog-walker and a jogger. She was taken to Lutheran Hospital, where a huge bruise was found on her right side, and choke marks were found on her neck. There were also injuries to her head and lips. She didn't know the name of her assailant, but she did provide cops with a description. She remained in the hospital, under police guard. Assistant Brooklyn DA Michael Vecchione, the prosecutor who credited Clemente with helping him get a murder indictment against DeVecchio, believes the attack is linked to the former G-Man. "Let's put it this way, it's not unrelated," he said. Vecchione also would not discount the possibility that the murder attempt was the work of DeVecchio sympathizers, some of whom are former FBI agents. Earlier this month, Vecchione complained in court that some witnesses had been harassed by DeVecchio's FBI buddies.

In time, Angela Clemente recovered from her injuries; however, a few months later, she lost her colleague and friend. In August 2006, the courageous Dr. Stephen Dresch, who worked tirelessly to publicize and illuminate Gregory Scarpa Jr.'s work for the government, and the subsequent FBI cover-up, died of lung cancer.

37
SAY GOODBYE TO
ADMAX

On Wednesday, December 4, 2006, Gregory Scarpa Jr. woke before dawn. Standing outside his cell was a corrections officer. Without emotion, the CO instructed Gregory to get out of bed and pack his belongings.

"You're being transferred," he said.

Momentarily stunned, and still trying to emerge from the fog of sleep, Gregory thought perhaps he had misheard. Was this a dream? A joke? As his head cleared, reality began to sink in. Finally, after all these years, Gregory was getting out of ADMAX. A wave of conflicting emotions suddenly washed over him.

"Although I was thrilled to be leaving AD-MAX," says Gregory, "at the same time I was preparing myself for the nightmare that always occurs when you leave one prison for another."

A federal prison transfer usually took

about three weeks. After placing his meager possessions in storage, the inmate was assigned to a holding cell while awaiting the arrival of a bus or plane from the U.S. Bureau of Prisons. Then he was strip-searched and given traveling clothes (usually khaki pants and a plain blue or white shirt) before boarding one of the BOP's five Boeing 727 jets, each of which carried fifty to one hundred inmates. The plane would snake across the country, picking up and dropping off inmates at different prisons. At day's end the plane landed at the Federal Transfer Station, a seven-story building in a remote part of the Oklahoma City Airport. There, the remaining inmates, leg- and waist-shackled and black-box handcuffed (the black box goes over the handcuffs and immobilizes the hands), entered the BOP area while heavily armed federal marshals stood watch. More than ninety thousand inmates passed through the transfer station each year; typically, they waited in cells for a period of one to three weeks before boarding a flight to their new home.

Gregory's farewell breakfast at ADMAX was a hearty one: two slices of bread, two fried eggs, oatmeal, and sausage. Waging an ongoing (and losing) battle with his weight, Gregory usually picked at his breakfast; on this day, however, with a long trip ahead of him, Gregory ate everything on his tray.

Prisoners usually were transferred without advance notice or explanation, and this experience was, in that sense, not unique; however, it didn't take long for Gregory to realize that something about the trip would be different. After the other inmates awaiting transfer were taken to the pickup area, Gregory was left alone in the holding cell. A corrections officer briefly entered the cell and packed Gregory's bag lunch and legal documentation; before exiting the cell, the CO informed Gregory that his escort (a federal marshal, Gregory presumed) would be arriving shortly. In another room, Gregory was strip-searched (this, of course, included a probe of his anal cavity, a degrading aspect of prison life that had never ceased to anger him). The search concluded, Gregory retrieved his clothes as two men entered the room. One of them nodded at Gregory and said, with what Gregory felt was an odd degree of restraint and respect, "Hello, Greg. My name is Patty."

"My pleasure," answered Gregory.

The corrections officer, in keeping with transfer protocol, invited Patty to join in the fun: "He's yours to strip-search."

Patty shook his head, smiled.

"That won't be necessary. Get dressed, Greg."

Gregory was happy to dress without bending over first. Then, to his amazement, Patty asked the CO, "You got a jacket for him?" The CO was perplexed. *Was he kidding?* A common humiliation of transferring inmates involved standing outside without the proper clothing — even in the dead of winter.

Patty repeated, "Please get me a jacket for him. It's freezing out there."

Gregory was surprised to be treated so nicely by Patty and his partner, a man coincidentally named Greg. The surprises (and pleasantries) continued when he was taken outside to a large SUV, assigned a seat in the back, and introduced to two more men, Bill and Dennis. All four escorts, as it happened, were from the Brooklyn district attorney's office. Gregory soon discovered that he was being moved to the Metropolitan Correction Center in Lower Manhattan. The reason for the transfer: There was a chance that Gregory would be asked to testify at the trial of Lin DeVecchio.

"The car ride was fantastic," recalls Gregory. "It had been nearly eight years since I'd actually been outside in the world, and eighteen since I'd ridden in a car with a couple of other guys. We were all talking and getting along great, laughing about the CO and the jacket."

The astonishment continued, as Gregory quickly realized that the SUV was traveling not to a prison airport facility, but to the Colorado Springs Airport. "You're traveling with us, in style," Patty explained with a laugh. For the first time in twenty years, Gregory was going to get on a plane with "regular" passengers, ordinary folks traveling on business or pleasure. The anticipation, for Gregory, was almost overwhelming

At the airport, Patty sat Gregory down in a wheelchair and placed a jacket on the inmate's lap to cover his handcuffs, chains, and shackles. Again, to Gregory, who was accustomed to being treated like an animal, this represented a profound degree of sensitivity. The men wheeled Gregory through the airport, and as they moved, Gregory's head turned as if on a swivel. After eighteen years surrounded by the dull grays and greens of prison life, Gregory was amazed to see the different colors in the stores and fast-food restaurants. And the women, of course. Everywhere he looked, there were beautiful women. Gregory closed his eyes and inhaled deeply, letting the smell of freedom (if only temporary) fill his lungs.

At the security station, while other passengers suffered the numbing indignity of post-9/11 air travel — luggage searches, shoe removal, and the like — Gregory and his handlers were waved on through. How ironic, Gregory thought, that a convicted killer posed no threat. Patty slapped him on the back and laughed: "You're like the president, Greg."

They boarded first and sat in a private section at the back of the plane. An attractive flight attendant with dark hair and brown eyes offered Gregory a choice of beverages. He ordered a 7Up, his first soda in eleven years; as the carbonation tickled his mouth and the sugar cramped his tongue, Gregory could not believe how good it tasted. The meal, a hot barbecue chicken sandwich, was even better.

Gregory couldn't get over the TV screens on the back of every seat. Patty offered to pay five dollars for Gregory to watch a movie, but he was too excited watching the real people on the plane.

"If the COs at ADMAX or the feds knew I was enjoying myself this way . . ." Gregory said, letting his voice trail off. He shook his head, and laughed. "Fuhgeddaboutit!"

When the plane landed in Houston, the

flight attendant approached Gregory. To his shock, she smiled at him and offered words of peace and encouragement: "I don't know who you are or what you did, but there is something good in you, and I am going to pray for you." Almost speechless, Gregory whispered a thank you. He watched the flight attendant walk up the aisle away from him, and immediately became consumed by a fantasy. *Maybe he'd get out of prison one day and meet her. Maybe they'd fall in love. Maybe they'd marry . . .*

Here, at this moment, almost anything seemed possible.

After changing planes, they flew to La-Guardia Airport in New York, got into another SUV, and arrived at MCC around midnight. Once again under the heavy thumb of prison authorities, Gregory found that the pleasantries ended. His travel clothes, including the jacket, were replaced by a thin jumpsuit; he was locked in a small, cold, steel-walled cell that was illuminated by lights twenty-four hours a day; no exercise or recreation was permitted, aside from shivering to keep warm. The COs even refused to give Gregory the newspapers that his family had arranged to be delivered. Two cameras, often monitored by female officers, observed his every move — from taking a shower to using the toilet. When Gregory asked for a shower curtain to prevent water from spilling out onto the floor, his request was denied. "No curtains," the officer told him. "And don't cover the cameras or you'll get a ticket."

The morning after his arrival at MCC, Gregory was brought to the office of the Brooklyn district attorney. There his shackles were removed, and he was offered a comfortable chair at a conference-room table. He was encouraged to relax; a "big surprise" awaited him.

Moments later the door opened, and in rushed some of Gregory's family: his mother, Connie; his son Gregory; his brother Frankie; and Frankie's girlfriend, A.J.

"The kisses and the hugs and the crying were just unbelievable," says Gregory. "My mother couldn't stop sobbing." Gregory was overwhelmed at seeing his son, and continually kissed the boy even though he was very shy and sat away from his father. "I didn't want to force my attention on him, but it was difficult for me to let him go," says Gregory. "I just wanted to hold and kiss him."

His baby brother, Frankie, big, muscular, and almost totally tattooed, was also crying.

Frankie had been prosecuted on the same RICO indictment as Gregory, but had served only two years in prison (followed by five years of probation). After being released, Frankie had gone straight, developing a new life in the construction business. His wife had divorced him and he had met A.J., a loving woman who worked in his employer's front office. The two were madly in love and planning to marry. A.J. had been writing Gregory for years (because writing had caused too much pain for Frankie), so Gregory felt as though he already knew her. "We all laughed at a nice Jewish girl marrying into the Scarpa family," he said.

Connie opened shopping bags and began pushing food toward Gregory: paper plates overflowing with bagels and cream cheese, butter, smoked salmon, and a dozen different types of pastries. The reunion, filled with laughter and tears and hugging, lasted several hours; to Gregory, however, it seemed to have ended in a flash. The sadness of their departure, though, was tempered by the continued consideration of the DA's office, which promptly served a vast Italian lunch, the kind that reminded Gregory of his teenage years in Brooklyn. He hadn't eaten this well in more than two decades.

Food, of course, was the narcotic used by the DA's office to induce cooperation from Gregory. He understood the arrangement, knew that he was being pampered to foster goodwill, and to facilitate the transfer of information. But he didn't care. After so many years behind bars eating lousy prison food, Gregory was perfectly content to go along for the ride. And the ride, whenever Gregory visited the DA's office, included both breakfast (three eggs over easy, bacon, and home fries) and lunch (veal or sausage and peppers; pizza or take-out Chinese food). He went twice a week to answer questions about his life in the Mafia, questions that always focused on two subjects: Greg Scarpa Sr. and Lindley DeVecchio. He talked slowly, pausing often to gather his thoughts — not so much because he wanted to exercise caution, but simply to extend the visit, and to keep food coming.

Gregory had seen the feds' orders, and he was sure that, if they knew he was eating well and entertaining his relatives, the special treatment would have ended. DDA Vecchione had told Gregory that the DA's office could do nothing about Gregory's prison treatment. The feds owned Gregory and would have to approve any deal. The court had finally responded to Gregory's many pro se appeals (those where he represented himself) by appointing Georgia J. Hinde, a New York appeals attorney, to represent him. DDA Vecchione promised that if Gregory told the truth, he would write a letter to Hinde to present to the court outlining the help Gregory had given the prosecution.

So Gregory did something he had never done before. He told Michael Vecchione, Noel Downey, and others from the district attorney's office the unvarnished truth about everything, including the murders that he had committed himself. This was no small concession, given that Scarpa Jr. eventually copped to having killed more than twenty-five people. He had no immunity agreement, and naturally was concerned that he could be indicted for the murders (many of which had remained unsolved). He also was worried that by testifying truthfully, he might hinder his appeal; after all, he had lied in his original appeals. Worse, because his father was dead, Gregory had blamed all of his own murders on Greg Scarpa Sr.

If any of the ADAs expected remorse from the son of the deranged Mafia kingpin, they were sadly disappointed. To them Gregory revealed only the face of a wiseguy and murderer. What they did not know, and what Gregory would never have given them the satisfaction of knowing, was that when he returned to his cell at the end of a day of interrogation, he often reflected on the sadness and horror of his own life. He wondered what it would have been like to have been able to legitimately support his children and watch them grow up. He thought about the men and women he had murdered, and the pain he had caused — not merely to his victims, but to their children, grandchildren, parents, wives, friends. Gregory, of course, did not see himself as a monster; rather, he was a man who had the misfortune to be born into a business in which human life was a currency of little value. And he had proved adept at taking care of business.

That was the rationalization, anyway. But at night, after those soul-baring sessions at the DA's office, as he lay on his thin mattress with the lights shining above him, he would turn his head to the wall and hold his pillow tight, so that the cameras and the corrections officers couldn't see his contorted face, and the tears he sometimes shed.

38

DeVecchio On
Trial

On October 10, 2007, the trial of Lin De-
Vecchio commenced in the court of the
Honorable Gustin Reichbach of the New
York State Supreme Court in Brooklyn,
New York. It's hard to imagine that Judge
Reichbach, because of his own student
activism, would have been DeVecchio's first
choice to determine his fate. The walls of
his courtroom were adorned not with photos of men who meted out justice, but rather
with victims of injustice. Among these were
riveting images: Paul Robeson, the African
American actor persecuted for having com-
munist sympathies, testifying before the
House Un-American Activities Committee;
and Nelson Mandela, the South African
antiapartheid activist who spent twenty-
seven years in prison before becoming the
country's first postapartheid president. Near
the judge's bench were the scales of justice,
depicted in a bright red-and-blue sculpture.

On the very first day of jury selection, De-Vecchio waived his right to a trial by a jury of his peers and asked that Judge Reichbach serve as both judge and jury. DeVecchio wanted to be tried "in front of an impartial, intelligent individual who can assess the facts the way they are presented, which will mitigate in my favor."

Flattery notwithstanding, Judge Reichbach would not be so easily swayed.

"I'm a great believer in the jury system," he replied. "And in the common wisdom of citizens." He called DeVecchio's type of request "a generally unwise step."

This latest legal maneuver may have been due to the hostility that jurors had shown to DeVecchio during three previous Mafia trials in Brooklyn, or because New York City jurors were thought to harbor resentment toward law enforcement officers. Moreover, in the event of a conviction, DeVecchio may have planned to accuse Judge Reichbach of an anti-FBI bias; however, the judge scuttled this plan by disclosing that in the late 1960s, while a Columbia University law student, he had been under FBI surveillance, and he was described by agents as an "extraordinarily powerful speaker" with "strong, charismatic appeal," and as "one of the most dangerous" members of Students for a

Democratic Society, a radical, anti–Vietnam War group. Reichbach told DeVecchio that despite the surveillance, he had "no personal animus," toward the FBI and that he was "obliged to be fair and impartial."

This "bench trial" was merely the latest in a series of tricks that DeVecchio's lawyers had attempted to employ. They previously had claimed that the charges against their client be dropped, because they had arisen from DeVecchio's work as an FBI agent investigating the Mafia. When that didn't work, they had wanted the case transferred to the federal courts in the Eastern District in Brooklyn, assuming the feds would go easy on DeVecchio. When that ploy failed, they claimed that investigators had used DeVecchio's immunized testimony from previous court proceedings to obtain the indictments against him. All three attempts were unsuccessful.

Not surprisingly, given the sensational nature of the trial, the courtroom was packed with reporters; also in attendance were several former FBI agents who supported DeVecchio, including Joseph D. Pistone, whose undercover work infiltrating the Bonanno crime family became the basis for the best-selling book and acclaimed film *Donnie Brasco*.

"We've all worked with Lin since the early 1970s," Pistone said. "We're all veteran street guys. If anyone could smell something bad, it would be us. And with Lin, we never smelled [anything] bad."

DeVecchio and his supporters claimed that the agent was a victim of a conspiracy by prosecutors, law enforcement agents, investigators, journalists hoping to capitalize on the trial's story, and, finally, mobsters either holding grudges or hoping to get their own convictions overturned (if DeVecchio were found guilty, all of his testimony in previous trials would be considered suspect).

In his opening statement, ADA Joseph Alexis portrayed DeVecchio as a high-ranking supervisory agent with a prodigious appetite for money and power; he not only traded FBI intelligence information for cash, gifts, and prostitutes, but also became Greg Scarpa Sr.'s informant, resulting in significant criminal activity, including homicides. Because of the statute of limitations, only the murder charges could be brought against DeVecchio.

ADA Alexis alleged that DeVecchio had provided Greg Sr. information that had led to the murders of at least four victims: Mary Bari; Joseph "Joe Brewster" DeDomenico;

Patrick Porco; and Lorenzo "Larry" Lampasi.

"The information that the defendant gave this crew was dead-on," said ADA Alexis. DDA Michael Vecchione added that Gregory Scarpa Jr. would also testify that DeVecchio often provided privileged FBI information to his father. But the prosecution's star witness would be Scarpa Sr.'s longtime mistress, Linda Schiro, who would testify under oath that she heard DeVecchio giving Greg Sr. information that had resulted in the four murders.

Declared ADA Alexis: "Linda Schiro knew all of Greg's secrets."

In his opening statement, Douglas E. Grover, DeVecchio's attorney, countered that Linda was "totally lying." He added, "These were horrendous crimes, and what she's done here is taken real facts and real crimes and she has planted Lindley DeVecchio right in the middle. She's framed him."

Grover depicted DeVecchio as an excellent agent whose tireless, courageous work had helped put dozens of the city's most reprehensible gangsters behind bars. Now, tragically, the agent had been betrayed by a scheming gangster's moll who, because the Colombo crime family had cut her off financially, wanted to "cash in on a book deal." He also revealed that since March 2006, the Brooklyn DA's office had been paying Linda $2,200 a month for food and rent.

Grover also pointed out obvious cracks in the credibility of the prosecution's star witness; for example, in the mid-1990s, when DeVecchio had been cleared of corruption allegations following an internal FBI investigation, Linda had testified that she "never was close enough to overhear the conversations" between Greg Sr. and DeVecchio. The prosecution argued that during that probe, DeVecchio utilized the services of an intermediary to threaten Linda outside the FBI building. Linda, fearing for her safety, had taken the threats to heart, and had not complied fully with the FBI.

The prosecution methodically constructed its case, starting with the testimony of three FBI agents. They said that during the Colombo War they had become convinced that DeVecchio was leaking secret, confidential law enforcement information to Greg Scarpa Sr. Special agents Raymond Andjich and Jeffrey Tomlinson testified that they were "shocked" by DeVecchio's relationship with the elder Scarpa. Although they were supposed to be involved in meetings between DeVecchio and Greg Sr. at Scarpa's home (to avoid even the appearance of impropriety), DeVecchio made the agents wait in another room while he met with the mobster. Not only that, but DeVecchio had an odd and disturbing habit of raising the volume of the television in Scarpa's home while they met — presumably to drown out the conversation. As a result, Andjich testified, he could clearly hear only snippets of their meetings, including Greg Sr. saying "murder" and "hit." Later, they testified, DeVecchio had asked the agents to say that they had sat in on the meetings.

By 1992, the agents had become so suspicious that they opted to keep from DeVecchio information about the impending arrest of Greg Sr. Andjich stated, "I was concerned that Mr. DeVecchio might tip off Mr. Scarpa."

FBI Special Agent Christopher Favo testified that he had seen DeVecchio, his former boss, use the "hello" phone (the special phone reserved exclusively for conversations with informants) to alert Greg Sr. about another mobster, saying, "I don't know what he's saying about you; the Brooklyn DA's office has him." After that Favo stopped sharing certain information with DeVecchio.

Favo also testified that when he had

informed DeVecchio that Larry Lampasi had been killed, DeVecchio said, "We're going to win this thing," and slapped his hand on the desk.

Favo had told DeVecchio, "We're FBI agents; we're not on either side."

DeVecchio's attorneys asserted that many people had access to the information that their client was accused of leaking; additionally, they claimed, DeVecchio couldn't have provided Lampasi's whereabouts to Scarpa, because neither DeVecchio nor anyone else in the FBI had any information about Lampasi until after he was killed. (This argument was debated throughout the trial, as the prosecution later provided evidence that DeVecchio had, in fact, known Lampasi.)

Mobsters Carmine Sessa and Larry Mazza provided the Mafia side of Greg Sr.'s relationship with DeVecchio, and it did seem to dovetail neatly with FBI testimony. Arrested on the steps of St. Patrick's Cathedral in 1993, Sessa had begun cooperating with authorities immediately. He had testified at several trials, and had served a total of just six years for thirteen murders.

"I didn't know anybody to operate so openly," Sessa said about Greg Sr., who had often talked brazenly of his criminal life in front of his girlfriend and daughter. Scarpa had also talked openly inside Wimpy Boys, despite the ever present threat of surveillance equipment. "I thought it very odd to talk inside the club, especially about murder," said Sessa. Once, Sessa even found what appeared to be a listening device inside Wimpy Boys, but Greg Sr. had dismissed the discovery with a laugh, tossing the bug in the trash as he continued to speak openly.

Several Colombo members had long suspected that Scarpa was a rat; however, the frequency with which he committed murder ("work" it was called, in Mafia parlance) deflected concerns. Strict federal guidelines prohibited registered informants from engaging in violent crime while they worked for the FBI; thus, it seemed impossible that Scarpa could be such a skilled and eager killer while working for the feds.

"How could he be cooperating?" asked Sessa. "That was the question."

Larry Mazza testified that he'd been Greg Sr.'s "right-hand man. I was very, very close to him." Close enough, apparently, to have formed a wholly unflattering opinion of the Grim Reaper, who was, according to Mazza, "just a vicious, violent animal, but unscrupulous and treacherous, just a horrible human being." Mazza remembered Greg Sr. boasting of his relationship with a law enforcement officer (referring to the officer as his "source"), and during the Colombo War he had heard Greg Sr. talking on the phone to someone named "Lin."

Mazza was a colorful witness — perhaps, though, just a little too dramatic for his own good. While recalling the year he had spent at John Jay College of Criminal Justice studying police and fire science, Mazza began crying. "I was planning to follow my father," he said, referring to the man who had not only raised him, but had also been a lieutenant in the New York City Fire Department. Removing his glasses to wipe his eyes, Mazza apologized: "I am sorry." When he continued crying, the judge called for a brief recess.

Under heavy cross-examination, though, Mazza conceded to defense attorney Grover that his tearful breakdown had occurred at virtually the same point when he had cried while appearing previously before a grand jury.

"That's a tough point in my life," Mazza said by way of self-defense. "I'm very close to my father, and that's the day I screwed up my life." The defense attorney then pointed out that in a wiretapped prison conversation, Mazza had once told his father, "It's when you start talking about your family and friends, and get very emotional, that you can win over the jury. Juries are stupid."

Another prosecution witness didn't help the case. Reyes Aviles, who began cooperating after serving three years for his part in the murder of Dominick Masseria, testified that Patrick Porco himself had told the Scarpas about his encounter with the cops. But the prosecutor strongly believed that DeVecchio had also talked to Greg Sr. about Patrick Porco, and that indeed it was DeVecchio who issued the equivalent of a contract by suggesting to Scarpa that Porco be killed.

Despite his status as an unreliable witness (he was an admitted perjurer), Gregory Scarpa Jr. was also scheduled to testify. The defense considered calling their own mobsters, including, posthumously, Greg Scarpa Sr., who, in a deathbed affidavit, had claimed that DeVecchio was not his law enforcement source.

Although the prosecution repeatedly tried to assassinate DeVecchio's character, the weight of the case ultimately rested on the slender shoulders of Linda Schiro — the sole remaining living person who could testify to having heard DeVecchio assist Scarpa in committing the four murders for which he was charged.

On the stand, Linda was precisely the stalwart witness prosecutors had anticipated (and needed), testifying that Greg Sr. had given DeVecchio "wads of cash, jewelry, and other gifts." Then she fingered DeVecchio in the brutal gangland slayings of Mary Bari, Joseph DeDomenico, Patrick Porco, and Larry Lampasi.

Linda testified that she had heard DeVecchio say to Greg Sr., when speaking of Mary Bari, "You know, you have to take care of this, she's going to be a problem." About Joseph DeDomenico, she said he had told Scarpa, "You know, we gotta take care of this guy before he starts talking." Finally, according to Linda, DeVecchio had told Greg Sr. where Larry Lampasi lived and when he left for work in the morning; he had also provided Scarpa with a detailed description of Lampasi's balky gate, so that the mobster would know he was stationed at the right address.

After the Lampasi murder, Linda testified, Greg Sr. had complimented DeVecchio for providing "good information." Linda also claimed DeVecchio had told Greg Sr. that Patrick Porco was going to "rat on Joey." When she mentioned that she had loved Patrick like a son, Grover asked her, "Did you do anything to stop Greg Sr. from killing Patrick Porco?"

"Once Greg got information," she replied, "there was no telling him. You couldn't stop it."

Not surprisingly, DeVecchio's defense attorneys tore into Linda, attacking her credibility as well as her recollection. And, indeed, there were inconsistencies in Linda's testimony. For example, she claimed that DeVecchio had never paid Scarpa directly for his work; however, the defense produced Linda's 1998 sworn affidavit saying that DeVecchio had paid Greg Sr. frequently over the years.

Nevertheless, to many eyes, Linda was a compelling witness — every bit the showstopper the prosecution had promised. One veteran reporter sitting in the courtroom, Tom Robbins of the *Village Voice,* found Linda's "deadly story convincing." During a break he even polled other reporters as to their reactions. One said of DeVecchio, "If I was him, I'd be getting on the A train right now, headed for JFK and a plane someplace far away. He's dead." Another veteran crime reporter nodded in agreement.

Remarkably, though, Robbins had been holding information for ten years that would have a huge impact on Linda's testimony, and on the trial. He had never provided this information to the prosecution or the defense. After hearing Linda's testimony, he still didn't submit it to the court. Instead, he did what any good reporter with a scoop would do: He wrote a story.

At 4:00 P.M. on the afternoon of October 27, 2007, the *Village Voice* posted a riveting and revealing story by Robbins on its Web site. "Tall Tales of a Mafia Mistress" deconstructed the ongoing trial, including the "convincing" testimony of Linda Schiro and an informal poll of veteran reporters who had predicted the defendant's conviction. But there was a twist. Just as it seemed as though Robbins was about to paint DeVecchio as a crooked cop fated to spend the rest of his life in prison, the author laid waste to the reputation of Linda Schiro. In the process, of course, he provided an exit for DeVecchio.

In 1997, the story revealed, Robbins had been privy to a version of events from Schiro that had been "dramatically different." He and reporter Jerry Capeci, of ganglandnews.com, had intended to write a book with Linda about her life in the mob with Greg Scarpa Sr. During the course of their interviews, Linda had not implicated DeVecchio in three of the four murders. About

Mary Bari, she had told Robbins and Capeci, "All I know is they had word she was turning; she was gonna let information out," but she didn't mention DeVecchio as the source. She had said that DeVecchio had "nothing to do" with the murder of Joseph DeDomenico, and that DeVecchio "didn't tell Greg about Larry Lampasi."

Robbins admitted that, as the prosecution had claimed, Linda may have lied about DeVecchio because "she was frightened of him. The agent is a big man who served thirty-three years with the bureau, where he made powerful friends. Moreover, DeVecchio had already escaped punishment after an internal Justice Department probe of his handling of Scarpa."

But if Schiro feared DeVecchio, Robbins added, "it seems strange that she didn't hesitate at the time to put DeVecchio directly into another murder, that of Patrick Porco."

Linda had told Robbins and Capeci that DeVecchio had said, "The kid was going to tell the detectives what happened."

Robbins had sat on the information for the previous decade out of a sense of honor (and, perhaps, for contractual reasons): He has said that he and Linda had agreed that any information derived from the 1997 interviews "would only be used in a book — not in news articles," such as the one Robbins had just written for the *Village Voice,* and that neither Robbins nor Capeci would "attribute information directly to her." However, Robbins and Capeci felt that Linda had violated their confidentiality agreement by cooperating with the DA's office; additionally, because her testimony contradicted her previous statements, revealing those contradictions took precedent over "vows of confidence." Robbins concluded, "Lin DeVecchio may be guilty, or he may be innocent. But one thing is clear: What Linda Schiro is saying on the witness stand now is not how she told the story 10 years ago."

The story had devastating consequences for the prosecution. During a trial in which witnesses repeatedly contradicted one another, Robbins and Capeci offered more than just hearsay. They had Linda's contradictions on tape, and Robbins said so. Within an hour of the posting of the story on the Internet, both the prosecution and defense had subpoenaed Robbins's and Capeci's attorney for the tapes. The next morning Robbins and Capeci provided them to the court, effectively destroying Linda's credibility. After portions of the interviews were played for the court, prosecutors dropped the murder case against DeVecchio. Judge Reichbach warned Linda that she might be liable for perjury charges, and appointed a lawyer on her behalf.

Robbins later acknowledged a sense of ambivalence about his decision to come forward. "I did not know what else to do," he said. "No journalist ever wants to go against a source. It's against our creed." But, he added, "tell me what else I could have done? If you sit silent, then someone could go to jail for life. I chose not to live with that." Robbins claimed that he had "not followed developments in the case closely and had been surprised to see Ms. Schiro as the central witness." He hadn't realized "this case came down to her testimony."

Yet, for more than a year, nearly every article about the trial made clear that Linda was going to be the prosecution's main witness. Robbins's partner in the project, Jerry Capeci, had even written several of those articles for ganglandnews.com. Well before the indictments were announced, Capeci had written, "The linchpin of the case against DeVecchio, sources said, is Scarpa's longtime lover, Linda Schiro." Given their experience and level of expertise, it seems unlikely that either Robbins or Capeci believed Linda was going testify for the prosecution that DeVecchio wasn't involved in the murders.

In court, the frustrated prosecutor, Michael Vecchione, admitted, "Had we been provided these tapes much earlier in the process, I dare say we wouldn't have been here." The reporters accepted no responsibility for the unraveling of the case; rather, they laid the blame at the feet of the district attorney.

Noted Capeci: "At no time did the DA's office ever call me, contact me, or ask me at any point in any way, shape, or form if I had any information about what Schiro told me."

Robbins said that if anyone had asked him to give the prosecution a "reality check," he would have done so.

A prosecution spokesman admitted to knowing early in the investigation that Linda had spoken with Robbins and Capeci; the prosecution had declined to contact either writer because they didn't think the reporters would "share the information."

However, the previous summer, both the prosecution and the defense lawyers had issued subpoenas to Mr. Capeci, demanding all material in his possession related to the book proposal and talks with Linda Schiro, which would have included the tapes. Capeci had fought the subpoena, and Judge Reichbach had quashed it, citing shield laws protecting journalists. Mr. Robbins was not subpoenaed, but had he been, he said, he also would have fought it.

Linda angrily denied that she had lied on the witness stand. "I want the world to know I told the truth when it counted: under oath," she said through her new court-appointed attorney, Gary Farrell. "I feel horrible about this. I know how hard the prosecutors worked. I feel I let them down." She added, "Lin knew when he gave Greg a name of somebody what would happen. I lied to protect him. I thought he was going to protect me."

In his dismissal order, Judge Reichbach wrote that he was particularly struck by Carmine Sessa's testimony, in which Sessa described the mob's rationale for expressing skepticism over the possibility that Greg Scarpa Sr. was an FBI informant. It was unfathomable, Judge Reichbach had paraphrased, for "the FBI, charged with fighting crime, to employ as an informer a murderer as vicious and prolific as Greg Scarpa. Apparently, and sadly, organized crime attributed to the FBI a greater sense of probity than the FBI in fact possessed."

The judge then aptly quoted Nietzsche: "He who fights with monsters might take care lest he thereby become a monster."

If there were victors in this case, they hid their jubilation. For DeVecchio, there was only bitterness. The trial, he said, "has consumed me emotionally, drained me financially, and it has tested my faith in the system I spent thirty years of my life defending. I will never forgive the Brooklyn DA. My question is: Where do I go to get my reputation back?"

DeVecchio "celebrated" the dismissal with a dinner at Manhattan's Sparks Steak House, appropriately enough, a mob landmark: Years earlier, after all, Gambino family boss Paul Castellano was gunned down outside Sparks by henchmen for Gambino boss John Gotti.

R. Lindley DeVecchio was more fortunate — he walked out of Sparks a free man, and returned to his life in Sarasota, Florida. He resumed his duties as president of the homeowners association, and chatted with other residents about parched lawns and pest control. He and his wife, Carolyn, rode their motorcycles through their gated community and took long walks on the beach; they ate cottage cheese pancakes at their favorite breakfast spot, a place named Millie's. For a man who had been financially wrecked and emotionally devastated, R. Lindley DeVecchio seemed, at least on the surface, to be reasonably secure and content.

39
DEAD MAN TALKING

Gregory Scarpa Jr. was not as fortunate as DeVecchio. There would be no cottage cheese pancakes or motorcycle rides in his future; nor further confessions of murders or visits from his family. On December 9, 2007, after twelve months of spilling his guts to the DA's office about his life in the Mafia, and the relationship between R. Lindley DeVecchio and Greg Scarpa Sr. — twelve months of admitting to whacking guys he hadn't thought about in years (except in his dreams), and ratting out other wiseguys — Gregory was told to prepare for his return to Florence ADMAX. There he would spend the rest of his life.

And a short life it could be, given the vast publicity accorded the trial of Lin DeVecchio and the testimony of Gregory Scarpa.

"What happened at that trial was a sad joke," writes Gregory from his MCC cell. "I believe those two reporters, Capeci and

Robbins, knew exactly what they had on those tapes and waited until they could get the maximum publicity before they pulled that rabbit out of their hat.

"Lin DeVecchio was in it much deeper than even Linda talked about, because she only knew as much as she knew. He was my father's willing conspirator in everything he did: heists, hijackings, bogus credit cards, dope rings, and murder, to name just a few. He not only ignored my father's day-to-day criminal activities, he assisted in his professional success. He gave my father the names of other FBI snitches, so my father could murder them, while shielding his own illegal operations. He told [my father] where the FBI was placing wiretaps so he could avoid them. He informed my dad of pending indictments against his associates — in one instance allowing me to go on the lam before I could be arrested. He gave my father the addresses of my father's enemies during the Colombo crime family war so that Dad could track them down and kill them. DeVecchio also fabricated evidence against Vic Orena and others of my father's enemies, so they would be sent to prison," Gregory claimed.

"DeVecchio was in it for the money, the excitement, and the importance he gained in the FBI through his 'skillful' handling of my father and other Mafia informants. And, even though he is as guilty as any one of us wiseguys, he's the only one of us who truly got off scot-free, thanks to the protection of the FBI. I know I did a lot of bad things — when I look back I can't believe what I did — but I helped my country fifty times as much as DeVecchio, yet I'm going back to ADMAX, where I will probably be attacked or murdered by another inmate."

Gregory had quietly hoped the Brooklyn DA's office might consider mitigating circumstances, and assist with a transfer to a facility other than ADMAX — preferably, to a prison in which the feds would have a more difficult time enabling his execution. But, he was told, there was nothing that could be done. The feds owned Gregory, and they chose to send him back to AD-MAX, where, he says, "I'm afraid for my life, plain and simple. The feds hate me. They'll do what they have to do to shut me up forever.

"Nobody will ever know what really happened," Gregory adds, speaking of his own inevitable demise. "But, trust me, it will be bad."

POSTSCRIPT

It has been more than a year since the court dismissed criminal proceedings against R. Lindley DeVecchio. The world saw photos and video footage of DeVecchio and his wife exiting court, a sea of FBI cronies parting respectfully and approvingly as the vindicated former agent stepped into their midst. The agents jockeyed for air time and newspaper space, each more eager than the next to denounce the district attorney's office for indicting their friend and colleague.

DeVecchio was victorious, but never formally found to be innocent. For that to be true, the trial would have had to reach its logical conclusion, which, of course, did not happen. Whether Linda Schiro was telling the truth on the witness stand had become almost irrelevant; her integrity had been so severely compromised that there was no practical purpose in hanging a case on her testimony; and so the prosecutor, despite his belief in her honesty on the stand, pulled the plug, sparing taxpayers an enormous expense pursuing a verdict that could not possibly be achieved.

Was Linda telling the truth when she implicated DeVecchio in four murders, or had she been truthful ten years earlier, when she was interviewed by Robbins and Capeci? Personally, I've come to believe she told the truth on the stand, and I said as much to Leslie Crocker Snyder, the former Manhattan judge who had been appointed special prosecutor by the administrative judge for Brooklyn, Neil Jon Firetog, to investigate whether Linda should be indicted for perjury. I told the judge I believed that the sworn testimony given by Linda on the stand took precedence over the taped statements she gave to the reporters, because at the time Linda spoke to Robbins and Capeci she was still in mourning for Greg Sr. and her son Joey; and was nearly broke, heavily sedated, and, frankly, drunk. In addition to having a serious drug problem at that time in her life, Linda also drank frequently and heavily. There is some reason to believe she was inebriated at the time of the interviews with Robbins and Capeci — on the tape recordings one could actually hear the pouring of the drink and the clinking of glasses, as well as the slurring of words on the tapes. Linda was also in grave danger of retaliation from DeVecchio if she revealed then what she later said on the stand. Perhaps most important, she was extraordinarily vulnerable at the time, and therefore needed DeVecchio's support — financial, emotional, legal, and otherwise. She had no one else and believed he would be there for her if she was in trouble, the way he had always been there for Greg Scarpa Sr.

In the end, of course, DeVecchio wasn't there for Linda. But it would take time for her to realize the degree to which she had incorrectly assessed their relationship.

On October 22, 2008, former state judge Leslie Crocker Snyder released her long-awaited "Report of the Special District Attorney in the Matter of the Investigation of Linda Schiro," in which she wrote, "while the witness, Linda Schiro, testified falsely at times during the trial, about two of the homicides, notably her denial in court that she ever talked to Robbins and Capeci about the killings, a full review of the record and available evidence does not yield sufficient proof of the falsity of her trial and grand jury testimony to support a perjury charge."

While sparing Schiro, Judge Snyder

strongly chastised Capeci and Robbins for not coming forward sooner with the tapes, and for disrupting the trial. Instead of protecting their source, she wrote, "they disgraced her and exposed her to criminal investigation for perjury."

According to *Newsday* reporter Anthony DeStefano, "those remarks drew a quick riposte from both writers who said Judge Snyder was 'dead wrong' in her findings." Judge Snyder immediately responded to the two reporters: "I call it as I see it, let the chips fall where they may."

In a stunning turn, Snyder also renewed questions about the relationship between Scarpa and DeVecchio, his FBI handler. In a one-page addendum, she turned her attention to other key figures in the trial of Lin DeVecchio and the FBI's involvement in the so-called Mafia wars and wrote:

I feel compelled to raise some of the many issues which warrant further investigation by an appropriate agency or some other investigative body:

- Did DeVecchio pass information to Greg Scarpa Sr. regularly, setting aside the four murders charged in the indictment?

438

- Is there probative evidence that the FBI — or at least DeVecchio — knew that Scarpa Sr. was ordering, and committing, numerous murders and, nevertheless, allowed him to continue his status as a top echelon FBI informant?
- Was there an effort by the FBI to protect Scarpa and DeVecchio in order to protect/insulate/preserve numerous mob prosecutions and some convictions relating to the Colombo crime family?
- Were the FBI agents who reported their suspicions regarding DeVecchio shunned and ostracized?
- Why was DeVecchio allowed to retire with a full pension, despite the government's acknowledgment that he leaked information to a murderous informant, and why was he granted immunity after he invoked his Fifth Amendment privilege in postconviction proceedings related to convictions in the Colombo War?

There was more, including concern over whether "the witnesses, potential witnesses, or people who cooperated in the DeVecchio investigation and/or prosecution had been harassed by various agencies because of their cooperation, as many of these individuals now claim."

In the final paragraph of her report, Judge Snyder stated: "My mandate does not allow me to reach any conclusions as to these issues — and far more investigation would be required before any reliable conclusions could be reached. Nevertheless, a dramatic picture of corruption with numerous unanswered questions exists."

Greg Jr. is still at Florence ADMAX, one of the most brutal prisons in the country. He'll probably be there until he's eighty — if he lives that long — unless he catches a monumental break, and his new appeal is not denied, as all the others have been. He has a court-appointed lawyer handling his newest appeal, so something might happen. As a writer — as a person interested in justice — as someone who has gotten almost too close to this story — I hope so. I want the truth about Gregory finally told, both through this book and through the courts.

In the years I worked on this project, I learned a lot about the Mafia, the FBI, the district attorney's office, the press, criminal lawyers, and the court system; none of which I had understood very well at all before I began writing this book. I have been mashed and bashed by many of the above, for no reason other than that I held strong opinions about the DeVecchio case and the truth of the information Gregory Scarpa Jr. provided the government — information that might have averted the tragedy of 9/11.

I was also intimidated by one former FBI agent, a dear friend of DeVecchio who had called me a few times before and during the trial in order to "befriend" me and get as much information from me as he could, all at the same time. I remember him sitting in the courtroom, glaring at me, when I gave my testimony to the judge. I certainly didn't expect him to call me to wish me a warm and happy New Year's months after the trial, and then slyly tell me he and his partner were "watching" me when I dined at Elaine's, a popular restaurant located just two blocks from my apartment. So I was more than surprised when he appeared at my door a few months later, suggesting we go to lunch; he kept digging the entire time, trying to find out if I was still writing my book, and if so, what I was going to say about DeVecchio.

Now he knows.

ACKNOWLEDGMENTS

I want to thank Gregory Scarpa, Jr., who, from his tiny cell at ADMAX prison in Florence, Colorado, and despite the possibility of violent retaliation by guards, other Mafia members, and a number of well-known terrorists also incarcerated at the same prison, wrote me hundreds of open and honest letters about his life as a Colombo crime family Mafia capo, a government informant, and a long-term federal prisoner, in order that this book could be written.

I also want to thank Angela Clemente and the late Dr. Stephen Dresch who worked for years, tirelessly and without remuneration, to bring Greg Jr.'s story regarding 9/11 to the attention of many government agencies, and who were uniformly rebuffed for their efforts. Both shared much information with me for the purpose of this book.

Much thanks to my two wonderful agents, Joel Gotler of Intellectual Property Group and Larry Kirshbaum of LJK Literary Management, who together sold this book to Charles Spicer at St. Martin's Press. I feel very fortunate to have been represented by you two terrific guys. I will always remember the way you both stood by me professionally and gallantly in all ways during the years it took me to write this saga.

Thank you, Charles Spicer. How did I get so fortunate as to find you? You are an amazing editor and a true visionary. And, I must admit, you were always right.

Thank you, Yaniv Soha, associate editor, for always taking care of everything in the most responsible, intelligent, and dependable way. You never, ever disappoint.

Thank you Rachel Burd, a great copy editor who didn't miss a trick. I am so impressed with your work.

Much thanks to Rob Grom who designed the powerful cover of the book.

Thank you, Joe Layden, for all your incredible help and support in those last stages of the manuscript. You are the best.

Thank you, John Murphy, vice president and director of publicity, and John Karle, associate director of publicity, two gentlemen extraordinaire of St. Martin's Press who really know their business, and are great guys, besides.

An added thanks to James Rosenfeld of Davis, Wright, Tremaine — a terrific attorney who represented me during the DeVecchio pretrial hearing and helped protect my First Amendment rights.

Finally, I want to thank Michael Vecchione, chief of the Rackets Division in the Brooklyn District Attorney's Office, the lead prosecutor in the DeVecchio murder trial, for spending so much of his precious time answering my endless questions about the Mafia and the DeVecchio trial.